PUT YOUR DREAMS FIRST

PUT YOUR DREAMS FIRST
handle your [entertainment] business

THEMBISA S. MSHAKA

with a Foreword by
VANESSA WILLIAMS

BUSINESS
PLUS

NEW YORK   BOSTON

Copyright © 2009 by Thembisa S. Mshaka
All rights reserved. Except as permitted under the US Copyright Act of 1976, no part of this
publication may be reproduced, distributed, or transmitted in any form or by any means,
or stored in a database or retrieval system, without the prior written permission of the publisher.

Excerpt on page 20 from *All About Eve* © 1950 Courtesy of Twentieth Century Fox. Written by
Joseph L. Mankiewicz.

Business Plus
Hachette Book Group
237 Park Avenue
New York, NY 10017

Visit our Web site at www.HachetteBookGroup.com.

Business Plus is an imprint of Grand Central Publishing.
The Business Plus name and logo are trademarks of Hachette Book Group, Inc.

Printed in the United States of America

First Edition: April 2009

10 9 8 7 6 5 4 3 2 1

Library of Congress Cataloging-in-Publication Data

Mshaka, Thembisa S.
    Put your dreams first : handle your entertainment business / Thembisa Mshaka. —1st ed.
        p. cm.
    ISBN 978-0-446-40946-9
    1. Music trade—Vocational guidance.   2. Women entertainers.   3. Businesswomen.
I. Title.
    ML3795.M73 2009
    790.2023—dc22

                                                                            2008038085

Design by Meryl Sussman Levavi

For Umi

Fulani Mshaka

1949–2007

Acknowledgments

With eternal gratitude to the Creator, the Beneficent, the Merciful, through Whom all things are possible.

With everlasting gratitude and love for my mother. My first and most influential mentor, Fulani Mshaka, MSW. A woman of faith. A woman of service. A woman of late nights with a movie and lazy afternoons with a book. I am a writer as a direct result of being my mother's first daughter. She sat and smiled with the muses every night I showed up to the page. She taught the author every secret she should know. Umi, you are deeply missed and eternally appreciated.

To my incredibly supportive and loving family: My very closest friend, husband, Consigliere, Renaissance Man, and Real Estate Gangsta, Anthony Tmor Morris, thank you for being my rock and my soul mate, I am truly blessed. You are deeply loved.

My son and Fearless Cheerleader, Mecca J. Mshaka-Morris, for your light and your hugs. Love you, Noop!

My father, Daoud Mshaka, for showing me how to love and respect music.

My aunt Elena Bell and sister Sumiyah Mshaka for the ongoing counseling and emotional support that only the best social workers can provide!

My brothers Ahmed Mshaka and Jabril Nasrullahi and sister Daisha Mshaka, just for being you.

My grandma Edna Mae Greene Bell, for pushing me toward my dream by making me her Chief Correspondent.

My grandpa Dr. James Bell, the most progressive patriarch ever and model local and global citizen.

My paternal grandfather Leroy A. Dandridge and grandmother Blanche W. Dandridge, for spoiling me with an endless supply of laughter and love.

My incredible uncle James Bell for showing me you can't sweat the small stuff while you're changing the world. Go, Burns Institute!

To my best friend of thirty-seven-plus years, Dr. Maliika Chambers, I thank God for you every day, my Seasons of Life Summer Soul Sista!

My extended families, the Greenes, Bells, Allens, Bests, Dandridges, Gibsons, Morrises, and Joneses, along with family born of life not blood: Chris Metcalfe, Stephanie Rutherford, Mykah Gant, Johnny Richardson, Mark Liddell, Michelle "Jigga" Joyce, Angela Bailey, the Montgomerys, Longs, Duncans, and Lees, Adrienne Herd, Rabia Rodriguez and Posse, Abdur-Rahmans and Shareefs.

To all my Mills Women, especially Evette Brandon, Kymberly Miller, Tonda Case, Agbanyero Chukwudebe, Elizabeth Carter, Rachel Noerdlinger, Maggie Gabel, Lelalois Hudson, Laura Dickerson, Rashawn Gilmer, Donelda Smith, Artricia Moore, Onika McGriff, Algera Tucker, Kathleen Cleaver, Elaine Brown, and Congresswoman Barbara Lee: You've all shown me that fighting the power can be fun and fruitful.

To all my Westridge Girls, especially Dr. Maya Alvarez-Galvan, Susan Harrison, Lisa Everett, Jennifer Bradbury, Dr. Maie Abdul-Rahman, the late Dondi Johnson, and Inger Miller, thanks for showing me how to stand out and rock out instead of hiding out.

To Regina "Agent" Brooks of Serendipity Literary Agency, thank you so very much for taking this journey with me, because only someone who truly believes in her client would hang in there for a six-year sojourn! To my editor, Karen Thomas, thank you for seeing the vision. To Latoya Smith, editorial assistant to Karen, you are deeply appreciated.

To my *Gavin* assistants Ayoka Medlock and Jackie Jones and my author's assistant Mara Spiegel: My career simply would not be without the gentle stalking, gatekeeping, laughter, and support you've given me over the years. Mara, I am most grateful to you for taking on the mission of this book with me. Thank you for your part in its creation. Every author should be so lucky. Special thanks to Chris Nolan, my legal eye, and Trinh Dang at Fox Clearances. To Deborah Karpatkin, thank you for helping me make a clean break to this, my new chapter.

To every woman in this book: an eternal thank-you for embracing and kick-starting the Handle Your [entertainment] Business movement for empowering and enriching women in our business. I am humbled by your generosity and trust. If I have served as a secure vessel for your testimony, then I have met my goal. You have moved and strengthened me in ways beyond expression. It is truly an honor to be the author with whom you shared your story. For all the women who are not in this book due to scheduling, personal, and/or legal constraints, thank you for your interest, commitment, and contribution to our industries. It was my honor to make the request and my pleasure to meet those of you who are now new connections. And to the women I interviewed, surveyed, and heard from, your names may not appear, but your words helped make this book a reality. Thank you all.

I cannot thank Vanessa Williams enough for contributing the foreword for this book. She would not hear of anything less than writing it herself. Her voice sings on the page, soaring as it has everywhere from the steps of Pasadena City Hall to the Super Bowl. As a true star of every entertainment medium, she has risen like the proverbial phoenix. My admiration and respect for her have only deepened after meeting her. Thank you for your generosity of spirit and for being a woman of your word, Vanessa. You are the truth!

To Miss Johnnie Walker and the women of NABFEME: I literally carried the manuscript in my Charlotte conference bag while I crafted each chapter and searched through each interview, so you have all been with me every step of this journey as shoulders to cry on, stand on, lean on. Thank you. May God return the grace you have extended to me tenfold.

Special thanks to my art director and logo designer Charnelle Anderson of Creative Elevation, LLC, for wonderful presentation, and many thanks to my own personal Glam Squad as credited for my author photo: Andrew, Nancy, Guidone, Miss Ollie, and Nicole. You rock!

I would not be the writer I am today without the guiding, critical, and encouraging hands of my hugely influential teachers and professors: Juanita Mizuno, Mr. Kaplan, Mr. Fallon, Mr. Moran, Mrs. Connor, Mr. Lowe, Dorothy Tsuruta, Fred Lawson, and Linda Goodrich; my editorial mother Beverly Mire and editorial father Ben Fong-Torres; my Sony Music copywriter predecessors, the phenomenal Kim Green, Chris Wilder, and Deneen Wade; and the amazing editors for whom I have had the pleasure of writing: Kofy Brown and Nzinga Hatch for Grits 'N' Gravy (I ain't forgot my Oakland roots, y'all), Nicole Moore of theHotness.com, Billy Johnson Jr. of Yahoo! Music, Kenya Byrd of Essence.com and *Jewel,* Jesse Washington of *BLAZE Magazine,* Big Ced of TheIndustryCosign.com, and the original *Honey* brain trust, Kierna Mayo and Joicelyn Dingle.

To the Abundance Group, Echo Allen, Lana Garland, Lynette Gitonga, and Lenora Zenzalai Helm: You have lifted me from the depths of sadness and self-doubt to endless power as a writer, mother, and wife. I cannot thank you enough!

To the 191 Madison Wolfpack, Anika Burt and Esther Alix of Spiritguide Films, Lana Garland of Insibah Films, and Tmor of AM Luxe, thank you for putting your creative foot up my you-know-what when I had no idea how this book would look! See you when we sweep awards season, y'all!

To the wise and dynamic women who mentor me: Kelly Armstrong, Sylvia Montgomery, Terrie Williams, Sharon Heyward, and Isisara Bey: Thank you for nurturing my power, determination, and inner beauty with your own. To Sylvia Rhone, Maria Davis, Helen Little, Cobi Narita, Violet Brown, Julie Greenwald, Lisa Ellis, Sonja Bates-Norwood, Congresswoman Maxine Waters, Kathy Nelson, Suzanne DePasse, Sherri Lansing, Julie Dash, Kasi Lemmons, Alfre Woodard, Cicely Tyson, Ruby Dee, Mary Datcher, Janet Jackson, Tina Knowles, Melissa Etheridge, Marlo Martin-Jackson, Carmelita Sanchez, The Poetess, MC Lyte, Yo-Yo, Dr. Roxanne Shante, Jill Scott, Susan L. Taylor, Tina Turner, Toni Basil, Barbra Streisand, Whoopi Goldberg, Jada Pinkett-Smith, Celine Dion, Bonnie Raitt, and Oprah Winfrey, thank you for mentoring and inspiring me without you even realizing it. Your presence in our business matters a great deal.

To the village that helps to raise my child Mecca, your love and care for him made this project possible.

Special shout to my Health Squad: Thank you to everyone at Max Health of New York: Dr. Ruth Fernandez, Dr. Tany Sutera, Dale, Gloria, Blanca, Melissa for literally keeping me in alignment so I could withstand innumerable hours in the chair at the laptop. Thanks as well to Dr. Carmen Bosch, Dr. Ketly Michel, Dr. Bhagat, Nails NY II, and Equinox Fitness. A big kiss to Fatima and Jane of the J Sisters for making the introduction to Ms. Williams, and hugs to her entire staff for their tender loving care.

Special acknowledgment goes to Aliesh Pierce, Alexa Pagonas, Nefertiti Strong, Erika Conner, Abra Potkin, Gwen Quinn, Nomi Roher, Marjorie Clarke, and Monique Martin, whose passion for the book exceeded sharing their testimony and extended into helping me find more women to join them in these pages. Thank your for your championship!

I would be remiss if I did not acknowledge the men who have lifted me up as I walked the path of my career. I didn't realize how fortunate I was to have you in my life and in my ear until I spoke to all the women who wished they had male mentors and confidants they could rely on for something more than a tired come-on. The industry would have women think that secure men like you are a myth. The world needs to know you for who you really are by name. God Bless The Bishop of Hip-Hop Adisa Banjoko, Jonathan "Sway" Calloway & King Tech, JC Ricks, Troy Shelton, Russell Gatewood, Diallobe Johnson, Bruce Solar, Lupe DeLeon, Ibrahim "Ebro" Darden, Quincy McCoy, Shelly Tatum, Kashif, Hakim Green, Melvin Bacon, Rene McLean, Warren Peace, KRS-One, Crazy Legs, Corey Action, EA Ski, Rick Rock, Chaka Zulu, Chuck D, Lenny Berry, Jay Wright, Julio G, Masta Ace, Tony Draper, Eightball & MJG, Rich Nice, Davey D, Tim Hunter, Rodd Houston, Professor Pablo Whaley, Kevin Mitchell, Will Strickland, Martin Luther, David Belgrave, Kawan "KP" Prather, Erwin Gorostiza, Chris "Awstopsocks" Austopchuk, Brian "Brain" Freeman, Chris Feldmann, Derek Dudley, Pharoahe Monch and Prince Poetry, Rashied "Common" Lynn, Trevor "Busta Rhymes" Smith, Sam Sneed, Glen "G" Wallace, Brad "Scarface" Jordan, Curtis "50 Cent" Jackson, Mutulu M-1 of Dead Prez, Nasir "Nas" Jones, Sha Money XL, Colin Gayle, James Cruz, Eric Skinner, Kevin Black, Sean Taylor, Kevin Liles, Blue Williams, Paul Stewart, Michael Mauldin, Mike Kyser, Chris Nagy, Cornell "Nelly" Haynes Jr., Daryle Lockhart, Dan Charnas, Savalas Holloway, Marlynn Snyder, Steve and John Rifkind, James Andrews, Big Jon Platt, Terrence Chin, Barry Simons, Elan Masliyah, Michael London, Ron "DJ G-Wiz" Butts, Demmette Guidry, Michael "MC Serch" Berrin, Michael Tipton, Taylor Tosh, Zurek (fka Rick Party), Terrence Hannah, and Dr. Michael Eric Dyson. Special acknowledgment to my Hip-Hop Bo$$ Ola Kudu for signing off on my leave of absence and supporting my dream 110 percent, along with Yves Erwin Salomon who served as my leading "write" hand while I was away. Help your fellow men and put them up on this book, then give it to the women in your lives.

Thank you to Debra L. Lee, Kelli Lawson, Janet Rollé, BET Creative Services (the best team I've ever worked with), and the entire BET Networks family for making me feel welcome and appreciated. It is truly my honor to be the network's first copy director. Special thanks to Jeanine Liburd and Bobette Gillette for your stewardship with Debi's participation.

To each and every DJ, DJ crew and advocacy organization, record pool, independent retailer, and music or content programmer I have had the pleasure of working with and dancing to, from the stations and clubs around the world to my *Gavin* reporters: Great music lives because you keep it alive. Thank you for all the work you put in, which goes unrecognized far too often. I challenge one of you retail vets to change that and write the book on music sales.

And may God grant Lesley Pitts, Angela D. Pittman, Aaliyah Dana Haughton, Lisa "Left Eye" Lopes, Donna Moore, Dr. Donda West, Justo Faison, Hesten Hosten, Mike Futagaki, DJ Pinkhouse, DJ Screw, Bigga B, Randy Parker, Ronnie Johnson, Lou Galliani, Timothy White, Don LaFontaine, Johnny J, Shakir Stewart, Ron Archer, and all our fallen hip-hop soldiers peace as we carry their legacies forward.

To Tylibah and Peia, you two are next to make your mark with SEEIT Live. I'm inspired by you both.

To every reader—from the women this movement seeks to engage and support to the men who see the value and the vision for themselves and the girls or women in their lives: a thousand thank-yous!

To the Oakland/San Francisco Bay Area, love and gratitude.

To the Obama family, thank you for the sacrifices you've made for our nation and for a new shared history.

This project has literally been in the making since 2001, so there are many I needed to acknowledge who have helped me to fulfill this dream. Maybe the list will be shorter for the second book . . .

Ashé. And so it is . . . like *that.*

One Love

Contents

Foreword

Ladies,

Thembisa has written the definitive blueprint, journal, and guidebook to help women get a real look at the inner workings of the entertainment business. What you're about to read are true stories of struggle, sexism, and discrimination that all are an unpleasant part of being a woman of color in this business, or frankly any business. That continues to be the uncomfortable truth about struggling to make it anywhere in our world. The fact that we women still don't make as much as our male counterparts, and have to endure condescending attitudes and remarks just for not being a member of the boys' club, and of course the occasional sexual innuendo, comes with living in our skins as females.

I'm lucky to not have to make a living in just one arena. I have the luxury of dipping into a genre like television, film, or theater, with an outside view, then stepping away to another adventure. But my frustration with the lack of quality roles available to me early on in my career led me to my introduction and hard-earned success in the music biz.

My recording career began at Wing Records founded by Ed Eckstine, which was a label on PolyGram. My soon-to-be husband, Ramon Hervey, gave me the direction to pursue after he saw how difficult it had become for me to be taken seriously as an artist with a big fat *Miss America* title preceding my name. He assured me that I would have much more control of my image and show the world what I was capable of as an artist if I could secure a solo record deal. I had taken meetings over the past few years in New York and Los Angeles, but it was after I recorded with George Clinton on two tracks — "Hey Good Lookin'" and "Do Fries Go with That Shake?" — that I actually heard myself on the radio for the first time. Ed took a chance when everyone else thought I was a joke.

That team of Ramon and Ed were my warriors, the big brothers, the ones who had to buffer all the jokes, witness the rolled eyes, and shrug off the insincere pats on the back with my signing and presence at PolyGram. Now the challenge was to make the record and be legitimately in the game. Not many songwriters were eager to give me good songs; they wanted to keep them for other artists who were proven, and of course they'd never bank on my success as a newcomer fresh off a scandal. But Ed did find the artists who were willing to take a shot.

The Right Stuff was completed and its first video (for the title track) was to be made. Annette Cirrillo was the head of video. She was direct, funny, and reminded me of my New York roots. She hired a female director out of New York, and we shot in Malibu and Pasadena. We were all off to a curious start. We knew we'd get the music played initially because of the guess-who's-got-an-album-out factor, but the follow-through of longevity was what we were hoping for. We went from station to station across the country. I co-hosted morning shows, did record signings, and appeared on track dates, all standard operation for working a new album and new artist.

Each city and territory had its masters of persuasion to help get the record played nationwide at radio stations. And this is where I saw many women excel (too many to name), both as independent promoters and radio programmers. It was connections, relationships, and willpower that made them rule on the road. These women were respected for the goods they delivered, the acts they paraded behind the studio mikes for interviews, and the fire to keep the singles playing on air.

Back at the office, PolyGram head of public relations Dawn Bridges was my ally. She was the one woman I could go to and get the real skinny on what was going on within the company, what people really thought out in the world about my music career, and what needed to get done in order not to be a flash in the pan. Dawn remained in my life and career at PolyGram after I lost Ramon as a husband and manager through divorce, plus losing Ed Eckstine as a boss, producer, and visionary.

*

The record business always had a lot of transitions: new people heading up departments overnight, new agendas, and new musical flavors of the moment. It was very easy to get lost in the shuffle of new artists that were constantly being signed. Without true alliances, it was easy to not have a voice. So I always relied on who knew me the best and the longest, Dawn.

I lasted at PolyGram for nearly ten years and I am so thankful I had the honest, direct, and unconditional support of the women who helped make my time there a success. But it was also men like Ed and Ramon who embraced the talents of strong gifted women. The combination steered me away from disingenuous execs with bad opportunities, gave me the feedback to make decisions in my career on my own terms, and understood what it was like to struggle to be a success while working through pregnancies, juggling a marriage, and trying to look fly onstage!

So the bottom line is to use your resources. Seek out your alliances. Find the people who really listen to your ideas, dreams, and ways to achieve them. And then nurture those relationships. There will always be folks who think you don't belong and aren't worthy. It's up to you to create your own success and, with the help of true allies, shut them all up!

—Vanessa Williams

PUT YOUR DREAMS FIRST

Sister Swans

When a swan glides atop the pond, what we see is its mesmerizing grace, its striking beauty, its determined poise. That image is a familiar, fabled one. Consider now what's going on beneath the surface. The swan is paddling fiercely to stay afloat while moving ahead without the slightest hint of effort. The treading beneath goes unnoticed, but the ability and stamina required for the task are immense.

Women worth their salt in the entertainment business are swans. Smooth and beguiling at first glance, yes. But upon further examination, they are puttin' in serious, continuous work to maintain their presence. Their position. Their sanity. Let's take the analogy one step farther and make the swan female: At turns exoticized and ostracized, depending on who's looking, she is now totally conspicuous *in addition* to being thoroughly exhausted. For the female swan, being watched makes looking good (literally and professionally) more important than natural law intends. The result? Unnatural pursuit of looking good, often at the cost of her dignity, her sexuality, her spirituality, her family, her very self.

Put Your Dreams First is a tour guide for the pond that is the entertainment business. I am your guide, but the true authors of the manual are the sister swans who call these tumultuous waters home. It is designed to relieve women of the exhaustion, resignation, and frustration this game seems to create especially for us.

This book is more about the intangibles of the game as women have to play it than the mechanics and the jargon of the game as it was designed. Like America itself, the entertainment business is still being run by its Founding Fathers and their descendants. The role of women was made peripheral to that of men. We were to be seen and heard, not respected. (Don't take my word for it: The lexicon of the industry says it all. *Exploit* is the accepted synonym for *sell*. And when something is being "exploited," this occurs "in perpetuity throughout the world." Standard.)

The most fabulous thing about the business is this: Upon reaching its shores, anyone really *can* achieve the American Dream. (If only that were so everywhere!) And despite all the -isms and obstacles placed before women, this is true for us as well. We can become millionaires before hitting twenty-one, like Missy "Misdemeanor" Elliott. We can break the record for Grammy nominations our first time out, like Lauryn Hill. We can have the number one album and film in the nation in the same week, à la Jennifer Lopez. You know what's equally impressive? That scores of us do this on a regular basis, one day at a time, one woman at a time. There are African American, Latina, Asian American, Native American, and Caucasian women giving industry pond scum a run for its money, going from intern to CEO or from college coed (hell, high school dropout) to self-employed success story. While it happens with much less fanfare, going largely unnoticed like the paddle of the swan, such stories are what power those celebrated by the media, like the aforementioned. Two examples: Mona Scott-Young, a black woman, manages Missy. Stephanie Gayle, another African American, supplied the marketing genius behind *The Miseducation of Lauryn Hill*. Yours truly created the ad campaign for it.

Are you getting the picture? We may not be calling all the shots, but we are the cornerstone of the industry. From Judith Jamison to Joan Baez, the galaxy of recording and performing artists sparkles with women, and certainly women of color, who have generated millions of dollars for our business — probably a few billion. I don't have enough pages to explore how many labels and studios retain and rely upon women as their assistants and life managers, keeping their gates and keeping everything flowing smoothly. Entertainment would not be the pervasive global force it has become if women weren't handling their business.

On today's ever-changing playing field, women are too eager to do anything, even if it's the wrong thing, to get in the game, with little thought to the impact of the undertow. These girls have confused adulthood for womanhood, substituting peddling themselves for paddling. And okay, I can't front: Some of them make it climbing up the ladder on their backs. It may even work for you, if that's the path you choose. But this book is for those who choose otherwise. For those who know better and were taught they deserve better. For those who'd rather not reinvent the wheel; for those who aren't blessed with a mentor's wing to shelter them as they take to the pond. For those ready to trade in these murky waters and take to the skies in pursuit of fresh aspirations. After years of bearing witness to how much paddling it takes to glide ahead, swim across, or simply stay afloat, I realized it was time the world was introduced to some of our Sister Swans. Some are known by name, others by their contributions. They all have incredible stories to share. Turn the page. Don't be surprised if you see yourself in their reflections. You're not crazy, and you're not alone. You're more than enough. And you're right on time.

*

A *note to parents:* Be advised that there is profanity used in this book. It does not diminish the value of the lessons for teens and young adults contained herein. In some cases, it underscores that value. As a parent myself I'd appreciate the disclosure, so I offer one.

CHAPTER 1

Getting In

....

Stephanie Abdullah ✳ Jennifer Coles ✳ Nefertiti Strong ✳ Nzingha ✳ Alexa Pagonas ✳ Tylibah aka Leebah Baby ✳ Vanessa Turman ✳ Yvette Noel-Schure

....

There you go thinking the grass is greener, but you don't realize it's Astroturf. You want my job, but you don't know what I had to deal with.

—NZINGHA, VETERAN MAKEUP ARTIST IN
MUSIC, FILM, AND TELEVISION

The burning question that fueled the creation of this book—and indeed, that fueled a movement for the enrichment of women in entertainment—is one that follows me to every seminar, panel discussion, roundtable, school visit, and media appearance of my life. "How do you get *in*?!"

People on the outside of our industry ask this of those of us on the inside as if there is one pat answer that fits all. I got in via an internship at a booking agency while freelance writing for indie music and lifestyle magazines. Some go to school for it and actually wind up earning a living in the same field in which they earned their diploma or degree. Others are born into it or grow up in it, with the benevolent hand of nepotism to guide their every step. Others still claw their way into it as a way out of a life of illicit activity. Some were discovered in music videos, talent shows, the Internet. There is no one way to enter the entertainment industry. There is, however, a wrong way: Using your self-esteem as your calling card because you left it in the heap along with your clothes, or set it down to get out your knee pads for that blow job. Women don't get the luxury of sleeping around to climb the ladder without painfully damaging consequences. It's a double standard as old as sexism itself. More important, you have options that don't involve abusing your body.

This book is full of testimony from women who are successful because they used their minds first. They honored themselves with basic operating principles grounded in personal integrity, then established boundaries for others to respect, whether those others shared their principles or not. This is not to say that their careers never suffered for it, that their lives were free of setbacks as a result, or that the boundaries were always honored. It simply means they took and kept a stand for themselves, something I see fewer and fewer women doing as I spend more time in the business. It's no wonder the song lyrics are so disrespectful. It's no shock that being an exotic dancer is the new career aspiration. It's no surprise teenagers want boob jobs and butt implants. We've allowed the boundary to be set by someone other than ourselves. The sooner we get back to the drawing board on parameters for r-e-s-p-e-c-t, the sooner we'll get it, and it'll be more than "just a little bit."

There are infinite answers to the question of how to enter this business successfuly. In this chapter, I am going to zero in on how getting in looks for the first-timers who are complete entertainment virgins, then explore how it can look for women who are moving to another area within the entertainment field. I'll round out the chapter with what's generally okay and what's generally a no-no. Just keep in mind that every instance differs. Honestly, the ways to enter the industry are illuminated throughout the book; the opening chapter is simply going to broadly outline the essentials. My objective is to relieve you of reinventing the wheel, wasting time, or straight-up playing yourself. I'll start out by taking you through my Top Seven List of Biggest Industry Clichés. The stars of the chapter weigh in on them, too.

....

THEMBISA'S TOP SEVEN LIST OF BIGGEST INDUSTRY CLICHÉS
....

1. It's Who You Know

Alexa Pagonas—manager of actors, models, stunt people, and fight chore-ographers for Michael Black Management—confirms that nepotism is alive and well. Being "grandfathered in" is more than just a euphemism. "The grandchildren don't necessarily see that the doors open easier for them,"

Alexa says with a laugh. "Hollywood is at this point multiple generations of nepotism," she continues. "It isn't to say [outsiders] can't get in, but it's a lot easier for those who are already in it. It's a built-in safety mechanism of dealing with people they know. An actor can break through, but the green-lighters don't change."

The who-you-know principle works at every altitude, even the lower ones. Alexa saw this at work while she was attempting to break in. Her example shows that sometimes, those outside the industry are connected to people of influence inside; the key is to always seek out and respectfully use those connections. Check out how this newcomer from San Francisco got a coveted internship spot at ICM: "Throughout college and law school and even in high school, I temped and got the basic secretarial skills—everything from answering phones to using the copy machine. I moved to Los Angeles wanting to get in the business. I kept submitting my résumé, but got no return calls. A woman who also went to Hastings that I didn't really know wanted to work for [politician] Jerry Brown. My mom grew up with him [and referred her]. She got the job and wanted to return the favor." Alexa smiles in hindsight at how fortune had smiled on her. "Her brother worked at ICM. He got me into the training program at ICM as an agent assistant for a great agent, Joe Funicello, who is one of the most stand-up, stellar agents in the business; he taught me a lot. It's not a formalized program, and it's over when you either leave or become an agent. Being someone who has working skills gave me the ability to focus my learning curve on what [I was] really there to learn. [Some interns] couldn't get the basic work done, so they had trouble learning the work of being an agent. Agents have a very specialized skill set. On one hand, they are stockbrokers selling a commodity at a fast pace. They have to have the ability to wine and dine clients and industry people and are spending eighty to a hundred hours a week at that high pace." Add to that consuming work schedule a very rigid and archaic workplace culture, and spending so much time at the office starts to make less and less sense, especially if you want a life outside the agency.

"On a wider frame, agencies are very patriarchal with a hedonistic attitude toward business relationships: *Get what you can now and get out,*" Alexa continues. "Not necessarily that they don't want girls to play, but the skills and attitudes they use are based on the male model with no enlightenment toward family issues. No child care, no flex time for caregiving. It just didn't fit me." I submit that's not going to fit many women, which is why so many agents are male. Alexa will talk in depth about working with men (among other things) in chapter 8, where I focus on television and film production.

2. You Only Get One Chance to Make a First Impression

Fanzine journalist turned über-publicist Yvette Noel-Schure has a great anecdote for women out there who think the route to a job is showing skin instead of skills. That may have worked when men did all the hiring, and there may be some pockets of Girl Friday fantasy lingering at independent companies run by chauvinist dinosaurs, but overall, *Ladies free before 11* attire is your enemy. Yvette describes an internship interview gone wrong for a scantily clad candidate. "It's not about being down, it's about business. The first impression is everything. And as a publicist you've gotta be dressed to close the pitch. You never know where you'll have to go, because a pitch may come up if a story falls out. I had an intern come in whose skirt was so short that I had to give her a scarf so she could sit down. When my male counterpart left [the room], I closed the door and spoke to her. I said, 'You're brilliant and ready to even be an assistant, but what were you thinking? I think you have the wrong idea about what we do here.' She didn't get the job."

3. You Never Know Who's Watching

Jennifer Coles wound up an agent after being disenchanted with radio, the field she thought she was destined to pursue after majoring in rhetoric and communications studies at the University of Richmond. Following an internship at a radio station, she accepted a sales job at a media company and spent a year there before she got her big break. And it came from a guy who didn't even have a job to offer her, only a referral to another position at an agency.

"Being at the station and working in every department from sales and promotions to dealing with the personalities, it became clear to me that as much as I loved it, everything was based around money. Talent had so many restrictions on them they were becoming machines. One of the station managers linked me up to a cable sales media company in New York. That opened my eyes to the different aspects of TV: how they find actors, researching the shows, learning the relationship between ad sales and programming. I was there for a year and though I didn't love the job, I learned a lot from it," she reflects. Though dissatisfied, Jennifer did not leave her job, she just kept hunting for her next one, which came from an unlikely source. "I applied for everything entertainment, be it PR or promotions. I got a call from a [senior staffer at] one of New York's larger stations, and he told me to sit tight. Then a week later he called me with an assistant job for a talent agency. It was so weird, but the guy was nice enough to refer me. We have champions and sometimes we don't know who they are. They see things in you that you don't think they see; our interview led to something better for me, and he must have picked up on that. You just never know who's looking, who needs you."

4. Gotta Pay Your Dues

Lyricist, Alvin Ailey–trained dancer, and self-published author Tylibah has been working to create and record her first album since she was a child putting on shows for her family in the living room. Once she finished high school, she began to meet established emcees, producers, and B-level managers, all of whom had sexual conditions they wanted her to meet in order to get any work done. Though it delayed her timetable considerably, those were the kinds of dues Tylibah was raised not to pay. "Words can't describe the level of resistance I encountered," she says, sighing. "I was surprised at these male celebrities who were already on but were standing in my way. Most people only want to help themselves." In Tylibah's case, they wanted to help themselves to a beautiful, naive twenty-year-old in bed with them. "My mother was the test. If I brought her around, would you still be down to help me? She brought out the fact that people's intentions weren't right to begin with. One of my mistakes was being too hungry and anxious. People would manipulate that energy and desire to be famous."

Tylibah's definition of paying dues is a powerful one. It takes all the perceived drudgery out of it, making it an opportunity for development. "Paying dues is acknowledging that you are a baby that wants to grow up. It's paying homage, not being diminished. It is sitting at the elders' feet and asking intelligent questions and showing appreciation for who they are. Paying dues is not disrespecting myself for you."

Stephanie Abdullah, personal publicist to Bobby Brown as well as US Army Entertainment Division liaison, makes a salient point about the whole dues-paying thing. "The higher up the ladder you get, the more you want, so the more dues you end up having to pay to get where you're trying to go. As you ascend and achieve, the doors won't go away; you'll just [have] the keys to open them from the dues you've paid. Just like membership dues, the dues we pay create access." Speaking of access . . .

5. Honor the Keeper of the Gate

I came into the business as a booking agency gatekeeper, first for Lupe DeLeon at DeLeon Artists, then for Bruce Solar at Absolute Artists. It is absolutely true that your success in contacting the boss is in direct proportion to the good, kind treatment you lavish upon the Keeper of the Gate. Which also means that the more of a dismissive pest you are with him or her, the more likely you are to be dropped into the voice-mail abyss, never to be heard from again. Being nasty and condescending gets you nowhere with gatekeepers, period.

To be clear, the treatment itself need not be lavish, but you must lavish good treatment upon gatekeepers. Usually, speaking to them like human beings with lives is all it takes. Ask their names. Note these in your database. Use them when you call. Be friendly. Don't be nosy or long-winded — gatekeepers are fielding hundreds of call each day — but find out what matters to them and make it a point of connection between you. Find out how best to communicate to the boss, and follow those instructions. Be among the people gatekeepers look forward to hearing from, and your request or message will work its way up the To-Do or Return-Call list. And when they help you get on the phone with the person they are guarding, acknowledge gatekeepers with a note or token of thanks, especially if you wind up getting the face-to-face meeting you've always wanted. At that point, it is a good idea to come bearing gifts, no matter how small, from a Starbucks or Container Store gift card to a bouquet. You can take it a step farther and sing their praises to their boss. One of two scenarios will come from creating good rapport with gatekeepers, who are sometimes also assistants or managers. They'll either keep their gate for what seems like an eternity no matter where their boss ends up working; or they'll move on and remember your kindness, whether they end up keeping a different gate or becoming executives in their own right. No matter how you slice it, exercising the Golden Rule means a slam dunk for you!

On the other side of this, gatekeepers who abuse their power run rampant. There are few things as uncool as a nasty gatekeeper who gets off on condescending to cold calls and wielding the power of *no*. These people would do well to bear in mind that they could be the hot assistant one week and jobless the next.

I recommend that when you encounter fire-breathing monsters at the gate, try slaying them with kindness. If that fails, I say go over their heads and lovingly share your experience with said dragon with decision makers. If they want dragons keeping their gates, fine—but no one likes being disrespected or missing a potentially beneficial opportunity. In the rare times I run up against situations like this, I express myself to the dragon's boss. Don't feel like a snitch: The gatekeepers told on themselves with their stank behavior!

6. Hey . . . Stranger Things Have Happened

The magic of our business is that you just never know how the opportunities will present themselves. If you subscribe to the Law of Attraction—most recently been popularized by Rhonda Byrne's *The Secret*—then you understand the idea that what you speak into existence is what the Universe will conspire to deliver right at your feet.

Vanessa Turman, Universal Music communications director, whom I have dubbed the Wireless Pimp, has worked in A&R (artist and repertoire) administration, marketing, and management for MCA, Epic, and C&C Music Factory, respectively. Hers was the most unlikely turn of events imaginable for entry into the business. And it holds true that yes, stranger things have happened, so don't be surprised at the twists and turns that characterize your entry point.

"I ended up in the music business after listening to Jody Watley's hit song 'Looking for a New Love.' I was in the United States Navy. While home on leave, a promoter was handing out her vinyl single on 125th Street. I went back to Puerto Rico and when I heard it I thought, *Oh my God, this is a hit!* Once I had her whole album, I thought to myself, *This girl should get a Grammy*," recalls Vanessa. What she never anticipated was that she'd go from listening to Jody's album to standing right next to her. "How blessed was I that once I came out of the navy, I got a job at Radio City Music Hall. My very first big production was to be Jody Watley's escort at the 1988 Grammys! I remember her telling me she wasn't going to win Best New Artist because Terence Trent D'Arby was a shoo-in. When she won, I screamed louder than anyone in the place. At that moment I knew I was [the next] Berry Gordy," Vanessa says, laughing. "I had found my calling."

Stephanie Abdullah recounts how she literally declared herself into becoming the publicist for the Bad Boy of New Edition. "When I was in college, my *dream job* was to work for Bobby Brown. That was when Bobby

Brown was on top of the world. Nobody was bigger than him. I was like, 'I'm going to be Bobby's publicist.' I even knew him at the time. I've known him since probably the beginning of his career, but saying that I want to work for Bobby Brown as a college student . . . you don't ever really think that that's *really* gonna happen. By the time it actually happened, I had gotten away from that dream, I wasn't chasing that particular thing anymore. But I had already put it out into the universe, so the universe was already putting things into effect for me for that to manifest." Stephanie bumped into Bobby at an event and, out of habit, started introducing him to people and getting him photo ops. It was 2004, and although Bobby's top-of-the-world status had long since been usurped by crooners half his age, he was now on the verge of becoming Black America's next top reality star. Stephanie's stars had aligned at last. "By the end of the night Bobby said, 'I want you to be my publicist.' I was like . . . *'What?!'* I was completely thrown off, forgetting that this is what I said I wanted."

7. Don't Mix Business with Pleasure

Nefertiti Strong has been in the business since she was fifteen years old. I think she's occupied every entertainment position there is, except maybe personal manager. No, really. She was a rapper turned actor long before most emcees had the idea, starring in *Panther.* She got bit by the movie bug and took her talents behind the camera, working as music supervisor, film director, set designer, screenwriter, and vice president of development for Patriot Pictures. After the deaths of her good friends Tupac Shakur and Christopher "Notorious B.I.G." Wallace, she put down the mic, saying, "If this is what hip-hop is, I'm out." She didn't record again until 2006, collaborating with Latin alternative rock band Kinky on *Reina,* which garnered a Latin Grammy nomination. If that's not hitting the bull's-eye on the first shot, I don't know what is.

With all the circles she runs in and serves as a connector for, Nefertiti has had infinite opportunities to mix business with pleasure, but—as she is prone to do—she flipped that script, too. "Mixing business with friendship and great energy is a yes because people like to do business with people that they feel reflect themselves. Trust is key in the business," she offers. "You have to make people feel that they're important and give them a reason to want to involve you in their endeavors. I think if you come at if from a sexual standpoint, you really limit yourself. Mixing business with pleasure is always a no-no. Always keep yourself professional, trustworthy, true to yourself and to others." Reputation is the ultimate currency in life as well as business, but especially in the entertainment business, where credentials are subjective at best and negligible at worst. Since there is no unified qualifier for being in the game, all you really have is your name, your word, and your work. The business–pleasure mix can sully your reputation irreparably, and if you're just starting out, you need your stock to go up, not down.

GETTING IN ALL OVER AGAIN

We've sufficiently covered the basics of getting in for the first-timers, but what about when you're already in and you seek entry to another area within the entertainment world? Usually at this point you've gotten older, and your ambition, hunger, energy level, or all of the above have taken a beating from time served to date. More to the point, you're grown and have commitments to maintain: mortgages, relationships, families. The whole fifty-hour-a-week unpaid internship thing is *so* not hapnin'.

Nzingha, makeup artist and CEO of ZFACE, Inc., is probably best known for the indelible beauty mark she left on the urban music world. She beat the faces of Mary J. Blige and Lil' Kim for M•A•C's Viva Glam campaign, and has counted Janet Jackson and Aaliyah among her celebrity clients, working on music videos or on tour with the biggest names in the business of hip-hop and R&B. She describes her transition out of music into film and TV makeup as critical to her survival. She had seen the business start to deteriorate in the late 1990s, and the abuse she experienced as an entourage member was chipping away at her spirit.

"I believe God moved me from music to film. I did not pursue film or TV; that was not on the front burner. What I saw was part of the future [of the music business] and it didn't look lovely. It didn't treat people well. And the artists were changing. When you have people around you that say yes to you all the time because they want to keep their jobs, their attitudes change."

Nzingha got her Exit Stage Next wake-up call while she was on the road. She hit her emotional rock bottom. "I was in Germany. I was on tour with a hip-hop/R&B artist. I woke up in the middle of the night in this beautiful bed and hotel room, crying my eyes out. I was crying because I had been disrespected publicly, I was treated poorly, I was exhausted, and I was on call twenty-four hours. If the artist moves, you gotta be there so they can look 100 percent. You're in your PJs, ready to go to bed—and they're ready to go to the club. And the next day I have to be up hours before them to prepare. It was a miserable experience. The hairstylist and I were sharing a room. And as I was crying, *she* was crying. And I asked her what was going on. She was like, 'I can't do this anymore.' And I said, 'You know what, neither can I. Once we leave Germany I'm done.' She stayed on for a while, but not everyone has the same revelation you have at the same time; they may need to get a little deeper into whatever that thing is. She wound up shooting a music video and they put her off the boat and left her. *In the water.* And she could not swim. She dog-paddled back to shore. And I was the first person she called because my number was very easy then. She said, 'It's officially over.' And she was devastated. But I wasn't surprised. That stylist is completely out of the industry. She went back to the salon and has her sanity and life intact."

Even though it felt like she was starting from scratch after a twenty-year career as an A-list music industry makeup artist, Nzingha welcomed the opportunity to get her own life back with open arms. She went without working for more than a year before she was hired as Diana Ross's makeup artist for the TV movie *Double Platinum.* The toughest thing about the transition, however, was her personal loss, not a professional one. "In the same year I was making my career transition, I lost my mother and six other people," she explains. "Two of them were my financial advisers, one of them was friend and client Aaliyah"—who perished in a plane crash after shooting "Rock the Boat" in the Bahamas along with eight other victims, including label staffers and entourage members. Nzingha was almost on that shoot. "I had gotten a call to work on the 'Rock the Boat' video, but I was unavailable because my mother was going through chemotherapy. So I really began to look at what I thought this life was about," she says, blinking back tears. "Then it was thousands of people lost in the World Trade Center and the war on the economy. I had to examine what was a necessity and what was a luxury."

Nzingha also took a noticeable pay cut in the transition, something we all must be prepared to do for the more important end goal of changing lanes. "It was a huge shock that I was making in a week what I used to make in a day," Nzingha says. "The music makeup artists were also shocked that I crossed over. They knew I was pulling in more money in music that I was on any film. What they didn't know was that I was crying in my hotel room in

Germany. The money is substantially different, but I actually have time to have a life." That life includes a new career in makeup with credits like *Project Runway, Wifey,* and *The Sopranos* for television, and *Spider-Man 3, I Am Legend,* and *American Gangster* on the film side. When we spote, she'd just wrapped *Push,* Lee Daniels's film adaptation of Sapphire's best seller starring Mo'Nique and Paula Patton, produced by Lisa Cortes, who shares her story in chapter 9.

Stephanie Abdullah has a truly miraculous story of survival in transition. While she was a publicist in civilian life, she has been an army reservist for nineteen years, which included a two-year tour in Iraq. Like Nzingha, Stephanie had an epiphany about her career handed to her by the realities of the world around her. "My major in college was nursing," Stephanie notes. "My first ten years as a reserve soldier, I was a medic. I met a woman who was in the Sixty-third Regional Readiness Command. She was in public affairs, and here I had been in the army for about ten or eleven years at this point, [and] had never even known that this existed in the army! Here I am being a medic, miserable, because I had changed my major from nursing a long time ago. [Meeting her] was my a-ha moment. I immediately started finding out how I could re-class from being a medic to getting into public affairs. I transferred into an actual mobile public affairs detachment."

While in Iraq, she served her country by documenting the experiences of her fellow soldiers with written and on-camera testimony, reporting her findings back to the Department of Defense. "Suddenly, my civilian life and my army life were somewhat parallel, except that in the army when they're talking public affairs, you're doing the whole shebang. I'm the media person, the journalist, interviewing the soldiers, writing the articles. My two lives started to marry, and I began to actually enjoy being a soldier. I'm at the US Army office of the chief of public affairs in Los Angeles now. It's the army's entertainment liaison office. I love it and they love me. And in my civilian life, I'm an entertainment industry publicist. I'm just in awe. It's beautiful. I feel captured by grace."

....
RELOCATION, RELOCATION, RELOCATION
....

Whether, when, and how to pack up, leave your hometown, and make your mark in the entertainment world can be a real source of fear and frustration. It's fraught with so much tension because when you do it, it not only represents a huge leap of faith, but also bring you face-to-face with your own fears of both failure and success. For me, I had a nationally recognized position in the heart of beautiful San Francisco, truly the best of both worlds. I was the rap editor for the *Gavin Report,* an industry trade magazine of charts, features, and reviews whose positioning line was "The Most Trusted Name in Radio." And while I was very powerful in the worlds of radio and music trade publishing, I started to need a bigger challenge at about the three-year mark. The rap editors before me, Brian Alan Samson and Kelly Woo, both wound up moving to Los Angeles to take promotions jobs. After being the one promo reps and publicists alike pitched to and schmoozed, I had no desire to be on the pitching side. And therein lay my dilemma. I was at the top of the Bay Area music scene's food chain. To stay in the business on my level as a music industry writer, I was going to have to take my show on the road, either back home to Los Angeles or all the way out to crowded, crazy, snowy-in-winter-and-humid-all-summer New York.

The conclusion I came to was that I if I was going to move, I needed a job to move to, especially if I was headed to the Big Apple. I had been there on business trips. For me, New York was a heady mix of exhilaration and overwhelm that—as a laid-back Cali girl—I had a tough time imagining as my daily existence. I wasn't opposed to the idea, but I definitely wasn't moving there with a polka-dot bag on a stick living on people's couches like you hear about so often. And since I refused to quit my job and relocate to LA, where I could have always moved back in with family (*not*), I waited for the right job. Well, I ended up waiting more than two years. That was the downside; the excruciating hours, unforgiving weekly deadlines, and increasingly urgent need to produce advertising revenue at substantial percentage increases were taking their toll. And then one morning I got a call from a cat named Chris Wilder. He was an associate director of advertising for Sony Music. He wanted to know if I'd be interested in interviewing for an advertising copywriter position! My prayers were being answered! I took him up on the offer to apply, though the only ads I had ever written were in-house *Gavin* pieces, plus a couple of label ads. I forwarded what little I had with my résumé and flew to New York for the interview. Did I mention I would have to move to New York? That was a requirement. Despite Sony having plush Los Angeles offices, the advertising and creative services departments' headquarters were rightfully on Madison Avenue in Manhattan. It looked more and more like I was going to wind up leaving my heart in San Francisco, just like Columbia/Sony recording legend Tony Bennett.

I interviewed over a wonderful lunch at the Red Eye Grill with advertising directors Steve Sussmann and Michael Schwartz. I nailed the interview, and fortunately I had upward of five years' worth of weekly columns, features, and special issues as a columnist and editor to make up for what I lacked in direct advertising experience. Since I was on the Left Coast, we agreed that I would write ads as a test for a while so they could see if I could do the job—and I could see if I liked it enough to uproot my life. I was a newlywed. My husband was going to school full-time while running an independent music marketing and street promotion business as the Bay Area representative for several major labels. He is a San Francisco native. Aside from Los Angeles, the farthest he'd lived from the City by the Bay was just across the Bay Bridge in Oakland. As ready as I was to leave the job I had, I was gonna have to really like this copywriting gig.

The first ad I wrote was for rapper and Fugees affiliate John Forté, whose first single was "Poli Sci." I realized while I was creating headlines for it that I enjoyed the work. To my surprise, they selected one of my lines! The ad ran in all the trade magazines, including *Gavin*. When the test ad I wrote appeared next to my own column, I knew God was trying to tell me something. I listened. Then I talked it over with my husband. He said, "If you get the job, I'll follow you, babe. I can go to school anywhere." After a few more test ads and a few weeks of negotiating with Sony human resources, I got the job. They would not give me money to relocate, but they did increase my annual salary. I announced my resignation and flew east to find an apartment.

Upon my return, Geoffrey Peete threw my husband, Tmor, and me a huge star-studded send-off at his popular nightclub, Geoffrey's Inner Circle. We packed everything we owned into a Ryder truck with my Ford Escort hitched to the back. I dropped the car off in LA with my sister. I didn't want to bring it just to drag it back if things didn't work out. Outside of a stop at the Grand Canyon, my husband drove for nine nights straight, give or take the hour or two I contributed every other day. When we reached our Jersey City apartment, I was grateful for the New York friends I'd made through *Gavin*. The late rap promotions guru and Mixtape Awards founder Justo, music marketer James Azor, and his homeboy Mark, were literally outside waiting to unload the truck. "Welcome to the N-Y, baby!" Justo bellowed with a hug for me and a pound for Tmor. If he had told me then that we would live and work here for more than a decade, I would have never believed him, but that's exactly what happened.

While my relocation was very measured, strategic, and protracted, that of host talent agent Jennifer Coles was the opposite. When she made the cross-country leap from New York to Hollywood, she had no place to live, and in hindsight she realizes she stressed out more than she needed to. "I asked friends for direction on real estate agents and neighborhoods to expedite the move. I was subletting, but I set a maximum of seven days in the sublet," she says. "That motivated me to be proactive in my search. Having friends where you're going is a big help." The one thing she did make sure of was that she had a paycheck waiting. "I felt like I had to have a job to come from New York to LA. It would have been hard to move and find a job," Jennifer says. "Trying to get adjusted without one is scary."

Stephanie let that fear of the adjustment stop her for years before she moved to Los Angeles from Oakland. She realized she had "allowed her fear to paralyze" her during an e-mail exchange with a girlfriend. "I was kind of just muddling along in the Bay. I was doing okay, but I really wanted to be doing it bigger and better. My [relocation] a-ha moment was over e-mail with a high school friend of mine who was living in Los Angeles. She was just telling me all these things that she was doing in LA. I was thinking, *What is going on here? Why haven't I taken the step?* Literally, one day over e-mail I'm typing to her and I'm saying to her what I had been thinking, what I had wanted to do for all these years because I graduated college in '95 and now it's August of 1998. I remember that as I was typing the e-mail, I just changed my sentence from 'I've always wanted to do this' to 'I'm getting ready to do this, I'm going to move to Los Angeles and I'm going to pursue my dream of being an entertainment publicist.' From that day, I went from thinking about to talking about it and being about it! I mean, I'm talking apartment searching, the whole thing. It took probably about five or six months but then I landed here, started the LA hustle, and bam—here I am. You know . . . I could've not done it . . . I could've still been in Oakland. [I] probably would've had a decent job and made an okay living. But now I can say that I had a dream, I thought about it, I talked about it, I prayed about it, and I'm actually doing it."

THE WORK–LIFE BALANCE MYTH

Yeah, I said it. Balancing work and family is a myth. While PDAs and laptops allow us to seem like we're in many places at once, in the physical realm we have yet to clone ourselves. Until that day, we're left with the choice to make our passion for work *and* our love for our spouses, partners, children, and families both work. As a wife of twelve years who has seen many an industry couple implode, and as a mother who has been the ear and shoulder for countless single parents, I am clear that *balance* in this scenario is nonapplicable. Once I discovered work-life *function*, I became a much more successful wife.

My choice to make a family and personal life work looked like me giving up my ninety-plus-hour-a-week job for one where I could actually leave the office at six o'clock without my boss looking at me sideways. Thankfully, you don't have to be a homemaker in the twenty-first century, but if you want to nurture a committed relationship and raise children, you do need to be home. And while I was working at *Gavin,* I was barely ever home. I was either in the office or out at clubs, radio stations, retail outlets, concerts . . . my professional life was my personal life. I was always in work mode.

Ironically, when I got to New York I was pulling down fewer hours a week. Outside of preparing for campaign presentations and shoots, my weekends belonged to me. Being home at 6:30 PM means being home for dinner instead of dinner meetings with a promotion rep. It allows for a date with my husband on weekend evenings when I might otherwise be networking at an industry event. Now that my son is here, my weekends are split between him and me, since my husband's the one working weekends in real estate. I am much happier running him from sports camp at Chelsea Piers to play dates and parties than I was making appearances at every event just to stay ahead of whatever and whoever was the next big thing. I still go out, but I am much more selective because my work as a tastemaker has grown and shifted. I'm not part of the underground anymore. I helped take it mainstream, so that's where I reside now. As a creative, I get my creative food from multiple sources: museums, theater, gardens, travel, community events. All things I don't have to leave the family to engage in.

Yvette Noel-Schure has made her work and home life function for over twenty-five years, but not without sacrifices by her husband and both their families to make sure her three children didn't miss out on their mother. This harmony we seek between work life and home life requires an orchestra of support from the village of which the African proverb speaks. Yvette describes how her family had gathered around her before her career took off, starting with "three people with one name, my husband, my husband, my husband. He doesn't have the hang-ups many have about roles. I got married my first year of college and had my son my second year. I would go to school four days and be home twice a week as often as I could. My husband ran an ice cream parlor in the Village at night. We crossed each other a lot on the stairs. As my career changed, we asked a family member to help with the younger children. After September 11, we vowed to change our lives and opted not to chase two incomes. My husband works from home and I am out gallivantin', as my grandmother says." She laughs. "I have the most unconventional job in the family and I have missed a lot, but not when it comes to the kids. When there's a boo-boo to blow, I blow it. I don't miss recitals or meets. I am on the five-thirty bus so I can be at dinner by seven if it kills me! The girls of Destiny's Child would tease me because I was always going home right after a job. The paycheck is not for me, it's for the family."

Nzingha has a wake-up call for us women who aren't keeping track of the time as we climb the career ladder. "All the stuff you want to do—get married, have kids—guess what? The higher you go, the more it ain't hapnin'. The fight gets harder, and you're fighting to keep your very life. I want to share a quote for those who don't know what they're getting into or how deep the rabbit hole goes," Nzingha adds. "It's from *All About Eve* where Margo Channing is talking to her friend Karen about climbing up the ladder." Here's that sage wisdom, from the 1950 classic by Joseph L. Mankiewicz:

MARGO

The things you drop on your way up the ladder, so you can move faster. You forget you'll need them again when you get back to being a woman. That's one career all females have in common—whether we like it or not—being a woman. Sooner or later we've got to work at it, no matter how many other careers we've had or wanted. And in the last analysis, nothing is any good unless you can look up just before dinner or turn around in bed—and there he is. Without that, you're not a woman.

As long the myth of balance is playing in your head, you'll be looking for everything to balance out. The truth is, creating a relationship and making the time to be in one is up to you. You have to put the brakes on to be available for your partner. Sure, he or she is going to feel insecure and intimidated if you're hardly there, because he or she barely knows you. Relationships need time invested, the same way careers do. If the only muscle you're flexin' is your career muscle, your relationship muscles will weaken and atrophy to the point that you forget how to even *be* in a relationship. That's how so many of us end up married to our careers, pushin' forty or more, lonely as hell, with all our self-esteem and identity intertwined with what we do to the point that when we lose the job, we lose ourselves. "I've gone to a lot of panels that are allegedly about balancing career and family," Stephanie says with a chuckle. "What I actually end up hearing is a lot of people having one or the other. You may have a very successful single mom because the husband couldn't stick around, couldn't go along with her drive. I think women can have both, but at different times. You have to choose which one you want." Stephanie chose family, and in her case, even after demonstrating her commitment, her spouse could not support her line of work. "I haven't had any children. I wish I had; I had a husband but he didn't stick around because it wasn't so much that I chose a career, it was the career I chose. He was very intimidated by it."

The pain we endure as we endeavor to make it all work is very real. In Stephanie's case, her marriage was crippling her career instead of supporting it, as was the case with Yvette. But her failure at the relationship itself almost took her under. Stephanie's divorce was devastating to her. In the darkness of its aftermath, she learned how strong she really was. "I went through an emotional breakdown directly related to going through a divorce," she reflects, "and right before [that,] I got laid off at the PR firm where I worked. Even though that was like a blessing because I didn't want to work there anymore, I figured I was out of a job and the whole marriage was collapsing . . . it was a very traumatic time. I found myself waking up laying in the middle of the floor crying every day. Eventually I crawled out of bed one day and ended up seeing someone at a mental health clinic in Hollywood. They gave me medication, told me how to take it, and said I'd start to get relief in a month. I was like, 'A month?!' With the anxiety and pain I was feeling, if I had to endure another four weeks I would not be around for the medication to take effect. I put those meds in my closet and never took them. I knew then I had to draw on strength from God. I had one friend who stepped me through all this, but I didn't turn to a lot of individuals. I turned to the power of prayer. I started to call my energy back and transform it. It was very spiritual, intense, very conscious and targeted. Once I changed the way I was thinking about my life, my whole life changed."

Stephanie's testimony is an offering to anyone starting out in the business. The lesson she learned in the middle of her career is one you can implement at the start of yours. Commit to making yourself work, however that looks for you—be it through religious or spiritual practice, self-improvement, wellness, mediation, yoga . . . the list goes on. The more centered you are, the better prepared you will be for the inevitable curve-balls this game will throw your way.

SUMMARY OF SECRETS REVEALED

WHAT YOU THOUGHT YOU KNEW:

This is a quick and easy business to get into.

WHAT YOU NEED TO KNOW:

The overnight sensation is a *myth*. By the time you're receiving a first impression of artists or executives, they've already been on the grind for years.

WHAT YOU THOUGHT YOU KNEW:

I don't have any transferable skills for a career in music or movies. My last job was as a cashier at Jack in the Box!

WHAT YOU NEED TO KNOW:

If Stephanie had believed that, she wouldn't be the player in publicity she is today, with Bobby Brown, one of the most controversial stars in music or television, as her biggest client. You gained something in that food service or retail job; you just have to pay attention and zero in on it.

Stephanie explains, "Speaking of Jack in the Box, [I worked at one in] Oakland on 76th and East 14th street, at sixteen years old. This is an area where drug dealers basically hang. Essentially [it] was their restaurant! I just remember a big gang of guys coming in all ordering things, this plus this, extra that . . . I did not get any training, I was just put straight on the register.

There was one person paying for everyone's food. Of course, his order was not right when he got it. He threw this hamburger at me over the counter.

"What I think I carried from that particular position is a thick skin. This is an industry where you have to have some thick skin. You also have to get into places and train yourself. There are not a lot of opportunities where people are babysitting you through your positions and your projects; you [often] have to come in and hit the ground running."

WHAT YOU THOUGHT YOU KNEW:

Since I'm new at this, I should learn by watching.

WHAT YOU NEED TO KNOW:

Most of what the best in the business know, they learned by watching and *doing*. Don't just stand there! Ask what's needed, then take the initiative to provide it.

WHAT YOU THOUGHT YOU KNEW:

I don't have as many transferable skills as I need to move into another area of the industry.

WHAT YOU NEED TO KNOW:

You absolutely do have enough to hit the ground running, especially if you are doing the same work. In fact, your level of expertise might surprise you once you get out of your previous bubble. That's what happened for Nzingha. "I definitely had to flex muscles I didn't have to in music," she observes. "There was a lot of humility involved. I had to create characters and effects whereas everything in music was always about beauty. I had to pare my makeup down and break down scripts." On the other hand, Nzingha brought a fresh level of skill to the film and TV side that made her a valuable asset and got her more work. "The other makeup artists on the set had never seen a face beat like I was beating them," she says, laughing. "I was servin' the Black girls and the white girls. The department heads just started referring me."

WHAT YOU THOUGHT YOU KNEW:

Since I'm just getting started, I need to work in an established area of the business for added security.

WHAT YOU NEED TO KNOW:

First off, security in entertainment is a rare gem. Don't go looking for it right off the bat; it will seriously hamper your search! Besides, the opposite may in fact be true. Going into a new growth area will allow you to gain expertise that sets you apart in the game without the added strain of heavy competition. Jen Coles is a host talent agent, a gig given new life by the explosion of the reality genre. "I'm not in a theatrical or commercial department where there are ten agents who [are] all trying to make their numbers. I work at one of the few agencies with a hosting division, and not a lot of people know the hosting end of the business."

WHAT YOU THOUGHT YOU KNEW:

I can balance it all — work, great relationship, family, children — and take care of myself, too.

WHAT YOU NEED TO KNOW:

You can make it all work. Balancing it all implies you can have all things equal. In the real world, however, you must choose where you will invest your time and commitment. This does not mean you go without the great career, sustainable relationship, and motherhood. It simply means you must be satisfied with being present to and focusing on each one in the moment. Hours spent at work mean less for your partner. Hours spent at home mean less time for work. That's the reality. Accept it and stop killing yourself for a career. The truth is, you want and deserve a symphony for a life, not just one note. Instead of work-life balance, strive for work-life function.

CHAPTER 2

She's Playing Your Song: Radio, Deejaying, and Turntablism

Cathy Hughes ✳ Cristal Bubblin' ✳ Darnella Dunham ✳
DD Artis ✳ DJ Kuttin Kandi ✳ DJ Mecca ✳ DJ Reborn ✳
DJ Princess Cut ✳ Monie Love ✳ Motion ✳ Jennifer
Norwood ✳ Raqiyah Mays ✳ Steph Lova

*Being female isn't the hard part. What's hard is remaining
open enough to show ignorant people that a woman can do
the work.*

—DJ Reborn

KICK IN THE DOOR

Quite honestly, there is no surefire way into radio. Yes, you can attend college for broadcasting and journalism, or trade school for engineering and TV/radio production. But many of the people I met in the radio industry came in just the way I did: by a fortunate turn of events outside anyone's original plan. Having a broadcasting degree no more guarantees you'll get into radio than having a degree in any field assures you'll pursue a career in it. My bachelor of arts is in international relations, and my booking agency internship steered me as far from that as I could have imagined, right into the record business. I ended up working at a radio trade magazine right out of college. I am the first African American female music editor and still the youngest rap editor the magazine ever had. The *Gavin Report* was a music trade magazine founded by Bill Gavin and based in San Francisco. Because Bill Gavin's credo was not to sell favorable record reviews and editorial in exchange for advertising, it was the one music industry tipsheet that broke artists because its music editors believed in them, not because their record label had cut a check. The *Gavin Report* also hosted legendary annual confabs for the radio and records communities called the Gavin Seminar, where independent and major-label acts alike had an equal shot at exposure to the people who controlled radio playlists: program directors, music directors, and mixshow DJs. Before its demise in 2002 due to steady declines in profit and a failure to sell the property amid consolidation of labels and stations alike, for an artist, being on the cover of *Gavin* for all the industry to see was up there with gracing the cover of *Rolling Stone* for music consumers. It was confirmation that you were next to blow—and that if you didn't, the music was not to blame. I took the power I had to take artists to their next level very seriously. I never wasted a cover. And with every cover, I exposed a side of the artist no other magazine would delve into. This gave me an editorial edge over my competitors, and it also paved the way for lasting relationships with people like Scarface, Common, and Chuck D. I am blessed to have worked at *Gavin* during hip-hop's explosion into the mainstream; a time when I can clearly recollect diversity of sound and commercial success within the genre. From 1993 to 1998, I witnessed the rise of Snoop Dogg, the battle between Common and Ice Cube, the off-the-hook lead single ("Dead Presidents") from a new Brooklyn cat named Jay-Z with his own label, Roc-A-Fella Records; I kicked off the solo debut of Busta Rhymes, picking up where my predecessor Kelly Woo left off in assuring the dominance of Wu-Tang Clan and the Fugees. I pumped my fist at the zenith of hip-hop girl power, from the first-ever gold album for Queen Latifah's *Black Reign* and the first-ever gold single for MC Lyte, "Ruffneck," to the arrival of Missy Elliott, Mystic, Lil' Kim, Conscious Daughters, Bahamadia, and The Lady of Rage, whom I was fortunate to interview exclusively for *Gavin* before her long-awaited debut hit stores. Shanti Das, then the director of promotion at LaFace, asked me if I thought "Elevators" by Outkast was a hit, and believed me when I said "Hell yes!" I had the foresight to give Common and D'Angelo their first national cover stories. I worked hard to get the exclusive trade interview with an unorthodox young producer out of Virginia named Timbaland who used babies, dogs, birds, and crickets in his beats. I eulogized 2Pac in print through his poetry when the national press vilified him in the aftermath of his own murder. Six months later in my San Francisco office, I watched Christopher "Notorious B.I.G." Wallace in rare form, a true master of the dozens, against Lil' Cease, over salmon croquettes and grits. I was snapping Polaroids with Biggie four days before six bullets stole his breath in Los Angeles. I still marvel at the fact that I actually got to kick it with Aaliyah, hip-hop soul's earth angel. I laughed hard, partied hard, cried hard. I was truly blessed to start my career getting paid to do what I loved all day, week after week, for five years: write about and listen to music. And though I was not in a radio station every day, I broke artists every Thursday with my charts, spoke to three hundred stations a week, and bridged the gap between college and community stations and the labels that needed them like oxygen, before crossover radio embraced emcees. My *Like That!* column set the standard for the hip-hop radio industry. And just like that, I worked in radio.

It was definitely tough in the beginning. I had to learn all the *Gavin* song coding chart technology—how to take reports from station DJs and input them into our chart program—in about a week, before my predecessor relocated to LA for his new label job. I had to forge relationships with all the national label reps in promotion, and all the urban marketing reps as well. Since I came onto the national music scene from Absolute Artists, a boutique Bay Area booking agency (read: out of nowhere for the rap music industry), I encountered some resistance from a couple of executives. Thankfully, *Gavin* management supported my way of running the rap format enough not to bow to the egos of advertisers.

As a female, it was important that I maintain a professional level of interaction with male promotion and marketing reps, and my bosses understood that. I was not going to be provocative or flirt with cats to get advertising. The column's integrity was going to do that instead. The one place I was underestimated by the higher-ups was in actually running the rap department. I made it clear that I was not going to be dominated by rap promotion execs who had to look good to their VPs. And yet, at the same time, I never made anyone wrong for having an ego that was out of control, or brandishing a sexist attitude that had never been brought to their attention, let alone challenged by a woman in a position of power relative to their own.

I had worked with serious OGs (original gangstas) in the music game by comparison in my previous job: people who *really* didn't take any shit. People whose name and catalog meant they didn't have to: Bootsy Collins, Stanley Turrentine, Shirley Horn, Bobby Hutcherson, Etta James, Junior Walker, Charles Brown, Gil Scott-Heron. While most of the time, these artists and their managers were great with me, some music veterans could be intimidating, condescending, and outright nasty, especially under the pressures of constantly being on the road, and in some cases—names withheld out of respect—almost constantly being under the influence of something. Granted, I was only twenty-one. But there was no way I was gonna let another twenty-something with a six-figure record company job put me at risk of losing my five-figure job. I worked for the subscribers (radio stations, DJs, and artists' handlers) as much as I did for the advertisers (labels). I made sure the record reps knew that. And that gave me credibility with the jocks, whom the labels always need, and who, at the time, used *Gavin* as their vehicle for exerting influence over or at least making an impression at radio.

Although I was well educated, had a vast knowledge of jazz and soul by virtue of my upbringing and my agency job, knew hip-hop backward and forward, and even had clips to demonstrate my writing ability, in the eyes of the senior management either my age, my inexperience at the magazine, or both necessitated the appointment of an older Black male "urban editor" to oversee both R&B and rap. I can dig management wanting to protect its investment, but only the irrational ignorance of sexism had me reporting about hip-hop music and culture to a man who, with all due respect, essentially knew what I told him about it. Never mind that I could go toe-to-toe with him about blues, jazz, and soul after working so closely with the luminaries mentioned earlier among others at the Absolute Artists agency. This cat was from the prototypical old school of straight R&B stalwarts with the *I have no idea what these rap niggas are sayin' and couldn't care less* attitude that so many post–Civil Rights Era Negro parents subscribe to. The difference between him and those parents was this: He was actually in a position to give hip-hop a platform as an industry tastemaker. Instead, he called it a fad and showed it the door, along with the majority of Black radio programmers and owners. The result? Hip-hop got swooped up by contemporary hit radio (CHR) and became a billion-dollar industry patronized by a demographic that is 75 percent white. By the time the people who ran these Black, now coded "Urban," stations realized they had a lot of crow to eat, they had lost touch with their own children, who in turn had lost respect for them for blowing off the creative contribution of "Generation Next"—as I called us on my first *Gavin* cover. This generation gap bogarded into the media's view with the rise of C. DeLores Tucker and Tipper Gore. While those two ladies were seeking parental advisory stickers and censorship, they had missed a crucial point that rap artists made with their explicit and, yes, admittedly misogynistic lyrics. This music was their way out of the cycle of poverty that Reaganomics had set in motion. 2 Live Crew, for example—the Miami bass group in Tipper's political crosshairs—represented hip-hop heads who were innovative and fed up, out for money, their sliver of power, and respect. Having been largely orphaned by elder musicians and major-label executives alike, emcees went for dolo, starting their own labels and marketing their music their way. As seminal emcee-DJ duo Eric B. & Rakim so eloquently put it, our generation got *Paid in Full*. But I digress. Back to the office poli-tricks I was dealing with.

My boss spent more time smoking weed than he did writing, and was in the sunset of his editorial career when he came to *Gavin*. The magazine's CEO, however, was completely oblivious to this. As far as he was concerned, he had just hired the HNIC, Head Nigga in Charge. The fact that he previously held a gig at a viable Black music tipsheet was all he needed to see.

In my case, since I didn't know many executives, it truly was *what* I knew that mattered. My music knowledge and my love for hip-hop got me over and through. I got to the magazine in December 1993. With the seminar taking place in February 1994, I had less than eight weeks to coordinate the rap portion of the magazine's national convention. I had the top executives and DJs on my panels. As the moderator, I encouraged everyone to speak the truth about what was happening in the business, so the panel discussions were lively and authentic. The daytime events were packed, and the evening showcases were standing-room-only. I put my Mills College organizational skills to the test and prayed a whole lot. My first Gavin Seminar was a great success. I had more paying guests than comps, a major feat for the rap format, where college DJs had trouble affording registrations and weren't always important enough for labels to sponsor in large numbers. I had proven myself by representing hip-hop well internally and to the industry at large. In the aftermath of the convention, the calls and letters poured in praising me for a job well done, with no mention of my manager. It was clear who was really doing the work in the rap department. By spring, I was out from under the urban editor, running the rap format on my own.

Another thing to understand about getting into radio is that there are just as many ways to work in it as there are to get in. I broke in from the margin. I had not come from a music retailer or distribution house; I'd never even set foot in a radio station as anything other than a guest of my DJ friends Sway & King Tech at KMEL. I started out working as an office manager at a booking agency who freelance wrote about hip-hop every chance I got. Radio doesn't just involve recording artists, DJs, and on-air personalities. There are also entire careers to be enjoyed in engineering, production, syndication, programming, research, consulting, community affairs, sales, promotion, management, and, yes, publishing. The number of actual jobs may be dwindling as commercial radio consolidates, but the kind of work you can do in the radio industry remains varied. Many women in radio have multiple skills to keep themselves viable and can produce, work an airshift, serve as voice-over talent for commercials, and program music. Sure, you can learn about radio in school, and there is a great deal of structure to radio technology and operating a station. However, radio is truly a hands-on field, one where improvisation skills are as important as the FCC rules. In this chapter, you'll hear directly from some powerful women behind the scenes and in front of the microphone: former gatekeeping commercial radio receptionist and top-selling songwriter-performer DD Artis; Canadian hip-hop radio icon Motion; journalist and firebrand shock jock Raqiyah Mays; controversial round-the-way personality Steph Lova, who stood up to Funkmaster Flex; veteran emcee, mother of three, London transplant, and morning-show DJ Monie "In the Middle" Love; music director, producer, community advocate, and *Radio & Records Magazine* urban editor Darnella Dunham; New York college and digital radio pioneer turned Music Choice programming manager DJ Mecca; Jennifer Norwood, one of an elite few African American women winning with hip-hop as a director of crossover music promotion; KPTY—Houston midday jock Cristal Bubblin'; and the unflappable single mother and self-made media mastermind (she humbly refuses to say she's a mogul quite yet), Cathy Hughes, CEO of Radio One and founder of TV One. They all came to the game equipped with some combination of sharp mind, distinctive voice, street savvy, or formal education, and used it all to succeed in radio.

....

UNBREAKABLE
....

In the world of spoken word, she was a force to be reckoned with. Wendy "DJ Motion" Braithwaite is a CBC 2002 National Poetry Face-Off winning poet and Canadian Urban Music Award nominee. But emcee turned radio vet Motion had no prior radio experience. Fortunately, she refused to let that stop her. "I was never trained on the boards; I just had to go for it. I literally learned *while* I was on the air. I got my engineering lessons from John Bronski, who was supposed to be the alternate host. We just ended up working together each week, and DJs were hugely instrumental in teaching me the technical aspects of sound. Eventually, I was self-producing the show." Motion co-founded and hosted CIUT—Toronto's world-renowned mix-show *The Master Plan* for ten years straight, every Saturday night, *without pay* until her son Akir was born in 2003. So fear not: You can come to radio from any career that requires interaction with people on a deep personal level, one where your communication and analytical skills and intuition are utilized.

Since most people work to make money, you probably want to ask why Motion did it so long for free. The first thing to know is: It's highly unlikely that college radio budgets can support paid staff; when they can, payment goes from the top down, rarely trickling to DJs. Moreover, college radio is a place to cut your teeth and get professional broadcast training. But Motion's reasons extended beyond catching a check. "At the time, there were no other outlets for hip-hop. We did it out of pure love," she muses. "The compensation came from having any platform at all, having my own program, not having to ask if music could get play, not to mention the best networking imaginable. We became an institution." And though she made her money self-publishing her book *Motion in Poetry* and performing all over the world, you can definitely get paid in radio, monetarily and otherwise.

DJ Mecca, programming manager for digital music network Music Choice, was a probation officer for the city of New York for eight years during the day. At night, she interacted with emcees and artists as the DJ and host on college station WNWK and Harlem community station WHCR. She had to keep those worlds completely separate—and at times they almost collided, because some emcees have the kind of rap sheets that have nothing to do with rhyme books. POs aren't even supposed to know these cats, let alone interview them and spin their records. "No one ever said I couldn't be on the air," Mecca recalls, "but I couldn't talk to any of my artist or radio contacts by day. I didn't want anyone coming to my job. There were a lot of artists on probation. It got to the point where artists wanted me to be their PO, because I understood their need to travel for touring and recording. Artists actually wanted me as their PO because I was young and down with hip-hop! Cases were assigned at random, but if I got an artist, I would switch cases. I loved the music too much."

Mecca moonlighted as a DJ on two stations during her time as a city employee. Then the chance to program music at Pseudo's 88 Hip-Hop came along. Mecca had advanced to senior probation officer at the remarkably young and practically unheard-of age of thirty-one. But hosting the ground-breaking feminist hip-hop show *Queendom* was such an unprecedented opportunity, Mecca couldn't say no. This was women spinning hip-hop online for the whole world to hear! "It was hard to imagine doing what I loved with benefits, and the pay was comparable to that of a PO. I did both jobs for four months, then left my job with the city, only to have my music director gig eliminated another seven months later."

Leaving a bird in the hand for radio was a turning point in Mecca's life. "I felt like a scorned lover. I had just bought an apartment and was paying my school loans back. I was so angry and mournful. I felt like I had been duped. Suddenly I had no money and couldn't go back to the city job. Budgetary issues kept me from being rehired. My friend Belviana Toddman referred me to music industry veteran Sharon Heyward. She gave me a job temping for Herb Trawick, Brian McKnight's manager at the time. That job was neces-sary, but it was so humiliating. I went from being in control of radio programs to being in control of nothing. Sharon realized I was older than I looked and encouraged me to put a tape together for WBLS. She couldn't watch me go through that anymore. It could have been my pride or my fear of rejection, but I never did [make the tape]. That was a humbling experience." Mecca's path to a career in music is a certainly a lesson of humility—but more than that, one of commitment. When she was offered an opportunity, in the form of a temp job, she didn't let her ego get in the way of accepting it. Even as she took cuts in position and pay, she kept in mind that it was temporary. Here's a piece of wisdom that I'll refer to again later in the book: You aren't officially in the business until you get laid off or fired. That's when you see who's been watching you, who's in your corner, and who ain't shit.

Raqiyah Mays, now with New York's WQHT HOT-97 and KISS-FM stations and a former on-air personality for Power 105—New York, got into the radio game using her journalism background. In her roles as for-mat manager and on-air personality, she was a researcher and writer for Sirius satellite radio. She also repped hard as a fiery features writer for *The Source, One World, VIBE, Essence,* and *Billboard.* She had gotten a taste of radio at WOWI—Norfolk with veteran on-air duo The Buddha Brothers, who asked her to do a woman-centered hip-hop show. More city slicker than Southern girl, Raqiyah moved to New York in 1997 and took an internship at *VIBE.* After a few months at the magazine, the radio jones started to come down, and she went back to the airwaves. "I produced for Grand Master

Flash's show on Sirius," she says. "I used that experience to make an incredible aircheck and meet people. I met independent urban radio consultant and Earl Boston, Inc., CEO Earl Boston, who knew Michael Saunders, the program director for Power 105. Earl passed my aircheck on to Michael, and it got me hired. It usually doesn't happen like that." However, on-air layoffs are common. In less than a year, Raqiyah was relieved of duty over a controversial airshift. She made comments about interracial relationships and expressed her opinion of them in a manner that did not sit well with what she describes as "a mixture of the programmers, a few advertisers, and some white and biracial listeners." For the record, she adds that "the Black response was overwhelmingly supportive." Where Raqiyah's sass was too extreme for Power, it was right in the pocket for HOT 97. Raqiyah got the proverbial "dirt off her shoulder" easily in one of America's most cutthroat radio markets. Within seventy-two hours of her firing, HOT 97 snapped her up, and she still rocks their airwaves every Sunday afternoon. The former executive editor of *The Ave.*, a well-respected hip-hop magazine she co-founded, has now taken her radio skills to the stages of the Big Apple, starring in *Platanos & Collard Greens* and *Auction Block to Hip-Hop.*

I think radio is the closest thing to magic or wizardry that exists in entertainment aside from, well, magic and wizardry of the David Blaine variety. For starters, you can't see what's going on; you can only hear it. Your imagination has to do a lot of the work that film and TV do with visuals. Radio employs incredible smoke-and-mirror techniques, from the way it's programmed to the science of payola. (Payola, by the way, is a book unto itself; read *Hit Men* by Frederic Dannen.) It's also still coded by race, as urban America continues to be anything but black and white. For decades, the terms *R&B, soul,* and *urban* have referenced Black music, even if Justin Timberlake sings it. Across the tracks, the words *crossover, rhythm,* and *pop* reference white music, even if Darius "Hootie" Rucker is sangin' it. I am still wondering exactly what "white music" is in post-slavery America, considering that people of African descent stand at the root of *all* contemporary American music forms. The many sounds that people of color have brought to radio have been crossing over since the line was drawn, and yet we are still speaking in racial code. For me, that makes the radio game the slickest sleight-of-hand play since three-card monte. Whether it's wired or satellite, radio's still working the oldest trick in the book: provoking our minds by playing with our emotions, providing a private dressing room for urban America's constant identity changes. In terms of navigating the radio arena, you can play inside the station or outside and still be a vital part of the industry. In this chapter, you'll meet women on both sides of the fence, and a couple who play roles on both sides simultaneously. You'll also meet women who operate on-air and behind the scenes as corporate executives.

Radio is an unruly, unstable animal. Mentorship is hard to find. Friends are easily made, but hard to trust. Additionally, in today's radio age, marked by rabid consolidation tied to special interests, research technology, and the advancement of the satellite platform, it's business first, music second. Before you get discouraged, take note: Though radio is male-dominated like the rest of the music industry, opportunity is abundant for women, because commercial radio primarily targets women heads of households, and women know women. From management and programming to on-air, promotions, and sales, there are plenty of places to get in where you fit in. The key is learning what you do exceedingly well. As Monie Love asserts, "The world is full of interesting people, but not everyone can come up in here and know what to do with the opportunity. You focus on you and be about your shit 100 percent."

The competition is fierce in radio. It is actually used as fuel to keep the station hot, keep everyone there on their toes, and keep them on the edge of their seats about their future. Raqiyah describes the environment: "It gets real tense four times a year when the Arbitron ratings [a quarterly consumer-based research assessment conducted, documented, and distributed by Arbitron, Inc.] book comes out, or when a new hire appears because it means somebody's losing hours. Just about everyone in this field has a huge ego, and that can affect the vibe of the staff, even create personality problems between them."

Longtime hip-hop radio fixture Stephanie "Steph Lova" Saunders is living proof of the danger that ego can get a woman into. She got on the air in Washington, DC, thanks to her assertive, no-holds-barred personality, and those same attributes kept her servin' heat weekday afternoons on Power 105.1 — New York, the slot also occupied by Wendy Williams on WBLS and Angie Martinez on HOT 97. As of this writing, she holds down weeknights on WKYS-93.9 in DC and weekends at Power 105.1 — New York.

In September 2002, she was allegedly assaulted by former HOT 97 colleague Ashton "Funkmaster Flex" Taylor outside the station. In 2003, she reached an out-of-court settlement in a five-million-dollar civil suit against her former HOT 97 colleague. Regardless, Steph learned some valuable lessons.

"I dropped the lackadaisical attitude, the idea that I was bigger than the music," she reflects. "Radio's about the people. And this business is like a marriage. When it's abusive, you gotta get out, even if you leave with nothing. That's what I left HOT 97 with, nothing. I have no animosity, but I say *Leave me alone*. I don't want to be remembered by HOT, especially after I damn near sued everyone over there." HOT 97 is now under different management. Beginning in 1996, Steph cut her teeth in the game on DC Flava 1580 AM with DC hip-hop and house music icons DJ Kool, Doug Lazy, and DJ Flex (not the Funkmaster). It was HOT 97 PD Steve Smith, then a consultant for WPGC, who saw Steph's talent. He offered her a job at HOT 97, but he had to wait. "I had just re-upped my deal at Kiss down in DC, so I had to wait ten months before I could get out of my contract. I came up and worked part-time and on weekends at HOT 97. When I got there, I realized I had sold my soul to the devil. I felt like a college ballplayer who had been told everything was sweet—until he got to the league." After being shifted around the schedule and rarely doing the shows and interviews she made the move for, she went to MTV2 as a VJ for a year before being hired to give Angie and Wendy some healthy competition weekday afternoons.

So what does it take to "be about your shit" in a tank full of piranhas? In addition to Steph's suggestion of putting your ego aside once you're off the mic, Raqiyah Mays believes it starts with "being a people person. You can't be shy about talking to strangers, and you have to have a thick skin, especially in commercial radio. Unlike college radio, the commercial side is highly competitive." Former music director and morning show jock Darnella Dunham also knows you have to have heart to go with that thick skin. "You need a passion for radio, because it doesn't pay well. You need a sincere appreciation for the opinions of others [your listening audience] because you can't just program what you like personally."

Cathy Hughes's advice is two-pronged. She began as an on-air personality and invented the Quiet Storm format, a programming mix of jazz fusion, classic soul, and smooth contemporary R&B music, at WHUR, Howard University's radio station. Handling your business in radio requires discipline. "People think anyone can be on the radio. What they don't realize is that while it is not rocket science, it is the most tedious job anyone can have," Cathy says. "The challenge is to do the same thing every day, and do it better than you did the day before." When it comes to business in general, and media in particular, faith allows you to persevere, Cathy told me. "Believe in

God. When something is beyond you, and you don't have a commitment to a power bigger than you, you will surely give up on your vision." When Cathy set out to start her own station, she was denied financing thirty-two times. Had she not persevered, she would have never met number thirty-three on her team, Livia Colon at the Chemical Bank in New York City. "In 1980, she gave me my first loan, a million dollars." She recalls it as if it happened earlier this week. "Each time I got turned down, it helped me hone my presentation. I was so used to hearing *no,* she had already approved me, but I kept pitching! I walked out of the bank and felt like all the traffic in Manhattan had stopped. That day, I learned to never sell past the close." She put that million into WOL—Washington, DC, the boldest radio resource for information and empowerment of African Americans in the nation's capital and the station featured in Kasi Lemmons's film *Talk to Me.* Sixty-nine stations and fifteen million listeners later, Mizz Hughes's request to launch TV One was granted with much less resistance, to the tune of 1.4 billion in financing.

Having a solid grasp of the technology used in radio is a must for longevity at any station. Darnella, along with DJ Mecca and Jen Norwood, highly recommends learning how to use Selector radio scheduling software. You can be trained on it in a few days. Selector has been radio's primary means of playing and tracking records since it was introduced by Radio Computer Services more than twenty years ago. Prior to its emergence, jocks were actually logging airplay on index cards! In this case, what you know will put you ahead of the game better than how you look, or the level another woman may be willing to lower herself to in an effort to thwart your progress. Knowing the systems and knowing how they operate makes you reliable, marketable (in case the aforementioned Chickenhead wins the battle and you need to move on), and, more often than not, damn close to indispensable.

In addition to being a DJ or an on-air personality, you can program, operate, or even own a radio station (if not several). If you've ever picked up a copy of *Billboard,* you've noticed that music charts are formatted, meaning categorized by genre. In *Gavin,* fourteen radio formats were represented, including college and alternative, country, adult album alternative, rock, gospel, and the formats readily familiar to urbanites, smooth jazz, R&B/urban, rhythm crossover, dance, and top 40. You'll also find community stations, public radio, sports, talk, and even kids radio thanks to Disney. Generally, college and community outlets are not-for-profit. That's why they are constantly fund-raising to sustain themselves, along with relying on grants and other funding sources. Commercial radio, on the other hand, is exactly the opposite: all about the Benjamins. Its money comes from corporate advertising and leveraging of corporate assets like sister networks, performance venues, and friends in high places. For your purposes as someone in the market for a gig, let's take a closer look at what there is to do in Radioland.

Operations Manager (OM)

Oversees all staff and daily operations of the station. Answers to the owner of the station or, at larger conglomerates, the regional program director. Oversees all programming. Watches the charts like a hawk, and enforces the playlist like a warden. This person ultimately controls what gets played at the station.

Program Director

Oversees all programming. Serves as the leader, motivator, and mediator for the on-air and DJ staff. Styles vary, from research-heavy to staff-surveying to gut-level, or some combination. Program directors also have the pleasure of presiding over the coordination of the massive summer-jam-style concerts that are now all the rage. These now year-round concerts serve as a thank-you for the listening audience by bringing their favorite station's playlist to life in the form of live performances, and leverage the station's profile in the market by securing the hottest names for the bill. They also save the label the hassle of coordinating a live event for popular baby acts that may not sell out a venue alone, but alongside marquee names get promotion for their resources. Sage words from Darnella Dunham on this position: "The ones that win know research is a tool, not the gospel. Soul must be felt, it can't be quantified." Traditionally PDs also help on-air staff develop; after all, the jocks are artists to a degree as well.

Operations/Program Director (OPD)

A combination of the first two positions. Translation: Because daily operations have to be attended to, there isn't much time for programming duty. In this scenario, the APD is gon' be workin' like a hot slave!

Assistant Program Director (APD)

This person supports the PD in fielding information from as many sources as possible to create winning programming that research, charts, and numbers often miss: how the song bangs in the club no matter how many times in a row it's played, say. Or how the local or regional artist of the moment is selling CDs independently in the mom-and-pop retail stores at a faster rate than *all* the artists in *Billboard*'s Top 10. If there is a mixshow director, he or she relies on the APD to convey what's on fire in the streets and pass it up the chain of command to the PD.

Music Director

The front line for interacting with music promoters, indie artists, and the plethora of indie labels that beat down radio's door for those BDS (Broadcast Data Systems) and Mediabase music tracking to parlay spins into a joint venture or distribution deal. The MD also serves as a buffer for the PD, returning calls that the PD can't or won't, listening to tons of new music, et cetera.

Mixshow Director

This person is often also the APD, or should be and just isn't getting the promotion. He or she manages the mixshow crew: the DJs in the mix and on-air for specialty shows, weekends, holiday marathons, and so on. This job requires keeping mad egos in check and team spirit high.

Promotions Manager

Just what it sounds like: managing the contests, appearances of on-air talent in the community, listener events, giveaways, flyaways, and the like. If a contest idea is approved, the promotions manager makes sure it's executed. This person also works with the production engineer or coordinator to get the advertising for these events right and tight.

Receptionist/Gatekeeper

Though the job is not glamorous or well paid, the level of influence is high. Gatekeepers actually end up being pretty high up the food chain, simply because they control all the staff's interaction with the rest of the industry and the outside world. They choose who gets through and who gets voice mail. Who gets seen and who gets stuck in the waiting room. What music gets passed on to the PD, and what gets passed on, period. They know what the jocks do between shifts, what the latest internal drama is, what the programmers really think about promotion reps and artists. Because gatekeepers also get calls from listeners, their opinion about what does and doesn't work at the station is taken seriously. Besides, they're listening to the station forty hours a week.

Sales Executive

An account manager charged with keeping the advertisers and sponsors happy and keeping the business coming. Sales execs usually report to a director or VP who is the point person for massive multiplatform advertising from the larger accounts.

Production Engineer

Production engineers cut the spots that make the whole station bling: singing with "stationality" (station personality), assertion of marketwide supremacy, excitement, urgency, anticipation, and fun. Often on-air personalities are involved with the production process as well, from writing the script to performing the voice-over or, in a crunch, cutting the whole spot themselves.

Production Assistant/Coordinator

These thankless wonders do it all, from selecting music beds to picking up food for the jocks. They take audience calls, prep the studio for the show, pull press releases and news for the morning show crew, you name it.

....
AND SHE DON'T STOP
....

The focus here may be radio, but this chapter also offers a window into the life and lifestyle of a nonradio DJ, in addition to what women behind the scenes in programming and promotion experience. There are also careers outside radio that require heavy interaction with radio: music promotion and marketing. In this chapter, you'll hear from a radio executive whose expertise in programming helped her to become one of this generation's pioneer women—and certainly one of a select few women of color in pop promotion—Jennifer Norwood. Marketing is a beast all its own, so it will be covered in depth later.

I want to clarify one term that is thrown about loosely in the world of radio, especially by people who are on the outside listening, or folks who are trying to get in. That term is: *DJ*.

The term *DJ* is short for "disc jockey." It refers to the person talking over the air and playing the records (for decades, this was often the same individual). The DJ is the central figure in radio, the one listeners connect with and confide in; the person they rely on to tell them what's hot and what's worth buying, dancing to, or at the least talking about. It is this power that gave rise to the more recent term of *tastemaker*—an elite group to which the DJ belongs.

For decades, DJs juggled the playing of vinyl and speaking between the records they played. Though Black radio exploded in Harlem during the 1920s, there weren't female DJs until the 1940s. Martha Jean "The Queen" Steinberg, wife of a white jazz player and mother of five, became America's first Black woman radio personality when she was hired in October 1948 by WDIA—Memphis. Not satisfied with the "women's genre" of popular love songs, she played the jazz hits of the day. Immensely popular, she ended up being stolen by WJLB—Detroit. In 1958, Jackie Owens, a fifteen-year-old Caucasian girl, took to the tables on her own teen radio show playing Little Richard, Bo Diddley, Ray Charles, and—oh yeah—Elvis Presley.

Fast-forward to the hip-hop era. DJs remained the central figure of the culture's musical element. In hip-hop, deejaying wasn't just about spinning records. It was about speaking with your hands. The art of music selection gave way to the strategy of DJ battling and the science of turntablism—using the turntable as musical instrument for the artistic expression of the DJ him- or herself. Women have broken down the doors in this area as well. It is widely agreed that hip-hop was born in 1977 with DJ Kool Herc cuttin' up funk breaks at community center jams in the Bronx. Pioneering DJ Jazzy Joyce won the New Music Seminar DJ competition in 1983. By 1985, the original DJ Spinderella was cuttin' it up behind Salt-N-Pepa. It took less than a decade before the emergence of women turntablists, compared with the many decades it took for women to become radio jocks. In the turntablist arena, women level the playing field at a higher bpm (beats per minute). There are currently the following types of DJs: on-air personalities, mix DJs, mixtape DJs, and turntablist/composers.

....

THIS IS THE REMIX

....

Where do you go from here? Well, if you've been on-air, your voice is recognizable and marketable. The question is: Can you use it to sell products? If so, you have a leg up on a potentially lucrative career in voice-over. As a creative exec for Sony, I employed personalities like Steph Lova, Ananda Lewis, and Big Lez for music advertising. They were a natural fit, because they already had the ear and respect of music buyers. In fact, in Lez's case, she came from TV as the host of BET's *Rap City* and then reinvented herself as a radio jock in Los Angeles, moving on to syndication and satellite platforms. If voice-over is something you're interested in, invest in a few coaching sessions with a voice-over trainer or producer. You can even cut a demo reel using the resources at your disposal. A VO demo is simply the next level up from a radio aircheck, using actual general market commercial scripts with music beds.

When I asked the ladies I spoke with where to go from radio, the answers were varied. Monie and Steph are confirmation that you can step into television VJing from radio. Jen Norwood suggests real estate: "I'm selling music, and if you can get people to like you, you can probably get them to like a property you're selling." Honestly, you could probably get *any* buyers to a place where they're comfortable listening to you; on-air people create this intimacy on a minute-to-minute basis.

Radio is such a diverse training ground. It's like music industry boot camp. You work your muscles in every way, from resourcefulness, to thinking on your toes, to making everyday people extraordinarily happy. Monie puts it like this: "You could head up a department at a label coming out of radio, because you touch every aspect of the business over time." On the executive side, there is opportunity to make moves in other fields of media on every level. Cathy Hughes was looking for a way to extend her brand beyond radio. Her own television network catering to urban viewers was a natural progression. "Alfred [Liggins, her son and Radio One's second in command] and I knew we had to diversify, but we didn't want Wall Street to get jumpy. We have fifteen million Radio One listeners who we can tell what to watch on TV One."

DD Artis is taking a lot of what her gig as radio gatekeeper has taught her into the field of her dreams as a singer-songwriter. While she admits that "no job could have prepared me for this one," she's taking her vast set of contacts, her communication skills, and her ability to "get pit-bull on callers when necessary" into the recording artist arena. She vowed that radio receptionist would be her last day job. And judging from her résumé thus far as a writer for Anthony Hamilton and a backing or studio vocalist for Angie Stone, Nona Gaye, DJ Eddie F, and James Poyser, she meant it. DD relocated to Los Angeles in 2005 to pursue singing full-time and now tours with Justin Timberlake.

If you seek a position within the station, the challenge will be reinventing yourself for the staff who've come to rely heavily upon you as their gatekeeper, and limit their perception of your abilities to this specific job.

Though you have to know the functions of radio to do this job, the powers that be who are in a position to give you a shot may not want you to move. At which point, you must be prepared to move on.

DD actually looked into changing jobs: "Sales, programming, and marketing staff change, but management, engineering, and production tend not to. Initially, I wanted to be a programming assistant, but the format kept flipping and the pay wasn't even that good." Note: That's how payola came to prominence: wack salaries with little prospect of job security.

Darnella has great insight about where to go after radio. She reversed my path and went from radio to publishing with no prior experience, becoming urban, gospel, and rap editor for R&R (Radio and Records). She also likes the idea of being an A&R (artists and repertoire) executive at a label. "With all the grooming of local artists I've done at the station, I could be good at that." Making moves within the station has its trade-offs, however: "I could also go for a program director job," she asserts. "But for all the talk of how women listeners rule radio, there are so few women in programming. Besides, PDs get yanked in a heartbeat for doing what they were told to do [by an operations manager or research consultant] if that same plan doesn't win ratings." Ah yes, that tank-of-piranhas thing. "Being a city girl in Orlando for a year taught me that quality of life is part of the compensation. I'll take a less lucrative position for a market I want to live in, for a community I love. If I run the risk of losing a job, I want to be happy during every moment I can while I'm there."

Going into music promotion as a label executive is a natural career move after radio. Stability is still elusive, but national travel and an expense account are nice perks. Crossover promotion phenom Jennifer Norwood has most promoters beat, because she has enviable radio experience. Having worked in radio in the Mid-Atlantic and West Coast regions, she knows how to relate to jocks and mixers—she's in their world, too. She also understands the cultural nuances in several of America's key markets from living and working there. Most notably part of Sway & Tech's Wakeup Show in Los Angeles, Jen "Boogie" puts it this way: "Coming into label promotions from radio, you have the edge over your competition because you know everyone at every label. I'm a unique promoter because I know what the radio execs are dealing with, from 'Where's the van!' And 'Are the winners getting their prizes?' to 'What's with the morning show hate mail?'" Jen is the ultimate inside trader, able to use this understanding to her advantage and translate it into ironclad radio relationships and spins for new artists or records by known acts that need that extra look to break big.

THE TABLES HAVE TURNED

DJ means more than an on-air personality heard across airwaves and satellite feeds. DJs can also make an incredible impact showcasing their skills in lifestyle settings face-to-face with their consumers, or competing hand-to-hand in turntablism contests, furthering the use of tables as music-making instruments. And while there may not be millions of people listening to them at once, the commitment to excellence and the thirst for dominance are just as intense. Three incredible soundweavers give you a slice of their lives on the wheels of steel: DJ and theatrical music director DJ Reborn, champion turntablist and co-founder of the Anomalies Kuttin Kandi, and Japanese-born, Dallas-based chopped-and-screwed mistress DJ Princess Cut.

The act of DJing is recognized as mixing, scratching, or cutting two records to transition from one to the other during an event for dancing and listening pleasure. The practice goes back as far as vinyl itself, but has been given new life and broader access to listeners in the age of hip-hop and emerging mix technology. DJ Reborn defines DJing for herself as being "a sound architect. I feel like I am an artist. A Black woman constantly trying to utilize the medium to project my voice, to remind people of the power of music, have people reminisce, and make new memories in the presence of my DJing."

Reborn has made a conscious choice to avoid radio. "I don't want to be told what to play," she says point-blank. "I've really seen the death of radio in a way. With the elimination of competition [due to consolidation] comes this incestuous, repetitive radio play. Today's DJs are personalities first, who work primarily for white men that pump a lot of bullshit. I don't believe in that."

DJ Reborn has been able to generate a lively career and make a living as a full-time DJ without it. Thanks to the profile of the DJ being elevated via hip-hop and entertainment overall (even Ellen DeGeneres has a DJ), there are many more places to flex your skills. Reborn, a member of New York's Ubiquita all-female DJ collective, stays sharp by taking advantage of as many as possible. In addition to spinning in clubs, retail stores, museums, technical schools, and youth workshops as the program director for the Dub Spot in Manhattan, Reborn has served as a hip-hop theater DJ since 2002. She music directed Will Power's one-man show *Flow* and deejayed abroad as part of *Def Poetry*'s stage production. Reborn describes a very rigorous endeavor that she manages to make look easy on the theater stage. "Instead of an orchestra, I am pushing the story and characters forward with turntables," she explains. "It requires learning the full script and hitting my cues. Stretching and growing as a DJ in that way has upped my game in club settings."

She also took cues from her male counterparts on what not to do in club settings during routine observation she conducts to hone her own technique. "I'd go to parties and see guy DJs masturbating with the turntables; the mixer was their dick, the tables were their balls, and they would be DJing like there was no one there. DJing is about call and response, not just what you want to play. To be able to hold people's interest for hours on end from song to song is really challenging. You do what you're known for, but you have to please the crowd. You have to be prepared for whatever room you're in," she emphasizes. "There's always this moment of *Is the risk going to work in my favor? Will they trust me enough to stay with me?* Once the burgeoning DJ gets a taste of that [doubt], they see how much there is to it. Your hands, ears, eyes, and spirit are constantly engaged. You have to be on point and working the entire time."

Being an extraordinary DJ requires a vast knowledge of and openness to music, but it also requires a level of technical expertise. That's what distinguishes the ones who can command higher fees and maintain steady work in multiple formats when necessary. "[Women DJs] are still fairly marginalized, but there is still this idea that if you're female, that's good enough on the novelty page. The other part of it is constantly having to prove yourself, either to the audience, venue owners, or male DJs. I have to leave a space for those who have never even been exposed to a female DJ. I've had my headphones on with my hands *on the records* and someone will say: 'You're the DJ?' I get these questions that I would never get if you saw a man setting up with crates." She sighs. "But reputation speaks for itself. If you're good, you work." After fifteen years on the tables, Reborn doesn't sweat being female in the field so much. However, she does understand the double standard at hand and as a result leaves no room for being viewed as underqualified in the mix. She rocks vinyl, CDs, and Serato. She comes equipped to every gig with a laptop and a soundman. Being a woman DJ "is an opportunity to shift ideas and the paradigm of what deejaying is," says Reborn. "Because I've worked to become good at what I do, they can reimagine a woman doing this work well. I take on the responsibility of being technically proficient."

For Filipina champion turntablist DJ Kuttin Kandi, technical profi-
ciency is paramount. She took it so seriously when she started cutting that
she practiced in secret for two years on her late father's wooden mixer until
she was ready to unveil her skills in competition. "If you don't know the
foundation [of turntablism], it will kick you in the ass in the long term,"
she warns. "Deejaying to me is an art form: taking two pieces of vinyl and
re-creating the music by manipulating the sound to turn it into a whole new
song, by slowing it down, breaking it down, and making something new by
beat juggling and making different patterns. Scratching is its own language,
thanks to [DMC World Champion] DJ Qbert," she explains. She got the itch
to compete watching her ex-boyfriend DJ Roli and his crew, the 5th Platoon,
as they battled the X-Men, now known as the X-ecutioners. There were few
women on the circuit for her to look up to at the time. "When I first started I
didn't know if I could really do it," recalls Kandi. "But seeing Lazy K and DJ
Symphony encouraged me. Now women are coming up front more because
they've seen me, Jazzy [Joyce], or others who gave them courage to do it."

Unlike punching buttons to cue records for play on the radio, turntable competition requires a grueling regimen of training on par with that of
musicians who play instruments. Contrary to what jazz master and hip-hop
detractor Wynton Marsalis might think, turntablists are instrumentalists,
too. They practice, or "shed," just as intensely as jazz players, for hours a
day on a daily basis. Kandi gets specific. "When you practice to compete,
you have to know what your opponents will try to do and beat them at that.
You study other DJs so you don't bite. You've got to do your routine in a new
way that is ten times better," she advises. "You also have to know the legends
who came before you. Then you hear the music for a while and listen to the
horn, bass, and kicks and imagine how else it can sound. Then you come up
with your own patterns, scratches, and juggles. You try to imagine the music
coming together in new ways. It's hard to apply that to your hand move-
ments. It takes a lot of concentration for you to be able to use both hands on
the turntable, *and* get the records to the point on the vinyl the way you heard
it in your head. Sometimes, playing around gets you there. One thing I've
learned through a vocal coach is that even people with gifts have to practice,
because even they mess up. We practice day and night."

Kandi has transitioned out of competing to explore new ways of spinning and performing, walking a similar path to that of Reborn, but with a
twist. She let me in on a bit of a secret: Kandi does her thing on the written

page as well as the tables. "I also do spoken word and only a few people know that, so I'm coming out with it more. I combined the two and was wowed by the possibility of it. Now I'm putting a band together and another DJ on stage with me for a new level of turntablism. I'm also writing a play to blend it with theater," she reveals. "I want to take [turntablism] to new places."

DJ Princess Cut backed up the late Pimp C of influential Southern hip-hop duo UGK (Underground Kingz) before his tragic and untimely death on December 4, 2007. Princess Cut is a native of Japan who heeded the call of hip-hop and followed it straight to Dallas, Texas, more than a decade ago. "I just liked Texas's wide-open spaces and the fact that there isn't another Japanese person for miles. Where I'm from, there [are] a lot of people in a smaller area, so it's just more crowded and tense," she says of her unusual relocation choice.

Princess Cut is a competing turntablist whose specialty is the slowed-down, weighed-down chopped-and-screwed style created by the late DJ Screw. For her, his style was love at first listen. "When I heard Screw for the first time, it changed my whole outlook on the art of turntablism," says Princess Cut. "When I make my mix tapes, I use a lot of turntablism. I like to play what I want to hear and scratch, chop and screw, and whatever else I feel like. Not everybody is going to understand what I'm doing, and that's okay."

Enough of the masses understand where she's spinning from. Princess Cut was named 2007 Female DJ of the Year at the Southern Entertainment Awards (SEA). She has the respect of the Japanese back home, noting, "Japanese people look up to me because I'm making it in America. They respect that." When DJs step to her, thinking this petite Japanese chopped-and-screwed competitor can't possibly be for real, she just goes to work. "I just let them hear what I do and accept all challengers if they think they are better. Let the tables do the talking. If they ain't hatin', you're not doin' it right," she says. She commands what she calls a minimum of "a stack" (a thousand dollars) to create mixtapes or spin for an hour. And she's handlin' her entertainment business on two continents. "I have three managers, one in Japan and two here in America. It's not all fun and games and diamond rings, it's hard out here on these streets. No one's going to believe in you but you. Once you really believe and are determined, then others will follow. I've paid my dues now I'm tryin' to get paid, know what I'm sayin'?" Most definitely, Princess Cut!

AT THE END OF THE DAY

There are more than three thousand music stations in America, turned on by over 225 million listeners. Satellite radio firms XM and Sirius are providing a varied, commercial-free alternative to roughly eight million subscribers each. Merging of the two was approved but it will take some time, given the only two players in the market are vastly different structurally. There are also more than three million pirates out there who broadcast on the margins; imagine how many there are we don't know about. HD radio is a new format unto itself. MP3 players and the Internet have revolutionized the way the world plays music, turning everyday people into program directors. For decades, radio has been working the same ol' model, but those days are over. Trade magazines and tipsheets are not the lightning rods of fresh information they once were. Even television programs music now, thanks to cable music channels, music video, and strategic music placement in network series. I started this chapter by saying that you don't have to be at a station to work in radio. However, radio is the place to be if you want a bird's-eye view into how down and dirty the politics get, how passionate people are about music, and how the music business is more business than music.

True to her name, Cristal Bubblin', the effervescent princess of southern urban radio, has experienced the fallout from her love of music and from the job itself, engendering so much hostility from her own boss she wound up losing her job. Her show was the number-one-rated program in her time slot in her market, and she still got her walking papers. Now, ratings are what everyone in radio lives or dies by. When those quarterly Arbitron ratings hit, heads roll if the numbers drop. For Cristal, her numbers went up and she still got the ax. She thinks it happened because she was inherited talent that her middle manager, the assistant program director, had no say in hiring—and also thanks to her out-of-the-box success with listeners on the air.

Here's Cristal's perspective: "I came over with the program director from my previous station and he liked my work and all was cool for about eight months. When my first ratings book came out, my show was number one in the market! I didn't even realize how I'd done it. The APD's show took five years to get to number one, but it took me six months, and he hated me for it. My APD started throwin' salt on me after that. Here I was working to make him proud. I fell back and let him lead," she recalls, thinking that would smooth the road between them. But even that was used against her by her APD. "Then I was called a slacker who acted like I didn't want to be there. My PD even pulled me in the office and told me I was too aggressive, and asked too many questions about things that weren't my business." Cristal's Catch-22 went on for two years at the station, where she was damned whether she did something or not. "I became the assistant promotions director, but I wasn't allowed to be in the promo meetings. It was just another title so I did more administrative work; there was no additional pay," she adds. As a young on-air personality just getting into the radio game, she withstood the harassment because she was under contract. It was a lot to go through for one job, and she was holding down four at the time to pay for her student loans.

Cristal elaborates, "My wages were being [garnished] for my student loan to the tune of three hundred dollars a week out of seven hundred. I was broke. I was full-time at the station, part-time at a hair salon as a receptionist, a server at Applebee's, and working part-time at Gymboree. Being on the radio does not mean you're making a ton of money. It's about what you negotiate. The top 5 markets are unionized, but I was in market number 127. The bread and butter for radio jocks are appearances, where you get paid to appear by a sponsor. And anytime my PD felt I needed to be on punishment, he would tell the clubs and car dealerships that I couldn't make any appearances. I should have negotiated that my appearances be part of my contract, but I went on my program director's word about not being able to put them in. You definitely want a lawyer looking over your contracts because they are worded crazy! They basically say that you can be fired if you do anything the station doesn't like. I'd rather sign a bad contract in the beginning of my career than twenty years down the line." She laughs. "I got it out of the way."

Cathy Hughes has been in radio for thirty-five years. She was the first Black woman to graduate from Omaha's Duchesne Academy of the Sacred Heart, five months into a pregnancy she hid expertly by the end of high school. Her son Alfred has been in radio his entire life. "He thought everybody worked at a radio station until he was about nineteen," she says with a grin. Now they run Radio One as a family business. No surprise, considering that in the beginning, she "had no women to turn to, and the men said I was not emotionally suited to be in the business." I asked her what she'd learned that the old-boy network hadn't revealed to her. Her response was totally out of the box, just like her: "The old-boy network isn't really a network at all. They don't get up and have meetings to keep us out. They just have a strong preference for themselves. That's not a fault in my mind. We need to have that preference for ourselves like they have for themselves. Livia Colon was open enough to prefer a woman of color and give me a chance. And she changed the course of radio." Now it's your turn.

SUMMARY OF SECRETS REVEALED

WHAT YOU THOUGHT YOU KNEW:

Showing up for the job is enough.

WHAT YOU NEED TO KNOW:

Your personal and professional strengths. Mine were event planning, organizational efficiency, interpersonal relations, and a vast knowledge of recorded music.

WHAT YOU THOUGHT YOU KNEW:

It's okay to go with the flow and freestyle in the entertainment business.

WHAT YOU NEED TO KNOW:

You can only go with the flow as long as you know your craft. Mine was writing. It is at the core of my career, which has spanned publishing (*Gavin* magazine), records and technology (Sony Music Entertainment advertising), and now television (BET) and film (as an independent music supervisor through my own corporation, SEEIT Live, Inc.).

WHAT YOU THOUGHT YOU KNEW:

The things I haven't learned weren't necessary to get the job, so all I need to do is play my position.

WHAT YOU NEED TO KNOW:

Playing your position will keep you right there: so good in your lane that you'll have a tough time switching into another one. Learn what you don't know even if you don't need it for your job description. You never know when you'll be called upon to execute something beyond your function.

Observe what there is to know inside the station or job, then make a list of the things you don't understand or have experience with. Then turn that list into a list of newly acquired skills. For example, if you know you don't know Selector, but you want to program a radio station, learn Selector. Take the classes and get certified. If you know you want to be an on-air personality, study the ones on the air. Spend a few hours with a voice coach. Practice being on-air. Hire a producer to create a professional aircheck with you. Professional enhancement is always money and time well spent. I personally recommend Landmark Education. It's human being school. Nothing anywhere compares to its curriculum. My entire life has been transformed by my participation in its courses.

WHAT YOU THOUGHT YOU KNEW:

The people who hired me can see all the ways I set myself apart from my colleagues. After all, they hired me, didn't they?

WHAT YOU NEED TO KNOW:

Identify all your points of difference and use them. What sets you apart from everyone else you'd consider competition? In radio, these are the things that may win you audience loyalty, ratings, and the big bucks, baby! A unique-sounding on-air voice? Hometown advantage, having been raised in the market you serve? A way with words and people like no other? Great interviewing or writing skills? These are but a few examples. Whatever those points are, write them down and exploit them to your benefit!

WHAT YOU THOUGHT YOU KNEW:

Gossip is the most important thing to keep up on in the workplace.

WHAT YOU NEED TO KNOW:

Do not confuse gossip for strategic maneuvering. Sometimes gossip is employed with a political goal in mind, but gossip is the last thing you need to be engaging in. Dialogue with people who are smarter and more powerful than you are is a much more effective use of your ears and your time. Know the political landscape of your place of business, but don't get sucked up by it. Evaluate it and work your plan in line with your values. Integrity is a rare gem in the entertainment industry overall, but especially in radio. Integrity shines amid slime. This goes hand in hand with the next bit of advice . . .

WHAT YOU THOUGHT YOU KNEW:

Every little thing needs to be addressed or I will be perceived as weak.

WHAT YOU NEED TO KNOW:

Prioritize and fight the battles you can win. The low-level pettiness that gets under your skin is not worth the energy or the ulcer. Bigger issues, however—promotions, raises, increased responsibility on the job, acquisition of perks, or someone in the workplace gunning for you—are all worth your time and energy. In my case, instead of starting a mini war with my slacker boss, I just stayed on the grind in my domain. I knew that my work and the subsequent revenue my area generated would speak for themselves.

If something illegal is at play and you have reason to believe it may impact you, *document, document, document!* Important note: Write in your personal journal or keep a time line with specifics on your *personal* computer. Then ask an attorney any questions you may have—*not* a co-worker. And be prepared to lose some battles to entrenched co-workers, cronyism, or high-level incompetence. It happens. It's all about choosing to see it as another opportunity for you to excel and be appreciated elsewhere, if not on your own or in partnership with someone of like mind and complementary skill set. For more on this, see The Ten Severance Commandments in chapter 6.

WHAT YOU THOUGHT YOU KNEW:

If I keep getting rejected, I must not be cut out for this.

WHAT YOU NEED TO KNOW:

Don't give up your mission. You could very well not be cut out for this, but rejection won't be how you'll know; your indicator will most likely be the clarity that comes as the passion that fueled you along your walk dissipates. If you get rejected one place, knock on another door—make that several more doors. Cathy Hughes had plenty of reason to abandon her mission by the thirty-second *no* from a lending institution. But her relentless pursuit and her refusal to let go of her dream led her to Livia Colon, the loan officer who gave her the first million dollars that built Radio One.

CHAPTER 3

Mad Skills: Not-So-Plain Janes

....

April Silver ✷ Christine Yasunaga ✷ Fiona Bloom ✷ Joan Baker ✷
Kamilah Forbes ✷ Kim Cooper ✷ Lenora Zenzalai Helm ✷
Wendi Cartwright

....

I am best when I do it my way. I work doubly hard, but at the end of the day I can lie in my bed and live with it. I am definitely hustling harder than I ever have before.

—FIONA BLOOM, OWNER, THE BLOOM EFFECT

If the entertainment business did nothing else, it brought out my inner hustler. In our industry's lexicon, *exploit* is a good word! What the women who last in this business come to realize is that it truly is a game of exploitation; it's just a matter of what side you choose, that of the exploiter or the exploited. Each of the women in this chapter chooses to operate outside the system, determined to pimp the game on her terms. Not one of them could be confined to a traditional corporate gig; they had too many things they were great at, and too many things to accomplish with their diversified skill sets. Equipped with inordinate levels of resourcefulness, creativity, ambition, and perseverance, these women could not be kept in any kind of box, cubicles included. They are Janes of Many Trades. Where they might have been frustrated homemakers or corporate misfits in some other decade of American life, they are fortunate to be so well equipped during a time of such rabid, rapid fluctuation. With entire industries from banking and real estate to the analog music business hemorrhaging losses, Janes of their kind are not so plain. So many choices are available to women of means across an unpredictable landscape that their challenge becomes more about agility and clarity.

My experience of women in entertainment is that they know how to do more than one thing; if they have mastery over one area—say, dance—they have aptitude for dance across many styles within the form. Christine Yasunaga, for example, is adept at ballet, modern, even the traditional expression of hula.

Increasingly, layoffs, reorganizations, and full-time freelancing without benefits are the order of the day. Companies are actually laying off staff only to rehire the same folks as freelancers to save on insurance expenditure. And the shell-game shuffles are happening in waves so close together that just when you've survived one mass firing, you're bracing yourself for the next before you can exhale. In January 2008, EMI let go of two thousand jobs. Sony has laid off employees in its music division consistently since 2003 as it merged with BMG. In 2006, Island Def Jam pink-slipped the entire international division of Roc-A-Fella Records, Roc La Familia. And the Roc's founding mogul, Jay-Z, was the parent label's president. That's how cold this game of exploitation can get. Without warning, without explanation. No wonder the women in this chapter who spent time inside corporations read the writing on the wall and got out while the gettin' was good. They were all gracious enough to give me some of their very valuable time for some real talk on the heaven and the hazards of being a Not-So-Plain Jane.

I organized this chapter a bit differently because the stories here demand as much. These women have all done and know so much, the round-table format that dominates this book would have become a ball of confusion. So we're going to focus extensively on each for a while. This panoramic view of their respective journeys will hopefully give voice to you women out there who remain conflicted about your desire to play on several courts at once. You are not crazy, and you're not alone, but you do need some tips from women after your own heart to navigate this terrain. Wanna hear it? Here it go . . .

*

Kim Cooper is a young lioness, a multitalent with more than a decade in the business. She has had the coveted benefit of not one but two esteemed Black female mentors: publicist turned author Terrie Williams, and promotions executive turned NABFEME founder Johnnie Walker. But even their guiding hands have not been able to stave off the twists and turns Kim has faced. The myth she's uncovered along her journey is "that it's a meritocracy; that if you work hard you'll succeed in a linear upward fashion," she reveals. Instead, it's more about "managing your emotions, knowing when to pick your battles, and putting your game face on." The upward mobility also tends to show up more like a zigzag—less lateral, more jagged.

Attractive at a very ample build and standing nearly six feet tall, Kim struggled to find comfort in her own skin towering above all the "little petite girls. I didn't look the part, so I always felt like my work had to speak for me." And work she does. Experience at the Terrie Williams Agency, RCA Records, and Elektra Entertainment made her attractive to Vanguard Media, where she was appointed "marketing manager, then sales manager, and ultimately editor of *Impact!* magazine and organizer of its programs and panels." All this matriculation within the company is bound to pay off and turn into a six-figure salary commensurate with all these duties she's covering, right? Wrong. Vanguard Media, home to *Impact!, Heart & Soul,* and *Savoy* at the time, shut down right before Thanksgiving in 2003—as in the day before, November 25. Fortunately, Kim was able to keep from slipping on the rug that was pulled out from under her publishing career, but not without depleting her savings. "I had a nest egg and went solo doing PR for about a year, then it was time to get a job again," she says, sighing at the memory. "It was about taking all the skills I had gotten and using them. My career [carries] the perception that I have done so much fabulous stuff and always had a fly job. I'm the girl who always lands on her feet. But internally, I struggle with questions like, *Why didn't I get that job? Why couldn't I stay in a job longer?*" The self-doubts crept in when neither her salaries nor her titles changed significantly for the better along her way.

Armed with a arsenal of contacts and the support of the National Association of Black Females in Music and Entertainment—an organization she helped build with her own hands as its New York chapter founder and president—she was hired as a freelance copywriter for BET, where she wound up reporting to an old friend with whom she had Terrie Williams in common: me. As Kim's copy director, I respected her hustle, and wanted to make her hours there count for more than a weekly check. I charged her with co-writing the 2007 Rap-It-Up campaign, which was quite a hit internally and with young viewers confronted by the idea of getting tested for HIV/AIDS. Kim is now a successful advertising and promo writer, yet another skill she can add to her impressive list as she works toward seeing her income increase as well. Not that the money's bad, but money could always be better, longer, stronger — can I get a witness?! What Kim has faced head-on is the fact that it's all a process preparing her for the best use of all her abilities. "I am having to redefine what comfort means, having to exercise more patience with myself. I've learned that my career has never been enough. I was always so far ahead with the vision that I was never present in the moment."

This is a common trap that multiskilled women fall into: amassing knowledge of how and what to do without being present to the difference they are making or the opportunities before them where they are *right then*. The go-getter in them is prone to take over, which keeps them looking far ahead as a matter of survival. Meanwhile, treasures are being overlooked.

*

Renowned voice-over superstar (live announcer and voice for everything from ABC News to American Express and Olay), television actor (*Guiding Light, Saturday Night Live*), voice coach, and philanthropic author Joan Baker is the quintessential Jane of Many Trades. In addition to that short list of descriptors above, Joan runs a boutique advertising firm called Push Creative with her husband, former network production executive Rudy Gaskins. The irony is, Joan has been pushing herself to win in show business since she was a teenager. Her need to be a star was so great, however, that it almost sent her over the edge. "I grew up in a white neighborhood, white father, black mother. If there was any trouble [on our block], 'the Black girl or the Spanish girl did it.' I was just a nigger to them. I felt so unloved and unwanted by the outside world, my talent was gonna save me and people were gonna love me because of it," she recalls. As a biracial child of the 1970s who never fit in regardless of the environment, Joan moved to New York in 1980. "My dream was to join [Alvin] Ailey," she notes as she recites the laundry list. "After I made my mark there, I was going to be a movie star, and from there be a humanitarian. That was my plan for many years and I didn't see it any other way. That vision saved me from a childhood of being ridiculed." Which is why Joan's dream became a nightmare when it didn't happen. "It was supposed to heal me from my past, but nothing but that dream could heal me. I would turn down smaller dance companies that asked me to dance or perform dances for shows in small venues around New York City because it wasn't Alvin Ailey asking me. I had hopes that I would be asked to do something for bigger dance companies or Broadway. When things came my way, I completely dismissed them—when it might have been another way for me to achieve my dream. I would meet a director who would ask me to read for their play and I would think it would block a bigger play from coming my way as opposed to jumping on opportunities as a vehicle to perform. I just didn't quite understand how things worked."

With her dance career behind her, Joan turned to acting. She starred in *Guiding Light* for more than a decade. She signed with Don Buchwald & Associates for voice-over representation in 1991, taking acting and VO classes between auditions and bookings. Eventually, Joan's VO work overwhelmed her on-camera work. She live-announced the industry's trade conference, ProMax; she voiced for Showtime and countless commercial brands. I even hired her as the voice for the *Miseducation of Lauryn Hill* advertising campaign. She learned her lesson from her tunnel vision with dance. When her acting school invited her to teach voice-over, she had just been fired as a sports bar hostess (the one thing in life she was probably just okay at). "If I hadn't ended up losing my job, I wouldn't have taken it," Joan reflects. "I ended up loving it! I was experiencing auditions and jobs outside class, and I would go in and describe what happened to me all week at those auditions and jobs. It was therapeutic for me—and I was getting all the stuff I was teaching my students on a deeper level just from teaching it. I realized that I would miss [teaching class] if I didn't do it again. Now it's a major part of my career."

Joan clearly has a ton on her plate, but somehow she found the time to write *Secrets of Voice-Over Success,* now in its second edition. Her book allowed her to fulfill the dream of being a humanitarian; its proceeds go to the Alzheimer's Foundation in memory of her father, who succumbed to the disease. She conducts seminars that bring her VO how-to book to life with fellow actors, agents, and producers. She also built a boutique agency from scratch with the same guy she wakes up to in the morning, her husband.

What are the guiding business principles for Joan? Discipline. Streamlining. Joan went from networking through the night at events and clubs to putting in eight hours a day in her new office, which was literally a coat closet—by choice. "All I had was a phone, milk crate, and a notepad. I didn't want space or luxury; I just needed it to be bare bones so I could focus,"

Joan remembers. "I made call after call and got big results that way. One day Rudy made me a makeshift desk and put a laptop in there, which forced me to learn [how to use] it," she says with a giggle. "I wouldn't have written my book if I hadn't."

Then Joan had an ISDN line installed in her office, so she could record voice-overs via telephone with digital quality. This allowed her to record jobs across the country, which made it possible—and profitable—for her to retain another voice agent based on the West Coast. "I have two VO agents from two different companies. In a contract you can't have an agent within fifty miles of another one. Now that technology has changed, it allows me to do that. I can record anywhere in the world. More auditions mean more jobs." This move also meant less running around outside the office to audition and record bookings, saving her time, money, and stress while she brings in money drumming up creative business for Push. She also put herself on MySpace and YouTube. Joan continued to do many things at once, and, in the words of Daft Punk Kanye West, just got better, faster, stronger.

*

Jazz, blues, and opera singer turned college professor and teaching artist Lenora Zenzalai Helm has used her natural gifts to excel at entirely new ways of contributing to the arts, for both underserved urban youth and aspiring arts teachers. In so doing, she realized that she herself was in fact a teaching artist, part of an emerging field that creates community uplift and supplemental income for entertainers with people skills. An independent recording artist and touring jazz performer, Lenora got her start on stage as a backing vocalist for Freddie Jackson and Michael Franks. Her first taste of the industry day-job came five years later, after earning her degree in film composition at Berkelee College of Music. By day she was a bank teller. Come sundown, she was gigging in supper clubs, night weddings, and hotels. "My whole career has been a crisscross between performance, the business, project administration, and arts management."

Lenora is the prototypical artist and performer who makes a living out of making music, leveraging all the skills she has. She spent some time inside companies and sopped up the game with a biscuit, because they certainly were not where she planned to spend the rest of her working days. Those desk jobs didn't pay that well, but they made Lenora privy to invaluable information rarely (if ever) available to artists—information about pay structures, publishing, and recouping on sales. She handled contracts and got to know the fine print firsthand. "I answered an ad in the paper and got the job as an administrative assistant at the Norby Walters Agency in 1987. Walters was a huge rap agent, representing Big Daddy Kane, Eric B. & Rakim, and Public Enemy." What an incredible time to be working in hip-hop, when emcees were touring the world pulling down respectable performance fees without getting arrested on a weekly basis! "I learned how to manage my own group, Sepia—and how to negotiate a contract from that job," says Lenora. She also worked in the business affairs department of Sony Music, where she "learned what should be in the contract in the first place."

After signing to an indie label for her debut, Lenora opted to record for herself the second time around. She testifies to the role the Internet plays in her success, saying, "The Internet made having my own label possible. I maximize my profit as an artist in four key areas: recorded income, live income, merchandising, and publishing. I had my own shirts, sent out news-letters, and sold CDs at my gigs."

But as is often the case with the multitalented, something was missing for Lenora. She wanted the learning environment back. "Developing teach-ers and providing access to music for youth are passions of mine. I love mentoring young artists at the college level. I want to be the Oprah of arts education." Knowing what a tall order that is, Lenora co-founded Housing Authority Resident Musicians of New York (HARMONY), a nonprofit that provides free music instruction to the city's underserved students. What began as a program focused on kids in public housing ultimately served hundreds of young people without music in schools in Brooklyn, Queens, and Manhattan though Saturday and summer instruction programs. Leno-ra's knack for administration combined with her classical and performance training served her well as HARMONY's artistic director. Her journey as a recording artist also gives her a wisdom few arts administrators have, and a certain credibility with youth obsessed with music stars. "Managing myself when no one would take me on taught me what it takes to develop myself. I can show my students the road maps [whether they want] to be the next Beyoncé or the next arts administrator," she says, smiling.

What is this Jane's secret to flexing her many trades? Personal devel-opment through Landmark Education, a series of seminars specializing in how human beings work that, for many participants, yields incredible results around career, relationships, and personal power. "I feel I can be a change agent through the ability to enroll others that I learned in Landmark," Lenora notes. She also took some notes from Quincy Jones when she enrolled in one of his master classes. His words have stayed with her throughout all her reincarnations as a musician. "Quincy said, 'Find out what interests you, then go about perfecting your ability in those areas so you can become the most bankable one there is.'"

*

From the ways Kamilah (*ka-MEE-lah*) Forbes has become accomplished as an actor, playwright, theatrical director, television producer (HBO's *Def Poetry*), and founder of the Hip-Hop Theater Festival, you'd think she was in Quincy's master class, too! In fact, Kamilah led a double life throughout college in an attempt to please her parents, for whom the only acceptable disciplines were medicine, law, and engineering. Well, Kamilah ended up "going to Howard University to study biology, and got bit by the theater bug. I had this idea that I would balance it all to make my mom happy. I almost got disowned." She invokes the words of thinkers Myles Horton and Paulo Freire. "With entertainment, we make the road by walking. I've had to be creative about my career. I changed my major, and once I graduated in theater, I went on to a post-graduate program at Oxford University with a concentration in classical text." She traded in biology for the classics in her balancing act, reading the canon by day and flowing in ciphers in the clubs by night. Seeing hip-hop theater artist Jonzi D sealed the deal for Kamilah. "I was in rap groups in DC, and that was the culture I identified with. I was blown away by Jonzi; inspired to the point where I wrote *Rhyme Deferred*. I came back to the US knowing this was a genre in the making. Mixing deejaying and text on stage was always bubbling in my mind. I created a theater company called the Hip-Hop Theater Junction."

It was this endeavor that turned Kamilah into a producer. She and her company of actors did the research necessary to create a nonprofit so they could apply for grants, with her friend Nyakya (*nia-kia*) Brown sharing upfront costs. She worked as a bartender and an aerobics instructor (yeah, I'd like to see you try that) to pay her rent, pay her actors, and pay for costumes to put up the play in theaters. The company would split the door proceeds with the theater, then split their share among the company. "If we made a grand, that was a big payday," she recalls. The success of the Junction led to the creation of the Hip-Hop Theater Festival with performing artist and playwright Danny Hoch, who is a card-carrying member of what I call the Bad White Boy Association, which also counts Elton John, George Michael, MC Serch, Bobby Caldwell, Michael McDonald, Hall & Oates, Freddie Mercury, Boy George, and Eminem among its members.

While Kamilah now has help from Hoch, she is also taking more on. The festival grew from one city to three locations in one year. And her eye for screening festival talent won her a job as a talent executive for *Def Poetry*. There was no passing up the opportunity to work on a nationally televised show that celebrated theater arts and spoken word. And being Kamilah, well, you guessed it — she was promoted to producer, and she thrived in her expanded role. "I was able to give more input and become more of a stakeholder in the process," she beams. "I was able to vision for the future. We started to move from just [showcasing] poets to specializing on each episode. We had an episode about Katrina with poets from the Gulf. We even had DMX and Carole King perform."

Okay, reader, let's count up everything Kamilah has going on. She's running a theater company and a hot new multicity festival, she's producing a hit television show, and she's still acting every now and again. Kamilah's biggest mistake was one many Janes confront: Doin' Way Too Much. Well, all this ground to a halt before an acting gig she had in Denver. As we all know, the Creator and the body will conspire to slow you down when the mind refuses to. "I was literally in New York for a week, then San Francisco for three days, then back to New York, with no time for me built in. I was so exhausted, I had to tell them I couldn't do the gig and go home. I didn't realize how empowering *no* was; I didn't know how to say it," she explains.

Enter a critical lesson for all women, but especially you Janes out there: Say Yes to No. It was the biggest lesson of Kamilah's career. "Once I valued what I said yes to, that allowed me to be fully present to it. Even the people I said no to felt better about it, because they could see where my focus was — and I felt better because I could actually focus!" Saying no is sometimes really saying yes to you: your sanity, your health, and the value of your contribution. Now Kamilah slows herself down to keep from being scattered and spread thin. "When it's festival time, I lock down and do that. If I'm directing a show, I slow down on acting. I also work with a coach to help me see when my vision is shifting."

*

Like Kamliah and Lenora, Fiona Bloom is also a classically trained Jane of Many Trades. Now a new media PR maven and artist manager, Fiona has hosted cult classic radio shows, run an indie rap label called SubVerse, worked in urban marketing for EMI, been a hotshot music publicist at Zero Hour Records, and co-founded the "I Know You Got Soul" conference, a confab for independent soul artists. Born in London and surrounded by Black music, which she came to love, Fiona's inner hustler was set free after sixteen years of classical piano, from age five to twenty-one.

The biggest challenges for women with many skills are those of indecision and the inability to finish what gets started. Fiona uses herself as an example. "Philadelphia College of Performing Arts gave me a full scholarship. I studied very intensely, but was burned out, so I transferred to [the] University of Maryland. I practiced eight hours a day and I was good, but I had no life. I didn't finish there, either. I couldn't compete. I just couldn't take that pressure. My family felt so let down and disappointed after all the money and time invested. I led such a strict regimented life as a child that I had very little fun. But I wasn't a quitter . . . I didn't know what else to do, so I moved to Israel and went on a year-long kibbutz in Jerusalem. I just didn't want to return to London a failure."

Well, Fiona had only experienced her first taste of failure in what can be a decisively cruel business. "A wise woman once told me, 'You're not really in the business until you get fired,'" Fiona says. "And I used to scoff at that because I hadn't been fired and knew I was heavy in the game. I didn't fully understand the meaning of her statement until that point where it looked like I might get laid off. I was confronted with the idea that I would lose everything I had worked for up to that point and get sent home with a booby prize in the form of a severance if I was lucky." That's when it became clear that job security was an illusion—a bubble that could pop as arbitrarily as the kind that start out in a plastic bottle. And you're not fully in the game until you're made to face your contributions, the possibility of them becoming irrelevant, and the need to reinvent yourself to survive.

Fiona went through years studying music in school completely unaware that she was headed for her moment in the mirror upon relocating to Atlanta, transferring to Georgia State, and taking a late-night radio show slot on WRAS. The story she shared about being fired is a lesson in the downside of innocence and the importance of tact. WRAS is a college station with the wattage and audience reach of a mainstream station. Fiona hosted a popular jazz show, winning listeners over with her sandpaper-meets-champagne British-accented tone. Her popularity landed her a late-night slot at Star 94, where she became assistant music director at twenty-four. "I learned about dayparts, [music chart] reporting, programming, and schmoozing with labels. They worshipped the ground I walked on to get their records added."

Young, ambitious, and talented, Fiona was on the fast track—and she was feelin' herself. "I was very confident," she recalls. "I would speak my mind to the general manager—but that wasn't the wisest thing to do. I used to tell people at the station that I should be on during the weekends; that they should give me a break." When the break she felt entitled to didn't come, she took a meeting with the programmers of the competing station. What she never anticipated was that she was being watched, let alone being snitched on. "I was never even thinking of them as the competition, but people there called over to Star and said, 'She's a traitor! She's taking meetings over here!'"

Mutiny is the cardinal sin of radio. Needless to say, then Star 94 program director Tony Novia called her into his office. "He said, 'You made the biggest mistake of your career. I'm not happy to do this but I see no other way. You're gonna learn the hard way from this, but you're gonna go places.' Once I got fired, I was so devastated, I was crying." She went from the APD position at a commercial station to hosting *World Party* with her DJ, Lil' Jon, on WRFG, a renowned community station. But the pay was nowhere near the same, which led Fiona to events planning from retail in-stores to shows for Fat Joe and many other emerging emcees. After a couple of years on WRFG, she had become a "local celebrity: The girl who knows everyone in the urban community, has great passion, and throws great parties."

Her swagger caught the eye of Daniel Glass, who was top brass at EMI. He offered her a marketing manager position with a forty-five-thousand-dollar New York salary. Atlanta gave its adopted urban daughter a huge send-off hosted by Jermaine Dupri. She moved to Manhattan. She was a good-size fish in a small pond swimming upstream into the ocean of an industry mecca. Fiona put it simply: "I was thrown in with the sharks. I had no record industry training, and was never an intern. I busted my ass there, but I wasn't performing. I was flustered in meetings. They'd give me three minutes to present my updates because they didn't really care about Soulsonics, Gang Starr, Shara Nelson, Joi, or even Digable Planets. They were looking at their watches. And eventually, I got let go. Shortly after that, so did Daniel."

This kind of risk accompanies the relocation leap, or the leap to your first job with a serious salary. You are expected to hit the ground running and move at a heightened pace, a pace that tripled for Fiona coming from the sleepy South to the City That Never Sleeps. Situations like Fiona's earn you hard-won skills, but at a very humbling price. While she might have realized she was on thin ice at EMI, she probably thought she could appeal to the man who'd hired her in a pinch. Instead, the plug was pulled on her before she could even get her ducks in a row. In entertainment, you can only see where the guillotine is going to fall after you've survived a few rounds of layoffs. Even then, you can still miscalculate — and find yourself signing off on a package in HR.

As a new employee, Fiona's severance was paltry. "I only got three weeks' severance, and I had no money. But my pride wouldn't let me go back to Atlanta. I couldn't go from the hot New York job to temping. I was depressed," she recounts. "I got an offer to work [publicity] at an indie rock label. Ray McKenzie was a musician who had made a ton of money in finance. He quit his job to start Zero Hour. I had to take the job." Fiona's reinvention as a publicist was under way. Even though she had never done the work for a label, she told Ray she could. And there's no harm in that as long as you're ready to download the Chopper Flight Program like Trinity did in *The Matrix*. Fiona wasn't a rock chick at heart, but she put her foot in that job, going above and beyond. "I put him in every publication I could; he became the hottest guy in the business because of me. And I was becoming the hotshot publicist everyone wanted. He took amazing care of me."

Fiona returned the good look by introducing McKenzie to her former boss Daniel Glass, who had a new label venture, Rising Tide. "Before I knew it, they were behind closed doors with Doug Morris. They ended up doing a multimillion-dollar deal." She was given a bonus for making the introduction, but Fiona also seized her own opportunity and asked for a hip-hop imprint of her own under Zero Hour to run. McKenzie agreed, and her label 321 was born. The label's first release was *Connected*, a hip-hop and dub compilation.

She had the foresight to sign Blackalicious, now a veteran underground group with a following that stretches from its native Davis, California, around the planet. "When I flew out to Oakland to offer them a deal, their Soundscan was two hundred. They ended up selling seventy-five thousand copies of the *A2G* EP. The label 321 released *Nia* just as Rising Tide pulled the plug on Zero Hour; its rock acts were tanking and the label was hemorrhaging. 321 went with it. Sadly, Blackalicious had sold seven thousand copies of its album in the first week and was on tour when it happened. Suddenly they had no support." Fiona was being dealt another devastating blow. But the coldest thing about it was that she was the profitable line item on a sinking ship, and her earnings paled in comparison with the king-size losses of her parent company. In hindsight, after breaking several artists and contributing to the rise of hip-hop and soul for close to two decades, Fiona recognizes the impact of lacking more business acumen. "I'm a late bloomer and I've accepted it. People say to me, 'With all you've accomplished, you should be a multimillionaire.' I am, however, admired around the world for the artists I've discovered, and that goes a long way," she proclaims. "My parents call it the Bank of Thanks. I'm turning it into the Bank of Green!"

After doing some A&R consulting for a Swedish metal label, she started her own company, The Bloom Effect. She was being paid a great monthly retainer, but the label turned all her discoveries down. It was finally time to put her energy into the music and artists she believed in without a co-signer. This stop on her journey brought Fiona to a powerful realization about how she needs to work: on her own terms. "I am best when I do it my way," she says. "I work doubly hard, but at the end of the day I can lie in my bed and live with it. The Bloom Effect is a one-stop shop for lifestyle and branding needs in music: event production, PR, Web strategy. I will even shop artists at Midem or walk you in to the few A&R reps there are left. And the way labels are going these days has sent many artists and companies my way. In the next two years, the company will turn around a million-dollar profit."

This Jane of Many Trades imparts her hardest-learned lesson: "You will never make it if you take everything to heart. In business you can't wear your emotions on your sleeve. It's okay to cry, but don't let anyone see. I used to cry a lot. Now I'm hustling harder than I ever have before."

*

The hustle is second nature for Janes of this caliber: women who fight back, bounce back, and take back that to which the business world says they have no right. For April Silver—for more than a decade as an arts and community activist as well as the founder and president of AKILA Worksongs—taking back Black music and culture for the fiscal and spiritual uplift of its creators has been, in her words, "feast or famine. There were times when I had contracts big enough to buy a car or hire an entire staff; then there are times I'm calling home for help. I don't know any [small] businessperson who earns a hundred thousand or more a year who consistently has three months of reserves. Half the time, your big contracts help you catch up on bills and keep you afloat. This is partly the price that comes with being your own boss."

For April, activism and commerce are inseparable. As the founding president of Howard University's Hip-Hop Conference, the nation's first conference on hip-hop culture on a university campus, April helped to jump-start the conversation around hip-hop, empowerment, and artistic integrity—a conversation that, for members of the mainstream, began with C. DeLores Tucker, Rev. Dr. Calvin Butts, Tipper Gore, or Don Imus, depending on which rock they happened to be under. "We were the first to examine it academically, and we did it for six years," she notes. "There was a call for us to look at hip-hop from a position of owning it, not just performing it."

April counts author turned politician Kevin Powell and the Jena 6 among her most recent clients, but after college and some time in a graduate degree program, she attempted to tie her commitment in with labels from a place of partnership. She thought labels actually wanted to be accountable and contributive. She thought wrong. "My goal was to be the community affairs department for the labels," she recalls. "I had even convinced a few to do the right thing. But the money didn't come. I had contracts, and they stiffed me. Something that, naïvely, I never thought would happen. Within two months of leaving my job, I was working in the stockroom at Macy's. I lasted one day and gained a new respect for retail employees."

Janes of Many Trades, take heart. None of the women in this chapter resorted to hiking skirts up literally or figuratively to stay alive or viable in the business. Which means you don't have to, either. Additionally, April confirms that the next wave of Janes has an advantage she didn't have coming up: the Internet. "Technology has leveled the playing field a lot," she asserts. "It has given a voice to people who needed to be heard when the doors were closing to anyone who was not on the A-list. It doesn't cost thousands of dollars for a site anymore, but they do require work to maintain. As someone who beats the drum in the community, the Web has been a huge asset to me. And while it is not supposed to replace rallying, it keeps us better connected politically."

*

April chose to work outside the system to represent her community; former music licensing executive Wendi Cartwright did so in order to raise and preserve her family. As I've mentioned, I do not subscribe to the notion of work–life balance. I believe that eventually memories and moments will be sacrificed or missed, whether you choose to miss the listening party and screening, or the recital and Little League play-offs. Unlike music publishing, where the writer's share and the mechanical share equal two sides that each control their respective 100 percent, in the pie called family-and-career there is only 100 percent to go around, not 200 percent. The challenge, the key, the mission, is to make your career life and family life harmonious. In the context of family and relationships, *balance* is a setup for feelings of failure, guilt, and inadequacy for career women. I have simply chosen function over balance. As a result, my husband of twelve years and son of nine years experience me as much more present, relaxed, and fun to be with. I have left keeping balls in the air to jugglers at the circus.

Wendi took her cue from a devastating decision she made to forgo a planned trip to Paris with her mother and best friend at the request of her boss during one of those heads-are-about-to-roll periods at the major label where she was working. "During the time I was supposed to be gone, my boss came to me and said it wasn't a good time for me to go on vacation." She sighs as she relives the conversation. "He was looking out for me, and said that if I left, he couldn't guarantee that my job would be there when I got back. So my mom and best friend went without me. My friend died a few years later—and I was laid off anyway. I learned to follow my heart and let the chips fall where they may."

For Wendi, the chips wound up falling in the world of lifestyle modeling and commercial acting. She happened to get discovered in her jogging, sweat-drenched glory while pushing her newborn son during her routine run. "An agent stopped me, gave me his card, and said I had a great look and should consider acting or modeling. That same week, two or three other agents approached me. I talked to my sister-in-law, who walked me in to the agency where her son was signed. Five years later, I am still with that agent."

After years of doing licensing and clearances along with working in business affairs for companies like Priority Records, Virgin Records, and Rhino Records, dealing with everything from Ice Cube to show tunes, the flexible schedule and residual checks that came with acting and modeling were a welcome change. Wendi was even able to use her label experience to help her make the transition from sitting behind a desk crunching numbers to being on-camera talking to her wall over a bowl of cereal in a Terminix commercial.

Wendi breaks it down like this: "If you listen, are open, and follow direction, you will work it and give the client what they need. The work ethic is the same as having a budget and deadlines inside a label. My solid work ethic and understanding that time is precious, [that] people have expectations you must meet, and not to be nervous all help me on the acting side. I'm also really used to rejection from asking for rates working in licensing at labels. Actors would be so upset over how they got talked to or didn't get the job—and I couldn't believe it. They treat you like furniture to a degree. When you're being lit and made up, they talk about you like you're not there. But no one is feeling you up in a corner or spitting on you—it's so much more fun than the music industry."

Instead of her life in records becoming the straw that broke the camel's back on the home front, Wendi the actor-model turned the stress and overt sexism of the music business into positive fuel. "My attitude is different. I don't expect to be given the job, and I'm happy when they give it to me. And I already got the prize, which was a happy home life. That's why I show up happy and work as much as I do. I'm a firm believer in not swimming upstream. If you're ready when an opportunity comes, just try it. If it fits with what you want and works for your list of what you need in order to live, then go for it."

SUMMARY OF SECRETS REVEALED

WHAT YOU THOUGHT YOU KNEW:

I have to participate in everything that is presented to me—or else I will lose out, miss out, or be left out.

WHAT YOU NEED TO KNOW:

The power of no. As a Jane of Many Trades especially, your ability to be selective and discern what deserves your very valuable time, energy, and focus will be the difference between doing what matters and doin' too much. Further, it may rescue you from being associated with a disaster. Say Yes to No!

WHAT YOU THOUGHT YOU KNEW:

If I just keep working hard, I'll keep advancing.

WHAT YOU NEED TO KNOW:

If hard work was all it took to get to the top, some women wouldn't be working so hard on their blow jobs. Opportunities are taken more often than they're given. Don't just keep busting your behind looking for someone to confirm that you've done well only to give you a chance to keep doing well. Start by asking what you can do to get to your next level. Feel free to take it a step farther and create opportunities for yourself by taking the initiative to do something no one else ever thought of doing before you. Then own the result. If you succeed, you're a hero. If you fail, cry privately, clean up the mess, get the lesson, and keep it moving.

WHAT YOU THOUGHT YOU KNEW:

_____ *is what I know best, and it can't help me in another, totally unrelated field.*

WHAT YOU NEED TO KNOW:

No matter what you fill in the blank with, you have what it takes to make the leap, even if *what it takes* looks like recognizing that you need to learn more before you make it. Before looking from without, take inventory within: Make a list of all your skills, talents, and abilities. Then literally take your next goal or idea. Write it down at the top of another column next to the "Mad Skills" list. Draw a line from the skills that can be of immediate service to you as you move toward your goal. Circle the skills that may not be directly applicable but can create a bridge of access, knowledge, or leverage. Finally, create a short, manageable list of action items for the circled "Bridge List": someone you can contact to share your goal or request help from; a way to contribute without expectation of reciprocity; an event you can attend or relevant reading you can do to learn something new.

WHAT YOU THOUGHT YOU KNEW:

I am doing everything, but I am not experiencing any forward movement.

WHAT YOU NEED TO KNOW:

Take a break from all that "doing" and bring yourself to *being,* as in being in the present moment. Some skills won't reveal themselves as transferable until you are in the moment of transferring them. This is when it's critical to pay attention to your intuition, your first mind, or your heart—however you call Spirit—and take heed. For example, for years people would tell me I had a great voice. And for years, I said, 'Wow, thanks,' to them—and *Yeah, whatever* to myself. Until the day that my scratch voice-over on a commercial I had written was selected for the spot. Instead of seeing that as a fluke, I realized that those people were on to something, and so was I. So I took the steps necessary to turn voice-over into a new revenue stream and career. Besides, if Wendi can draw on the constant rejection she experienced during her music executive career to eliminate the defeating power of rejection as an actor, it's worth asking yourself, *What weapon in my arsenal has yet to be drawn?*

WHAT YOU THOUGHT YOU KNEW:

I'm a hustler, a go-getter.

WHAT YOU NEED TO KNOW:

It ain't hustlin' unless you're profiting from it. Stop collapsing hooking someone up with being a hustler! You have powerful resources, and hookups are not always reciprocated (read: waste of your resources). If you're helping other people make money, contacts, or deals without getting a piece of the action for yourself, you're not being generous. You're being hustled. Money is always great compensation, but it's not always available from a transaction. In these instances, exact your benefit by bartering for services, information, or an introduction—just like Fiona did when she parlayed her label imprint, 321. Your considerable skills can take it from there.

WHAT YOU THOUGHT YOU KNEW:

I can do most things myself, so I should just get it done on my own.

WHAT YOU NEED TO KNOW:

More isn't any good if it kills you. Don't wind up laid out in the hospital doing it all yourself. Look at your skills list, identify what you do with the least ability or joy on that list, and delegate. Or practice embracing the power of no. This is your opportunity to put the *work smarter, not harder* principle into full effect.

CHAPTER 4

Imaging: Beauty Is a Beast

Abby Dobson ✳ Aliesh Pierce ✳ Ashaka Givens ✳
Dawn Haynes ✳ Kimberly Kimble ✳ Leslie "Big Lez" Segar ✳
Mayasha Long ✳ Mimi Valdes Ryan ✳ Mystic ✳
Nzingha Stewart ✳ Traci Bartlow

*If I was a rock 'n' roll chick, no one would say shit to me.
Rockers can have their hair unbrushed with bare dirty feet,
all in the name of rebellion, and it's okay. Well, hip-hop is
rebellious, too, and my clothes should not determine the
value of my art.*

—Mystic

THE LIES WE BUY

The biggest lie we buy with respect to image, glamour, and style—be it in total or in part—is that we are not beautiful. I know, I can see many a neck rotate in disagreement, and yes, it's tough to hold up the mirror of self-doubt and look straight into it. But more often than not, we enter the glamour conversation heavyhearted with inner conflict. We tell ourselves that we're fly, sexy, and lovable, but what we *hold on to* is the conversation we kick about what part of ourselves we like least, want to change most, how many pounds we wanna lose, and why we're not _____ enough (you fill in the blank). I need not rehash the paucity of positive, edifying images of ourselves across all forms of media or rerun the script of worthlessness that the mixed messages of slavery, racism, sexism, and domestic violence have shouted and whispered over the centuries. Ultimately, we were lied to about being ugly, and it stuck with us. Whether it's wearing natural hair, becoming a vegetarian, being a size 24, or doing five hundred crunches three times a week, every day that one of us chooses how we look or takes ownership of her image in a powerful way, it is a victory over the Big Lie. Every woman I spoke to for this chapter is committed to exposing the true beauty we possess through her own work. Just as important, they're all determined to expose the next lie: that women in general—and women of color in particular—are the consumers or victims of image and style, not the creators and innovators.

Sisters are most definitely architects of style. While the worlds of Western couture and fashion have largely been sealed off from us, the music business has provided a space for women who were not necessarily white or wealthy to jab in the crowbar and pry open the door to create, be recognized, make a living, and influence the runways, especially with the advent of music video. Recording stars from Patti LaBelle to Erykah Badu look to their sistren to create eye-popping hair and captivating costumes. Knowing the disadvantages women of color face thanks to the limitations of cosmetics in the complexion department, our makeup artists have consistently created custom blends and regimens that are now being duplicated in earnest by beauty companies on a massive scale. While you pretty much have to be a supermodel or megastar to successfully negotiate your own black hair specialist in the fashion world, the notion that women of color stylists are among the best in the entertainment business is widely accepted.

Hairstylist, owner of Kimble Hair Studio, and Kimble Hair Care Systems product line creator Kimberly Kimble is by all accounts among the best. She is the stylist Beyoncé enlisted to take care of her hair (that's Kimberly's work whipping in the wind machine on Bey's "Crazy in Love" video). Mary J. Blige has credited Kimberly with bringing her hair back to life. But before she became the go-to hair stylist for music icons, she already had four years on the books working in film (Natalie Desselle and Halle Berry, *B.A.P.s*) and television (Brandy on *Moesha*, Garcelle Beauvais on *The Jamie Foxx Show*). Her point-of-entry story is very important because Kimberly took the whole internship conversation a step farther: She was discovered while volunteering her services to raise funds for her church. Sometimes it takes going beyond working for free to working for something bigger than yourself.

"I wanted to see if I could do theatrical hair, so I volunteered my time to do a play at the Church of God in Christ in Los Angeles. I did hair for *The Five Heartbeats* musical and all the proceeds went to building the church," she recalls. And you truly never know who's watching. This one's almost too perfect. "Robert Townsend's assistant was there, and we met. I kept calling her and stayed in touch, letting her know I wanted an opportunity. And a year later she called me for *B.A.P.s.*" Kimberly designed the outrageous hair-pieces Halle and Natalie rocked in the film, a huge showcase of her talent even though she was not the key hairstylist. It was her competition portfolio that caught the attention of Townsend, so those of you cutting your teeth on the hair show circuit are on the right track.

Townsend was so pleased with her performance that he sponsored her into the union on her very first film—a rare occurrence, mainly because the production has to pay for your membership. "Robert [Townsend] used to call me Cinderella. I've gone on to *Austin Powers*, *Dreamgirls*, and a host of other movies. I went from doing hair on the bus to taking private planes to go to work. I wanted it, I prayed for it, and it happened." It was surely guided by the hand of the Creator, but Kimberly did her part. She placed herself in a position of service for charity. She connected with someone in the industry, Townsend's assistant, and kept in touch for a year before seeing any return on her investment by nurturing the relationship. And when she got the meeting, she had an impressive body of work to present, demonstrating her contribution despite being completely unproven in the film arena.

There is plenty of room for more of us on the set of a shoot beating faces, whipping hair, pulling clothes, or calling shots behind the camera itself. Like Kimberly's measured but seamless transition from TV and film to music, and again from simply owning a salon to designing her own hair care products, on the music side some women of color actually get to direct and produce after succeeding in a related area such as talent. Choreographer Fatima Robinson now directs music videos. Not content to stop at being a recording artist, Lauryn Hill established her film production company, Zion Films, lensing clips for Aretha Franklin and Common. J.Lo is killin' the fashion industry with her clothing line of curve-sensitive, street-credible couture and a fragrance line that smells like money—all to the tune of more than three hundred million dollars in annual sales.[1] As of 2005, her fragrance line alone generated a hundred million a year in the billion-dollar business of celebrity fragrance.[2] Of all the stars with a scent, it's Jennifer Lopez who lays claim to 10 percent of its overall earnings. Beyoncé, Lil' Kim, Gwen Stefani, and Eve have followed suit with their own respective fragrance, accessories, handbag, and fashion labels. Foxy Brown even stepped in the arena with a line of furs.

The barriers to access have been broken. Today profit is the primary concern. And with nonwhite populations booming with increased disposable income, at long last urban skin, hips, and hair are in. Kimberly for one wants Black women to have access to education about hair health and the products that help them achieve it. "I felt the [beauty market] didn't have a lot for women of color, or women who had a lot of hair damage or dryness. Either products are too watered down, or too greasy," Kimberly observes. "My goal for every client with damaged hair is to get it to grow, be healthy, and look good. Great hair equals confidence. And I want to give that to all women." Kimberly refuses to allow being a woman of color who is also a master of hair of color limit the scope of her clientele. If women who aren't of African American descent want extensions, braids, and locks, what's wrong with a Black hair specialist reaping the financial benefits of providing these services, creating the hairstyles that are her birthright? Exactly. Absolutely nothing.

Another untruth pervasive about every field in the entertainment business, aside from actually being a recording or screen star, is that you cannot make a living at this. You probably hear it said all the time from family, friends, co-workers at your day job — or even inside your own head — that only the lucky ones or the connected ones can do what they love in the world of image-making and be more than comfortable financially. I mean, being paid to fly all over the world to dress or photograph people with no consistent schedule? To people who are governed by the rat race of set hours, wages, and sick time, it looks like tomfoolery or some pipe dream. To everyday people, it's too good to be true. Some professionals are too selfish or bitter to mentor others and *want to impress upon you* that it's too good to be true so you don't come knockin' on what they claim as their clients' doors.

But it's not the impossible dream — though you will have hard times, be they financial, spiritual, or emotional. This possible dream is a miracle that the women you'll hear from in these interviews experience on a regular basis, and it's available to you as well, if you are willing to embrace the work that accompanies the lifestyle. The pros only *make it look easy;* remember the swan's toil beneath the surface.

What's important to remember here is that as an aspiring style maven, you can enter from just about any point. There is no prescribed path to travel in the entertainment world overall, and the same is the case for the world of entertainment imaging in particular. The thing to get here is that every path winds a different way and has its own set of consequences. What may take one of you three years could take another three months. One thing is certain: Playing it safe is the equivalent to taking the scenic route. Risk taking, even the most calculated kind, opens up possibilities for your career.

Education is key. Anything you want mastery over requires knowledge and practice. This also applies to the entertainment biz. But expertise can come in the form of every type of education, from formal schooling to the School of Hard Knocks variety. Kimberly's education began when she was twelve years old, watching her mom do hair at Trina's on Pico Boulevard in Los Angeles, which led to her enrolling in beauty college and washing hair alongside her mom at sixteen. "I went to a lot of trade shows and took classes, but the best education was actually doing hair," Kimberly notes. "You learn from repetition; you also learn from your mistakes, which can often create good new looks."

Just like Kimberly's mom, an influential mentor can impart information that a college professor may never get across. Sometimes it's not even about whether or not you're in college, an MBA program, or trade school, but *what part of the world you're in when you're getting educated.* For the style professional, some time put in outside the United States can give you a powerful creative edge, especially since we count Paris, Milan, and Tokyo among the capitals of the style world.

Celebrity makeup artist, groomer, and esthetician Aliesh Pierce is a skin color specialist who has become a fixture in the Los Angeles beauty community, having worked with Golden Brooks and Eva Mendes, along with grooming Don Cheadle, Lenny Kravitz, and R. Kelly. She became a makeup artist by going to Europe as an exchange student. She credits her time abroad with giving her invaluable experience working with models, learning the fashion world, and, most important, confirming her passion for the work. "I started working officially in '87 when I moved to Milan and took makeup seriously," she says. "I went to Italy at twenty-one and stayed for five years; I speak fluent Italian. I think having a fashion background is the most important thing as a makeup artist. Doing time in fashion gets you respect from your peers."

Couture and performance designer to the stars — namely Erykah Badu, André 3000 of Outkast (yes, the poofy shake pants), TLC, Talib Kweli, and Imani Uzuri — Ashaka Givens testifies to the importance of getting out into the world before her career took shape. "I got my first sketchbook at twelve from my mom, and I had been sewing matching outfits for my friends to wear in grade school," she recalls fondly. "I always wanted to design clothes, but I put it on the back burner to become a CSA [computer science administrator] since it was the career trend at the time, and to make a 'decent living.' I was told by peers and society in general that because I am young, female, and Black, I couldn't make money doing fashion," she admits. "Well, I got into computers and was so bored that I went back into fashion. After attending three different colleges and studying abroad for one semester at England's Manchester Metropolitan University on exchange from Buffalo State, I finally completed my education. I studied tailoring in England. It was the best experience of my life and it opened me up to more than Rochester, New York. I finished up at Fashion Institute of Technology with degrees in fashion design, buying and merchandising, and fashion design with technology."

In contrast, Mayasha (*my-EE-shah*) Long knew she was a stylist before completing high school. Her plan was to attend FIT and live with her uncle, the late Toyce Anderson. You may not know his name, but if you remember Cameo, I know you remember that red lacquer cup Larry Blackmon was sporting like a futuristic jock strap in all his videos. Having Larry rock that codpiece over tights was the brainchild of Anderson, a brilliant stylist who brought couture to the streets in the 1980s — with a *codpiece*. Word up! But when her uncle took ill, Mayasha found that New York was not to be. Undeterred, she stayed in Los Angeles and took a retail job in the Beverly Center. She was eighteen when she got her first styling check as an assistant on an En Vogue shoot. "I got $350 per day for a five-day job; I nearly fainted! I knew at that moment it was my career."

Mayasha's big break as an assistant stylist came from a co-worker named Nonnja, who enlisted her to help her style her newest client, Will Smith. As the "hands-on assistant," it became clear to Mayasha that assistants are trading salary for experience, even when they do the majority of the work. "Assistants actually do the work of pulling clothes. Then the key [or lead] stylist comes in, looks at what I pulled, and styles the artist. Assistants have equal control minus the entitlement" of the key stylist, who can command two to five thousand dollars a day on the very high end. Of that, the assistant's fee is more like three to five hundred dollars a day. This spells a recipe for poaching of assistants by production companies, who would much rather pay a neophyte key stylist five hundred a day than four times that amount for an established key stylist.

After three years of assisting with the likes of Nas, Jay-Z, and Method Man & Redman, Mayasha was known and noticed by producers, photographers, and artist managers alike. She credits Pharrell with her first key job.

He hired her to style the debut N.E.R.D. album and promotional appearances after watching her work with Kelis. Mayasha's work with the taste-making genre-bending band led to her working with Shaggy during his diamond-plus (meaning over ten million sold) album, *Hot Shot*. She was initially brought on to style him for a few months. That turned into "four and a half years," she says, laughing out loud. "I traveled the universe with Shaggy a few times. Going on tour gives you that free pass—I had per diem [daily cash allowance]; my hotel and flight were taken care of. It was very empowering to see the world [as a working woman], without a man. I've been to Lebanon (and there's no going back there today), Jakarta, spent New Year's in Durban, South Africa, even Australia. My passport is insane."

And then there was her day-to-day job description—which is not to be outdone in the insane department—while she was on the road with the world's biggest commercial reggae star. If you thought tour styling was just about shopping and playing dress-up with live people instead of manne-quins, read this very carefully. Mayasha rattles off a laundry list of duties that will surprise you.

"Shaggy would have four shows a week. I was responsible for Shaggy. He had four dancers and an eight-member band. I had to see to it that each night, they had their clothing pressed with shoes and any accoutrement needed for their look. Shaggy alone had three changes per show. The band stayed in one outfit each night, but the dancers changed into their three looks per show as well." Wait, there's more. The tour stylist doesn't just make sure everyone's dressed, she has to shop for and fit each member of the entourage, who speak more patois than English. "The clothes were part of our cargo, put into crates for travel that I was responsible for. For the first six months I was spent. I had a hard time with their patois and my English clashing. Not having an assistant to help me was also very new for me—and it was extremely stressful. So at the six-month mark I requested a pay raise and requested that the band dress themselves, and that the dancers take more time out to help style themselves so I could focus solely on Shaggy. I figured out easier looks. I learned patois and enjoyed speaking it after a while. Once we worked that out, it became a lot easier."

Compelling photos or films of exotic, thrilling locations just don't hap-pen from your bedroom, even if you're nice with Photoshop. Wardrobe styl-ing from your closet in the mirror won't cut it, either. You gotta get out into the world, create those looks, capture those images, and make a portfolio or reel that will blow the competition away, ideally posted online. Like most things tangible in the creative world, portfolios have also gone digital. Place your photos on a Web site or on your home page with your social networking site of choice as soon as you can.

A critical pathway for successful entry into the entertainment industry universe is via internship, even in the beauty world. While it is not necessary, or any solid guarantee to realizing your career goals, it is as close to college or a post-secondary education as you can get without actually being in an academic setting.

In fact, many companies have reputations as revolving doors for executive talent, turning out the movers and shakers of the field after breaking an artist or sending a celebrity's career into overdrive. Independent companies that enjoy major-label distribution may be a training ground of sorts for fresh executive talent because they can't pay like the Big Four and most likely soon-to-be three: Sony BMG; the looming EMI/Warner Music Group, which is now also a publishing partner with BMG; and Universal Music Group. Others might say it's because these gifted human resources are inadequately compensated for their efforts—and instead of staying underpaid, the smartest interns simply use the company's cachet as currency to write their own ticket to the next level. In truth, either case could be made about any staffer at a brand-new indie record label, recording studio, or lifestyle magazine that created today's generation of entrepreneurs and industry leaders. I'm pleading the Fifth on that.

Anyway, the rep persists. Perhaps this is because the smart interns with a long-term vision who came for more than the shine are outnumbered. On the label side, companies perceived as such training grounds have included Bad Boy Entertainment (I mean, Diddy went from interning at Uptown to selling $300M in Sean John clothing!), SRC Records founder Steve Rifkind's Loud Records, the large indie that irrevocably altered the landscape with two concepts, the street team and the solo deals for Wu-Tang Clan; Tommy Boy Records, run by the gutsy and unflappable Monica Lynch; Arista Records, the house that Clive built before we were voting on *American Idol;* Priority Records, the street indie that gave West Coast acts distribution partnership deals before it was the norm; Jive Records, Barry Weiss's one-stop shop (label, publishing arm, and the iconic Battery Studios) that releases artists as disparate as A Tribe Called Quest and Britney Spears; and, rounding out the list, the mother of all hip-hop empires, Def Jam. For media, BET, Miramax, VIBE Ventures, New Line Cinema, *The Source,* and Sutton Broadcasting come to mind. In the fashion world, training grounds are less centralized, looking more like apprenticeships under one experienced stylist than entry-level positions at glam-related organizations (unless you intern at an agency that reps beauty professionals). Thus, turnover happens much more readily because:

- Style professionals are often independent contractors who turn into business owners.
- Rosters and staffs change around with trends based on who's best at delivering the styles of the moment.
- Most of these are boutique agencies or small operations.
- For the companies dedicated to urban music and/or fashion, there are only a few legitimate major players.
- New companies spring up, luring veterans to accept higher-paying or titled positions elsewhere.

These reasons drive home the vital role of internship. If you can get in and make yourself indispensable, you have a great chance of being hired and moving up, or being hired, picked up on the industry's radar as a go-getter who makes it happen, and moving on. Remember: This industry has no concept of job security. Everyone acknowledges this and job-hops accordingly. The business changes so swiftly, and start-ups morph so rapidly into serious competitors, that everyone is constantly going in the direction of the business, whatever that happens to be at that moment.

Unlike other areas of corporate America, a very small percentage of women executives work at the same entertainment company for the lion's share of their career, or go from mailroom to CEO. Even Universal Motown president Sylvia Rhone (former president of EastWest and Elektra Entertainment) and Cathy Hughes (CEO of Radio One) moved around between labels and radio stations, respectively, as they climbed the ladder of success to head up companies. Rhone got her start as a secretary at Buddha Records. Hughes was a sales manager for Howard University's signal, WHUR.

Now the editor in chief for breakthrough beauty magazine *Latina*, Mimi Valdes Ryan is a rare example of a woman who spent a decade of her career at one company in more than one post, ultimately ascending from editorial assistant to editor in chief at one of the best boot camps in urban entertainment, *VIBE Magazine*. In her view, there's something to be said for going above and beyond to demonstrate your commitment to the company's vision, not just what gets you paid every two weeks. It's also important to remember that careers aren't built in a day any more than Rome was. Meteoric rises to executive superstardom, or what Mimi calls the Puffy Syndrome, are a myth. I ask her to explain: "The Puffy Syndrome is when a person thinks they can go from intern to head of A&R at Uptown," she says, shaking her head. (By the way, it's probably not called Diddy Syndrome because he wasn't Diddy yet.) "People don't want to pay their dues; they just want to be at the top. It went great for him, and he worked hard, but that's unrealistic. That's not the norm, and so many kids think that they will end up writing cover stories just by making an impression.

"I liked that I held many positions as I rose inside *VIBE*," Mimi continues. "The only things I didn't do were research and copy. My goal was always longevity, and having that well-rounded experience of knowing every aspect of a magazine can't be taken from me."

Style professionals, especially trainers and photographers or directors, spend lots of time in the trenches working out or crouching backstage to get the right shot. Makeup artists are working with products and colors, moving from model to face with seconds to work their magic before the camera rolls. Stylists' arms are usually loaded with rented, expensive designer clothing, and their legs are bent kneeling to tape a hemline or adjust a model's position during a shoot. It is rarely about lookin' cute in the four-inch heels with hair whipped and jewelry on bling. In fact, that look can often scream *groupie* or *extra* when you want to convey *focused* and *professional*.

According to Bay Area–based and nationally renowned photographer Traci Bartlow, who cut her teeth assisting photographer Victor Hall shooting 2Pac, Too $hort, and Digital Underground, in addition to being functional, dressing down sends its own powerful message. "I would dress in dark colors and forgo being cute to get the shot and be able to get filthy," she notes. "It was really important that I not be mistaken for a groupie, and when I was backstage stepping to artists I looked like I was there to work, not catch. I realized that being cute wasn't gonna work for what I was trying to do as a photographer."

But according to stylist and agent Dawn Haynes, far too many young women have it twisted, believing the hype that they as glamour professionals help to spin. "I have interns and assistants now who are young girls. I just try to keep their hopes and keep their dreams and keep their visions going, but a lot of times I find that, even in my inner circle of women, immediate gratification is what they want. They want the Mercedes or the big houses or the long trips or they want to go shopping and the shopping isn't because they're passionate about styling or wardrobe. It's because they want to bling. It bothers me."

This is all the more disturbing when we as women examine the cost of placing material gain over our own personal development and success. The skewed priorities born of low self-esteem show up as choices that at best are unintelligent, at worst, life threatening. When has the blow job given to the doped-up rapper ever qualified as safe sex? Furthermore, even after all that whoring, you still need to have assets to live on and/or provide for children with. So pretty soon you'll be back at the drawing board trying to reconstruct a broken life. Consider building it right the first time instead.

First and foremost, recognize that in the words of fitness, dance, and media, renaissance woman Leslie "Big Lez" Segar — who has choreographed Mary J. Blige, danced the intro for Livin' Single in silhouette, hosted BET's *Rap City* for eight years, and co-hosted morning radio with comedian Steve Harvey — "Most overnight sensations happen the night *after* ten to fifteen years of hard work." The death of the intern or assistant gave rise to what I call The Microwave Mentality, or TMM for short. Sufferers of TMM think to themselves (then even have the audacity to say to others), "Gimme thirty seconds, and I'mma be *hot*!!" Well, you may be hotter than MIMS, but are you trustworthy, reliable, honest about what you don't know, and committed to playing your support position to the best of your ability? *Yes* answers to all of the aforementioned, especially the latter, are what matter. That's the kind of heat you want: an arsenal of skill and reputation that both anchors you and precedes you.

TMM also has the dangerous side effect of causing you to be too preoccupied with being fabulous before your time and despite a pint-size budget. Take the train to the shoot instead of asking for a car service. The longer you're in the game, the more adept you'll be at knowing what's doable in the name of fun and what's just foul. Hooking up your homies at the expense of your gig or the client is a huge no-no. And this goes for everything from autographs to haute couture.

Mimi shares a story about an intern who almost messed up on her job: "There was a girl who was an [editorial] intern at *VIBE;* we were covering

Diddy's cologne launch party. She saw Nelly and wanted a picture with him. I told her she didn't want to do that because she wouldn't be taken seriously as a journalist, especially as a female in this male-dominated entertainment world. You don't ask for autographs or have him call your sister. Y'all aren't hanging out, you are working. You need to be taking notes and setting the boundaries of getting your story. You want them to be comfortable and open up to you, so they give you the information they won't give another magazine. You don't want to be the groupie fan." Mimi noted that when she gave her that jewel, the intern looked confused, as if taking pictures of talent as a journalist was a perk of the job. That's what the photographers are for. Trust me, we are already perceived as groupie fans instead of the pros we are, no matter what we are wearing or how old we are, so don't add lighter fluid to that fire. "I'd be on video sets and the PAs, even the director, would all think I was on-camera talent—some video girl," says Mayasha. "But the tone of voice changes when they realize I'm here to dress the artist. Then they have to apologize for trying to grab my ass."

Credit is gold; do not abuse company accounts or, in the case of stylists, client credit cards. Mayasha elaborates. "Make sure the garments that have been used don't look it. Make sure you return everything because they are reluctant to let you borrow things. Unfortunately, stylists are known to be thieves, so don't play into that. The same people who work at Barney's talk to the people in the styling department at Gucci. And once your name becomes dirt, the doors will close on you no matter who you're styling. They want the fifteen thousand dollars' worth of clothing you borrowed back *the next day,* not a month later. Your bad behavior makes it harder for the next stylists to do their job if the reputations of too many of us in the field are faulty."

And another thing: Leave the friends and family at home. *You* don't need an entourage on the set; that's the client's department. And look, chances are that just when you're feeling salty about working like a hot slave in the summer, you'll get hit off with some goodies.

Now that the industry is all up in everybody's living room thanks to entities like Google, YouTube and Viacom, the competition to be down and get in is beyond fierce. I mean today, you've got kids going on shows *pretending* to be their favorite music stars in the videos they watch, or at least uploading them for the world to see on user-generated-content sites like Juice and YouTube. The point of being an intern or assistant is to learn so you can *become* the lead stylist or photographer; actually impact the game from the inside instead of being a consumer of the hype it generates. Doing the work (especially what looks like trivial work) without complaint and giving 110 percent is the highest form of respect for your mentor. It communicates that you are a player who's willing to be coached to win. Those players become franchise, clutch, and Most Valuable Players. This doesn't mean take harassment or abuse of any kind. Nor does it mean suppressing your feelings, especially if they include feeling taken for granted or resentful. The idea is to work hard and have fun doing it, not to have the stress of your silence work overtime on you. Acknowledge that payment comes in all forms, and that a place with room to learn and grow makes you one rich intern or assistant. Once your job no longer resembles such a place, it's time to speak on it and step up your responsibilities, or simply get to steppin' to your next endeavor.

This goes back to being a coachable team player. Practice is over when Coach says so, and not before. During my "twenty-hour-a-week" internship at DeLeon Artists, I was going to shows we booked that happened on school nights, staying late to clean the office, attending events on weekends. What's more, this is what working in this business really looks like: a 24/7 "pride-swallowing siege," as Tom Cruise's Jerry Maguire put it, until you can call your own shots. Period. Pamela Watson's take on this says it all: "If you've committed to be on set assisting me for a day, don't look at your watch and say you need to go when the job's not done. That's what's required. When it's your shoot, you won't be able to leave!"

Video director, MTV Video Award nominee (for Bilal's "Soul Sista"), and screenwriter Nzingha Stewart (more than thirty videos, including Common's "The Light," Ol' Dirty Bastard's "Got Your Money," and Keyshia Cole's "I Changed My Mind") is her own boss, so this piece of advice is critical to her success. She actually counted four vacation days to herself the year we spoke. "Every single job sets the stage for the future," she warns. "I am always in some form of pre- or post-production. When I'm sick, I still have to work. I drag the laptop into bed with me. As the director, if I'm too sick to work on the budget, then I lose the whole job." Nzingha also knows the cost of wasted energy, especially in the form of negative self-defeatist thought. "I expected to be king of the world. When it didn't happen I would get discouraged, blame it on being a woman or whatever . . . I realize now that thinking was crazy. Nobody owed me anything. I wish I had spent that time focusing on being the best I could be."

Kimberly got a similar wake-up call while she was on the hair show competition circuit. "I did a lot of shows and competitions and [when] I looked at my competitors, I would find myself losing. I was losing focus on what *I was doing*. When I started focusing on what I was doing, I started winning."

Whether this is about finding new designers for your stylist to pull clothes from, experimenting with color on the makeup side, or scouting locations and doing research for a visual artist or director, realize that your resources—however limited they may be at first—will only expand and contribute if they *differ* from those of the people you work for or with. You make yourself indispensable by being the eyes, ears, sounding board, or inspiration of your mentor. You also sound like someone who could handle something big on her own, and sooner rather than later.

I worked in the Bay Area hip-hop industry for ten years before relocating to New York. By the time I left, I had held a nationally recognized magazine editor position after years of working on a grassroots level in the community with artists, publications, and label clients as a writer and co-founder of my own street marketing and management company. Now, I may be on the conservative end of the extreme, but the Bay is far from a wack secondary market, and it was tough to leave that beautiful place. In fact, the San Francisco/Oakland Bay Area is ranked fourth among urban markets for entertainment consumption, not to mention ripe with entrepreneurial and creative innovation. More important, I wanted to make sure I had done all I could there before I packed up my life, left my family and friends, and ran the decathlon of rat races in the Big Apple.

That said, before you follow the Yellow Brick Road, really look to see if you've done everything possible (short of selling your body) to advance your career. If you're in a secondary market (for music, that means anyplace in America other than New York, Los Angeles, Nashville, and increasingly Atlanta) and it's time to jet, take a deep breath before you go off the deep end: Send out the mass e-mail to your contacts and tell them what you seek to do and where. Send your letter with a résumé of paid and unpaid experience attached to people with hiring power. In your letter, share your dream, what you want to learn, and your aspirations. The key is to convey is that you're hungry, willing to travel, and flexible within reason on terms of employment to get to the next level of the game. The bottom line here is this: You don't categorically have to relocate to cut your teeth or to blow up—especially in today's digital world. It's a huge risk to move without a plan, and risks without a plan don't have a tendency to go well. In any event, stay committed to your goal, *not to how achieving it should look.*

....

BEHIND THE SCENES: GLAMOUR PROFESSIONALS ON IMAGE BUILDING

....

The people who make their living from making others look their very best are part coach, part psychiatrist, part parent, part best friend. In order to bring forth the best in their clients, they work to get inside their heads and win their trust, often with very little time. Being a stylist, makeup artist, choreographer, trainer, director, or photographer requires a peculiar balancing act: You must have a vision but be flexible; you must formulate an opinion but share it diplomatically; you must take a leadership role without standing in the spotlight. The masters of this tightrope walk called image-making are rewarded with referrals, fierce loyalty, and the respect of their peers. Celebrity, while not guaranteed (hell, what is?), can also happen for the glamour pro, but as chapter 7 on being a "supastar" reveals, true celebrity is elusive and fleeting, requiring a concerted, sustained team effort.

Glamour professionals don't agree on much, because their art is as subjective and open to interpretation as any. But the ones I interviewed love subjects who are willing to push the boundaries of what they perceive as visually pleasing—their comfort zone, if you will. The models, artists, and actors who are comfortable in their own skin are subjects that will light up the screen, make love to the camera, leap off the page with allure, mystery, confidence, otherworldly appeal.

Aliesh weighs in here on the importance of image and artist involvement. "I think the artist has to step up and say they will or won't. They may be perceived as a bitch; it's real pressure when you're in the situation [as the artist]. But they have to own that image because media and fans will hold them to it. If they don't match up to the image, the public feels lied to.

"I think everyone I ever worked with had a lot of say, and they are the ones I appreciate working with most," she adds. One thing that makes a glamour pro's job easier is the client's inner beauty. Their inner peace. And if you don't have that yet, at least know what part of your face and/or body you're insecure about and say so. "If you're so insecure about your nose that your 'makeup' means having two lines down each side of it, seriously consider having that nose job done," Aliesh offers. "If you'll never be all right with what you got, fix it. It's unreasonable to hope that a makeup artist will continually create the nose you've always wanted." But in the meantime and in-between times, while you *artistes* work to manage your insecurities about those imperfections, the off-camera talent needs a few things from you.

First, have the class to come to work focused on getting the job done. No matter what the short-term payoff may be for you as the star of the show, being high, drunk, or uncooperative is not cute for the person who has to battle your profuse sweating, dilated pupils, sunken cheeks, jitters, halitosis, or bitch-made irritability to make you look as together as you simply are not. You can traipse down that path of destruction for as long as the yes-men around you and the record sales or ratings will allow. As the real operating principles of the industry suggest, this path is bumpy and short. Mayasha has a short list of contrasting examples, choosing to mention by name the positive ones.

"I worked with an artist who, at his height, was my confirmation that the devil was present," Mayasha recounts. "This was during the big Ecstasy craze. Rap music was playing everywhere. Black folks were very debaucherous, lots of girl-on-girl action, orgies. This artist was the king at the time, and the white girls loved him — and he loved them right back, even though he was married. He had a mistress who knew every woman he slept with.

"The rapper had passed out for three days from popping pills, drinking, and getting blow jobs on set between takes. We were literally shooting the video around him — when he was awake," Mayasha continues. "He was blown out of his mind, incoherent during clothing changes, where he'd fall asleep. He even left over a thousand dollars in cash in a pair of pants. I found it but we had wrapped [the shoot], and the rapper and his producer had already left. When we handed it to him the next day, he had no idea that he'd left it. At that point, I walked away in complete disgust. That was just one of his videos, where I was assisting," Mayasha continues. "I was key on his next video.

"The R&B singer with whom he collaborated on the single was a complete dream to work with. But he and his producer were always missing. I had my assistant leave the clothing in the dressing room. And I opened the door to be greeted by the rapper's producer at the doorway with a woman on her knees, blowing him. And he spoke to me in a normal working tone, and asked me, 'What do you need?' In hindsight I think he set it up because he felt as the king's producer, I needed to see that. And two years later, his rapper lost his 'crown' to the next hip-hop king. It was a turning point for me as to how nasty men could be.

"A complete opposite from said unnamed rapper was working with Nas. Completely respectful to all women on set, be you video ho or craft services woman. He made sure all his goons were in check as well. If I walked in and they were all smoking and loud, he made sure they got quiet and told them all to 'chill in the presence of a princess.' There was one video where he read us Qur'an between takes. We all fell in love with this profound young man. He spoke only when it was time, and he was the dream rap artist to work with, by far my favorite rap client."

The second thing is: Artists, take care of your people! They take care of you, don't they? I mean, Aliesh for one is a real stickler for detail, down to your ashy body parts: "I always check knuckles because I am totally annoyed by a beat face and black knuckles, ashy knees, and a wrinkly neck. How does an artist get paid thirty-five hundred dollars just for the face? The face and body should match!" Well, okay, you had no idea they were lookin' out for you on that deep a level, but that's the whole point. Pay them, create an atmosphere of comfort, and show some appreciation for the fact that they give up their personal time to be on tour with you, in addition to a lot of other business they could be doing with other clients if they weren't on the road keeping you together.

"Another amazing man to work with is Will Smith, probably the biggest star we have," Mayasha reflects. "It was a ten-day music and film press tour for *Wild Wild West*. We were with him for New Year's on Capitol Hill. I was standing next to the Clintons as part of his twenty-five-Black-person entourage. After DC, we went to Germany, Paris, and London. Will made sure to throw us a party in each city. Will gave us per diem, put us up at the best hotels, and took us to extravagant dinners each night. Then he'd rent out a club and have Biz Markie spin for us!" You may not have Will's budget, but you can certainly take some notes on how to treat your entourage.

Finally, keep in mind that the style professionals are also beholden to more than one company or entity when they take a job. Not only are they there to bring a vision of their own to life, but that idea has to be congruent with that of the record label, product manufacturer, or media outlet. When image professionals are hired for a job, they are accountable first and foremost to whoever cuts that check. Granted, at day's end (or when the recoupment accounting for the project is done), artists usually pay the team that gives them their stardom. But on the front end, for example, it's Geffen Records, not Mary J. Blige, that issues that check. Of course when Mary's happy, everybody's happy. But if you're a new artist or do not have a long-standing relationship with the style pro, it's understood that the image professional's accountability lies primarily with the executive and the label that hired them. Artist, you're not the only face in town—hell, on the roster for that matter—in need of a touch-up. And be clear that the label offers a solid opportunity of repeat business once the artists on set today retreat to the studio or run into a PR nightmare that cuts their schedule short.

Take R. Kelly. In 2002, fresh off his top-selling album *TP-2.com* and "The Greatest," the uplifting hit single from the Oscar-nominated feature film *Ali,* his career was on a roll by all indications, with a new high on the horizon through his collaboration with Jay-Z on their *Best of Both Worlds* album. That is, until the sex tapes and the allegations that came with them surfaced. The album's debut was a flop for artists of their stature at that time, a mere 223,000 units sold. And this was at a time when CDs were selling well compared with today. Well, the shit hit the fan and splattered. The magazine covers were killed. The plug was pulled on the tour in support of the album. No new videos. No television appearances—with the exception of *BET Tonight*—in response to the scandal. Which means no work with R. Kelly for his veteran grooming and wardrobe principals, Aliesh Pierce and Pamela Watson, respectively—or any other self-employed creative artist affiliated with "The R" until further notice. Just like that. But through their work with R. Kelly, they can certainly continue their business relationship at R. Kelly's label and have a conversation with Jive Records about working with, say, T-Pain or Justin Timberlake because their bridge to the paying client isn't on fire: It's the one R. Kelly built with his public that's ablaze. Kellz has proven to be like Teflon to the justice system. The accusations and charges levied against "The Pied Piper" have simply been unable to stick. He rebounded from multiple charges of child pornography with successful albums, the latest being *Double Up.* He beat the case that has been following his career for the last six years, found not guilty by a jury and acquitted on all fourteen counts. So it's back to work for the glam squad. Pamela Watson is still his go-to stylist. Aliesh parted ways amicably and began to work with other musicians, including India.Arie and Yolanda Adams.

....

WHEN ARTISTS HAVE THEIR SAY

....

Photographer Traci Bartlow made a poignant observation about Lauryn Hill, an immensely gifted woman I am privileged to have worked with on an album that changed the lives of millions of women though its music and poetic exploration of heartache and empowerment, *The Miseducation of Lauryn Hill*. The difference in perception that accompanied her drastic change in appearance was a larger comment on the importance placed on glamour by the industry and consumers alike.

"Lauryn was the *one*. She opened the door for glamorous, natural black beauty. Sexy, natural, and dark-skinned. And with her second album, she is completely different: hair cut close, no makeup, dressed down. And the business has no sympathy for that. She showed her vulnerability and how brutal the business can be, and the audience has no interest in that. That's an unfortunate thing with image: We [as consumers] just want the outside to be attractive."

Now, had L-Boogie not sold twenty million albums, do you think she would have been able to determine how she looked or sounded on her sophomore solo album, *Unplugged 2.0?* Hellllllllll naw. But Lauryn was no longer interested in being controlled, and her numbers gave her the kind of leverage that entitles an artist to call some shots.

But what about the new or independent artists who don't have multi-platinum sales to use as a weapon in the fight for their image? Their struggle is no less significant. And without that leverage, the sacrifices made to preserve self-esteem become significant as well. I spoke to two recording artists about this in detail: Abby Dobson, a lauded New York–based soul performer; and Mystic, the Grammy-nominated Oakland-raised hip-hop veteran with a global following. Mystic's Bay Area sister Traci is impressed with how Mystic has been able to create her own look, which she describes as "very different: she's one part hippie, one part pimp." But Mystic's self-determination is hard-won in a business that exploits women with impunity.

"Imaging has been the most hurtful and confusing thing for me. For me, it's more than just an outfit. I always said, 'My image is I don't have one.' But that doesn't work in this business," she intones. "When it comes to women, there is a certain way we are supposed to look. You're either totally sexual with everything hangin' out, or you're a tomboy. In reality, women are much more diverse than that," Mystic emphasizes. "I've shed many tears about imaging, because to a label, it's marketing, but for me it's my life and body and I have to live with both forever." Mystic has been vigilant about the image she wants to get across, and she believes that being signed to a small indie label, Goodvibe Recordings, made some of those battles easier to fight—and win. "I've had a much better time than most women and I attribute that to being on an indie. Otherwise I would've lost my power and not have been listened to. I would have had to go into how being raped has impacted how I want to present myself, and that's not a conversation I want to have with white male strangers at a corporation. One person can't change the industry's preoccupation with image. So I simply keep an open mind, experiment with new looks, and at times I put my foot down and go for a velour sweatsuit as opposed to heels."

As a songbird who prefers to leave something to the imagination, independent R&B singer-songwriter Abby Dobson (heard most recently on Talib Kweli's "Get By") laments the wave of thugged-out imaging. "Labels' conception of Black music is one-sided. If you're not 'street,' you're not Black to them." She asks, "Would Alicia Keys be as successful as she is if she were not so hip-hop-oriented?" It's an interesting question; she definitely kicked down the door in cornrows, seemingly to offset her classical training and angelic face. And the braids came down a bit with every album, right up to her current best-selling third CD, *As I Am.* Touché.

Abby draws a direct connection from how she looks to her ability to remain authentic. "I sing because it's an expression of who I am," she says. "I don't want to feel like I'm living in someone else's skin while I do something I love. I would be open to suggestions, but I will be governed by my principles. I've said no to deals. Sure, I'd love to be signed and have a record out, but I prefer happiness to having that record out in a horrific situation."

....
LET'S TALK TURKEY
....

Even when there isn't money working in the glamour world, it's not bad at all considering that you're not licking envelopes or punching out for a coffee break all day. For assisting stylists, you do a lot better than your young peers in fast-food service and retail clothing on the mall circuit. The pay range for assistants can start as low as $150/day and go up to $350, which means Mayasha was on the high end right out of the gate with her En Vogue job. Runners—task-driven support staff—get less because they are responsible for less, and can make seventy-five to a hundred dollars a day. On shoots, a top assistant will get five hundred a day for a twelve-hour day.

Stylists just starting out will take a job for $750 a day to build the portfolio and database. Once your reputation, contacts, and work ethic get you into a rhythm and get you visible, your rate can go through the roof, commensurate with your experience, anywhere from $750 to $4,500 a day. Mayasha notes that there are a select few African American stylists surpassing that daily rate, and she knows because it's her job to have a general idea so she'll know when it's time to boost her own rates. You can also write the terms of your rate and dictate to the client when it goes up on a per-project basis. A day generally equals ten to twelve hours, followed by time and a half for up to six hours more. After that, clients can wind up owing you double time per hour based on your day rate.

On the hairy side of things, Kimberly outlines a vastly different pay scale. Some rates are set by the type of shoot you're on. "Editorial print can be as low as $150 a day for big-time stylists and new ones," she says. "Depending on the client and the production, and who's paying, it goes up to ten grand a day. But that ten grand is not usually going to African Americans . . ."

Kimberly also has sage advice for reducing on-the-job stress when it comes to getting paid: Don't negotiate directly with clients. Key hairstyling on sets or tours is a world away from the services menu at the salon! "When you get to a certain level, I recommend having an agent so you can make a living. I would do this for free, but that won't help me. I will do jobs out of love, because it's a great opportunity, or because it's a great-paying job; I choose who I work on and where. It's good to keep the financial and creative separate. I'm an artist, too, and I just want to focus on doing hair."

Aliesh echoes this sentiment. She took things a step farther. She was also very shrewd about percentages going to her manager. "Twenty percent commission is standard, but I was able to negotiate that if an artist is not their client, and I brought the work in, they only take 10," she says. Her rep would negotiate "a weekly/monthly rate [based on the client's needs]. If something comes up, I do the job. If there's nothing, I am free to do makeup for someone else. Under contract, you get paid whether you work with the artist or not." Everyone draws their own boundaries, however. "There are many makeup artists who choose to work freelance, or work on a relation-ship basis," Aliesh continues, "but I'd prefer to pay an agent 20 percent to avoid having to ask someone who has become my friend where my money is, whether management found the client or not."

Dawn Haynes, CEO of Dawn to Dusk Image Agency, represents glam squad members, and has worked as an image and wardrobe stylist in her own right since 1989. Her clients have kept the likes of Ciara and Vanessa Williams looking their best, and Dawn works personally with Jamie Foxx, Halle Berry, Usher, and Eddie Murphy in addition to her mentor, Quincy Jones. Dawn's been all about the Benjamins since she was a little girl orches-trating car washes at Thanksgiving dinner, splitting the profits with her cousins. She had a hustle for every season: pumpkins in the fall, Christmas trees in the winter, polishing teak on yachts docked in Playa Del Rey dur-ing the summer. She has some incredible pointers for dealing with money before you start making it:

- Avoid the credit card offers in college.
- Two years is the magic answer for the *how long* question, be it about employment or residency.
- Go after free money based on being female, of color, or both, among other things.
- Strive for a FICO credit score of 720 or better.

More from Dawn on money management as a business owner in chap-ter 9, I promise!

What's insane about women, particularly women of color, is that we will work like crazy, switching or even juggling several careers. Then we'll say we want out, but we don't have the millions we want to exit with yet so we gotta keep pushin'. Or we really mean we want out, but it's just out *into* something else. For Big Lez, she's pretty much out of her music video and dancing phase and on to her next career as a media jock. She's been an on-air personality since 1993 co-hosting *Rap City* on BET; she also had a successful run with her own program at Sirius Satellite Networks. What she is actively work-ing toward now is becoming heiress to Pam Grier's action heroine throne. Kimberly wants to open her own hairstyling academy. Aliesh has fortified her résumé by becoming a licensed esthetician. Though she gets more work than ever as a stylist, Pamela started a kids' apparel line. The bottom line is multiple streams of income, ideally passive income that makes money while you sleep. So whether you're just starting out, making moves from the inside, or looking ahead to life beyond entertainment glamour, what follows are some steps toward that end (or shall we say beginning).

....

SUMMARY OF SECRETS REVEALED

WHAT YOU THOUGHT YOU KNEW:

The image-making world is as glamorous and fabulous for me as a style professional as it is for my clients.

WHAT YOU NEED TO KNOW:

Nope! Style pros *do* have an image to maintain because they often are walking billboards of their ability to look good, dress well, stay in shape, or beat a face. However, when they are working, it's about being comfortable, tastefully professional, and usually minimally fabulous.

WHAT YOU THOUGHT YOU KNEW:

An internship guarantees me a job.

WHAT YOU NEED TO KNOW:

Be prepared to work without being paid by check. Your compensation is information, access, and hands-on experience.

WHAT YOU THOUGHT YOU KNEW:

If I'm not getting paid monetarily, I definitely don't owe them my evenings and weekends!

WHAT YOU NEED TO KNOW:

When you're on the job in this business, your time is not your own. We work nights. We work weekends and even holidays. And so will you, or you won't last.

WHAT YOU THOUGHT YOU KNEW:

I can achieve my goals and be taken seriously if I simply stand around looking cute, waiting for someone to hand me my Big Break. It is the beauty business, after all.

WHAT YOU NEED TO KNOW:

Don't stop at looking sharp: *Be sharp.* Think ahead. Anticipate your mentor's or boss's needs. Put all the energy of where you want to be into where you are right now.

WHAT YOU THOUGHT YOU KNEW:

The only way to make it as a choreographer, stylist, or makeup artist is to pack up and head for New York City.

WHAT YOU NEED TO KNOW:

It is possible for the business to come to you, but the business needs a reason powerful enough to do so. Amass as much power as you can in your world before you leave it behind for the next hungry go-getter in your market to dominate. Hit the glass ceiling in your hometown before moving to an entertainment mecca. And when you finally leave, if you aren't leaving with a lot of money or a job waiting at your destination, at least have a plan for where you'll stay and how long is too long to be without steady income.

WHAT YOU THOUGHT YOU KNEW:

This is a quick and easy business to get into.

WHAT YOU NEED TO KNOW:

The overnight sensation is a *myth.* By the time you're receiving a first impression of artists or executives, they've already been on the grind for years.

WHAT YOU THOUGHT YOU KNEW:

Since I'm new at this, I should learn by watching.

WHAT YOU NEED TO KNOW:

Most of what the best in the business know, they learned by watching and *doing.* Don't just stand there! Ask what's needed, then take the initiative to provide it.

CHAPTER 5

Before the Music: Songwriting, Music Making, Publishing, and A&R

....

Brenda Russell ✴ Cheryl M. Potts ✴ LaRonda Sutton ✴
Leah Harmony ✴ Marcella "Ms. Lago" Araica ✴
Meshell Ndegeocello ✴ Rachel Allgood ✴ Tina Davis ✴
Tomica Woods-Wright

....

I can see the music as it's going by. It's all reference; it's all audible math. To be good at anything musical, I just listen.

—MESHELL NDEGEOCELLO

The process of becoming beautiful for the world to see is a painstaking one taken largely for granted. Everyone loves looking good, but few have the ability to put colors and design together artfully. So it is when it comes to the process of making music: Everyone appreciates music of some kind, and many people can play instruments or carry a tune, but to bring notes, lyrics, melody, and rhythm together artfully takes being a gifted songwriter, lyricist, musician, and/or vocalist. This is not to say that there aren't recording artists in the world who are average and hugely successful; there definitely are. On the other end of the spectrum, you have those who are extraordinary and underrated. The reasons for this are myriad, from the sheer drive of the average artist to blow up by any means to the lack of marketing machinery for musical genius. And that's where the people who discover, develop, and direct the gifted artists come in: publishers, artist-and-repertoire execs, music producers, and engineers. This chapter will introduce you to women who have the gift, and to women who are pivotal role players in the music-making process.

We'll get into the *how to* and *why not* surrounding success for recording artists in the next chapter. For now, we're heading into what goes on before the music with women behind the sound. We'll get into the nature of the process, to the degree that such emotional creativity can be described in tangible terms. We'll also look at barriers to the creative process, be they self-imposed, external, or organizational. The reality is that once artists stop doing this for their friends and look to earn a living or (gasp!) become famous, music becomes business. And the industry becomes something to contend with as you seek to create, express, preserve, and protect your art. With the value of songs reduced to ninety-nine cents or less in the twenty-first century, this chapter's objective is to illuminate how much music still costs to make, personally and professionally. It damn sure ain't free.

....

THE WRITING AND PRODUCTION SIDE
....

Grammy-winning thirty-plus-year veteran producer and composer (her most recent work is the music for *The Color Purple* on Broadway) Brenda Russell can attest to the cost. She paid her dues in the studio as a session singer and arranger long before she got her first production credit or solo recording deal. Born to a drummer father and singer-songwriter mother, Brenda taught herself piano. "I write on the piano and play on my records, but I don't read a note," she reveals. The absence of formal education would not stop her, however. While she was backing up Elton John, Barbra Streisand, and Bette Midler, the studio was her classroom. "In some instances, it would have been good to have [note-reading ability], but it hasn't hurt me. I learned from the people working the machines. That was like going to school. Vocal work was my training ground," she explains. "I wasn't chatting between takes while we weren't on. I learned how producers worked with players and singers. Today's artists are so cocky, they don't even care about what happened before they got here. It's important to know your history, investigate where the music came from. You have to be able to learn from the people who are already doing what you want to do."

Brenda's career has been a marathon, not a sprint. Before becoming a producer and composer, she was a session singer throughout the 1970s, realizing her solo debut album in 1979. During that time, she was asked to arrange vocals for jazz artists whose songs had supporting vocals, which led to invitations to write songs for artists. It happened to be Aretha Franklin, the Queen of Soul, who handed her a standout lesson in songwriting.

"Aretha asked me to write a song for her, and I was a big, big Aretha fan! I thought about all her songs that I loved and wrote. She heard it, came back, and said, 'I *really* wanted a Brenda Russell song.' Time moved along so I couldn't write another song for her," she reminisces. Brenda's Aretha moment did, however, empower her to write for other luminaries, because she realized that she was in fact the key ingredient she needed to write songs for others. "I must always write for myself in the spirit of what I want to do," she notes. "That's why they ask for me. I should have written her a song that I wanted to sing, not what I'm projecting that they want or what they've already done. It gave me confidence to write." Brenda's newfound confidence led to hit songwriting, and some hard choices about what to keep for herself and what to sell for other singers to record. "'If Only for One Night' and 'Get Here' are songs I wrote for myself. I wrote 'Dinner with Gershwin' [for myself], but David Geffen heard it and made me an offer I couldn't refuse to give it up for Donna Summer." Eventually, "If Only for One Night" and "Get Here" became hits for Luther Vandross and Oleta Adams, respectively. Brenda recalls that she was careful to hold on to "Get Here" for herself initially. "The night I first performed it, a young executive came up to me and asked for the song for a young artist. I said, 'I think this will be the song that gets me a record deal.' The artist was Whitney Houston. It got me my deal with A&M. And Whitney was still all right," she says with a smile.

Brenda is among an elite group of woman producers who have sustained careers over time. That is doubly the case when you take into account that she is African American. She came up in a time when sisters of any color in control of their musical ideas were few and far between. Producers like Beyoncé, Missy Elliott, Meshell Ndegeocello, Erykah Badu, and India.Arie truly walk in the trail blazed by Ms. Russell. "When companies are spending so much on albums and they're having a hard time making money, they might not want to gamble on an up-and-coming woman," she says. "Linda Perry is a well-respected producer, as is Patrice Rushen. I call the players, organize the studio, and am running the show in the room. I love producing myself, even though it's a big job."

Brenda began co-producing with Andre Fisher early in her career, and experienced being marginalized by what she calls the "boys' club attitude in production" firsthand.

"It wouldn't matter that I arranged, wrote, and sang the song; the musicians that came in would always direct their questions to Andre. Or they'd talk about me like I was invisible. He'd just say, 'Ask her—she's right here.' It took me establishing myself as an artist to make projects work without that resistance."

Her songwriting has topped the charts on successful albums, and Brenda has also had a considerable amount of her work appear in film, including *John Q, Liberty Heights,* and the score for *How Stella Got Her Groove Back.* In writing music for film, Brenda encountered the resistance that is common to this distinct form of artistic collaboration. "Most times, directors have no clue about how music people work, or have no knowledge of music. I would create something for them, but they would have no idea what they wanted, which could be frustrating. The directors who know what they want make [film work] rewarding," she says. Brenda reflects on a film opportunity missed because she judged the movie by its script. "I got this one script," she says with a chuckle. "I wasn't moved by it. They came to me so early that I passed. That movie was *Flashdance.* I've been kicking myself ever since. I should have asked for some scenes. The actors made the movie—along with the songs. Now I'm more open and not so quick to judge. I try to feel where the movie is going."

In the case of *The Color Purple* on Broadway, she had the opportunity to feel where a stage adaptation from a preexisting book and film was going for five years. She and co-writers Allee Willis and Stephen Bray spent five years composing the music for the show. So for those of you songwriters who think this is something you do alone in a room in a vacuum, think again. You have to be committed to creating and sustaining—for grueling hours—a level of trust and respect that can create brilliant work. Brenda elaborates: "There was no script at the beginning. What happens is we'd get together and we'd write the music, then Marcia Norman would write scenes and bring them to us. We did this five days a week all day long. We ran it in Atlanta with live audiences for a few weeks, then go back to the drawing board, constantly rewriting. It's not writing a musical, it's rewriting! I got into the music business so I wouldn't have to have a day gig but here I was with a real day job." Being so completely invested in this process made it important for Brenda to fight for songs as the show went though multiple rounds of changes. The group dynamics she participated in for decades along with her producer knowledge informed what battles she undertook, and how she went about it diplomatically.

"They [show producers] would want to toss a song. There were times when they were wrong, and I'd risk getting fired to keep it in. I couldn't sleep at night if I let them do it, so I would express my belief," Brenda recalls. "If I was going to the wall, they better reconsider because I wouldn't do that often. I wasn't always going off, and because of that, they listened. I fought for 'Ms. Celie's Pants.' And the crowd loves it."

Adapted from a novel penned by Alice Walker and executive-produced by Oprah Winfrey, with music co-composed by Brenda Russell, *The Color Purple* on Broadway is a testament to how powerful a production can be when it is generated by and helmed by Black women. And though Brenda has experienced some incredible victories in her own career, she looks forward to a landscape where more African American women step up and assume authority over their creativity. "What disappoints me is that there are not enough Black women doing the songwriting and producing," she laments. "Guys would smirk when we come in the studio [sitting] behind the boards. We desperately need more women mixing, doing sound for stage."

....

THE ENGINEERING SIDE
....

Born to Colombian and Nicaraguan parents in Miami, recording and mix engineer Marcella "Ms. Lago" Araica (whose engineering credits include Timbaland's *Shock Value* and Britney Spears's *Blackout* and *Circus*) caught her unfair share of smirks as she matriculated through school at Full Sail in Orlando, Florida, where she was one of six females in her class of more than two hundred students. The smirks turned into outright sabotage from her male counterparts once she began interning at the Hit Factory.

"When I first started working at the studio, the clients would be like, 'Oh it's a girl!' and it was exciting to them. The other interns and engineers were hating, like, 'Ooooh — it's a girl,'" she recalls. "I assisted staff engineers and interned at the same time. That was a first at the Hit Factory. I really wanted to learn and fit in, but a lot of them didn't accept me and felt threatened by me. And looking back, I know they were." What they didn't know about Marcella was this: She was obsessed with being a successful engineer, propelled by an ambition that went unsupported by her family. A few interns weren't gonna stop her. In fact, she ended up turning the hate to love with her dedication, ultimately winning one over as a friend. They now work together on artists like Timbaland and Nelly Furtado. "Demo was really mean to me in the beginning," she says, laughing. "And we talk about it now when we get together. We had to paint and clean up [the studio]. He'd have me do it all while he sat and watched. I never complained. He appreciated that I wasn't this prissy girl who couldn't get her hands dirty. And one day, he invited me over to do some sessions at his house."

Ironically, it was a woman client who engendered the hate Marcella encountered. Fortunately, master recording engineer and Hit Factory staffer Jimmy Douglas was hateration-free. He became a mentor to Marcella, allowing her to sit in on his sessions with Timbaland during Missy Elliott's *Under Construction* project. Missy and Marcella clicked as friends. The interns, a boys'-club-in-training, resented sisters doin' it for themselves, but money talks. "Missy wanted me to be on all her sessions, and she was a big client. The studio manager wanted to make her happy since she was doing sessions seven days a week at the time," Marcella recounts.

At a specific point in your career, you will have everything you've done and learned to that point put to the test in a real-world situation. Marcella's test was engineering for Missy. Once she actually engineered a session for her, it was a real test of Marcella's mettle, their friendship notwithstanding. "Working one-on-one with her was completely different," she says. "When it comes to her, she's so great at what she does that you have to be quick. She's creating at a hundred miles an hour, and I had to keep up with her on the computer! It didn't go well. She was hard on me in a good way. It kept me on my toes and made me want to be better for her. She saw me when I first began. So today, I have something to prove to her because I was just wack then." She giggles.

And you don't go from wack to dope without jitters every now and then. As long as you have your skills with you and your wits about you, you'll be fine, as Marcella attests. "The first time I engineered for Tim[baland], I was—oh *gosh!* He won't be afraid to tell you 'get out the chair.' He was so set in his ways with Jimmy and Demo [his main engineers]. Demo would say, 'If I go to the bathroom, just sit in the chair!' One day, Demo was a few hours late to the session—and I had knots in my stomach, but it was flawless. I worked with Tim in the room so much that I knew how he worked—and technically I was hooking up all the keyboards. I think I was just nervous about being rejected."

Just as Marcella's rise as an engineer has been a process, recorded music undergoes a process of its own. It is not something that the artist just performs that gets played on the radio right from the studio. The artist has to be *recorded*, captured and immortalized on a listenable format. This ability to fully hear music is something that, up until the emergence of the digital platform, was taken for granted. Now, however, we can hear the much flatter sound quality of an MP3 file compared with the warmth of vinyl or the pristine clarity of CD. Regardless of the delivery method, the music now must withstand the transmission of its frequencies on MP3 players and phones in addition to home and car audio systems.

The engineer is the guardian of the recording process, ensuring that the very best is recorded from the collaboration between artist and producer. He or she is monitoring and optimizing the recording levels using all the equipment in the room. In so doing, the engineer lends their individual ear and touch to the process. Hence, all engineers are not created equal. Marcella breaks it down: "It's an understanding of sound, its frequencies, and how each frequency works with all the others. It's about how instruments work together; how to EQ elements without taking the body out of them."

After the song is captured, it must be mixed. This is the deliberate balancing of all the tracks on a record to elicit the sound desired by the producer and engineer, ideally one that is rich, evenly layered, clear, and vibrant. Wikipedia describes audio mixing this way:

> Audio mixing is done in studios as part of multitrack recording in order to produce digital or analog audio recordings, or as part of an album, film, or television program. An audio mixing console, or mixing desk, or mixing board, has numerous rotating controls (potentiometers) and sliding controls (faders which are also potentiometers) that are used to manipulate the volume, the addition of effects such as reverb, and frequency content (equalization) of audio signals. On most consoles, all the controls that apply to a single channel of audio are arranged in a vertical column called a *channel strip*. Larger and more complex consoles such as those used in film and television production can contain hundreds of channel strips.

Marcella is a mix engineer in addition to being a recording engineer. In fact, mixing is her specialty. It's one thing to monitor the controls while the song is being captured. It is another entirely to handhold what was captured and take it from session-quality sound to commercially viable sound in the mix. Most engineers do one or the other, not both, as they require vastly different levels of temperament and patience from the engineer. "[As a mixer,] you go one-on-one with the producers and A&R executives," Marcella elaborates. "I was recording for a long time and no one noticed me—it was when I was mixing that people started to pay attention to me. Mixing takes a special type of person—someone who understands sound. You can spend twenty-four hours or nine days on a mix, however long it takes to get it right. There's a different respect level for mixers. It's the finishing touch before mastering and going on the radio."

Bay Area–based production and mix engineer Rachel Allgood has been behind the boards for more than ten years, and has played piano for eighteen of her twenty-nine years. She's got the ear, the passion for music, and the patience to perfect it. The vast range of genres she works in is a testament to her versatility: She's recorded with New Order, Vanessa Carlton, former Guns N' Roses drummer Brain, and Third Eye Blind frontman Stephen Jenkins. A champion of "organic sound," Rachel believes that "compassion, multitasking, and nurturing come in handy for this job. But it's something that chooses you," she confirms. "Recording engineers are notoriously single men." She laughs. "I'm combating the myth that the 'female thing' will close doors on me and once I want to have a family that I'm gonna peter out. I could have easily been married to the job because of my personality, but I'd be really bitter if I did that. But if I didn't pursue this career, I'd be bitter about that as well. I want to push through without losing my husband."

Rachel confirms Marcella's assessment of time being elastic when it comes to the back-end part of the recording and mixing process. It can often lead to unrealistic expectations on the part of artists—and worse yet, disappointment when it takes longer then they envision. This is a particularly daunting reality check for independent or self-financed artists whose budgets may not be able to support the cost of the sound they wish to achieve. Rachel elaborates: "With indies, they are [often] both artist and businessperson. They have a conflict between the vision they have and what they have money for that they have a hard time reconciling. Mixing and mastering takes a lot longer than most artists think, especially for artists on their first record. There are a lot of things that go into the process that they can't even imagine. There's so much work and [so many] hours that the producer and engineer put in (especially when I wear both hats) compared to the [time spent by the] artist playing, commenting, and leaving me to implement things. And depending on how well versed they are in the process, they are disheartened that they left for five hours and I'm still working on the drums.

"I've worked with a lot of singer-songwriters over the last few years, and [they'll say], 'It's me and my guitar, but make me sound like a band,'" Rachel continues in disbelief. "Which means they're used to just playing alone and they have a vision of what their songs would sound like with all the other instruments; or they've brought in musicians for shows and some [songs] work with those musicians, while others don't. Or the band members they do shows with are also doing their thing on the writer's song—and that frustrates them. I end up being a bit of a psychologist. But as this happens, the songs start to change; it changes the time line, especially if they want to add instruments and complicate things. This is an emotional journey for the artists as they deal with their song evolving. I am always trying to help them juggle being fulfilled with the end result and staying within the budget. I can take someone's garage recording and make it sound great, but I can only do so much for people before I start pulling my hair out."

Point taken. There are steps engineers can take to preserve ther sanity so they can do their best work. And there are measures artists can take to preserve their creative vision and ensure the best recording experience possible. Whether you sit before the console or behind the mic, Rachel and Marcella have some real talk for you on studio etiquette.

Studio Etiquette for Engineers

Rachel encourages engineers to look past the current session and create a long-term vision for themselves and their careers. "When you tune in and ask the universe, *What should I be doing right now?*—that's when things happen. I don't want to work on something famous for the sake of that, but I'd be selling myself short if I didn't have a dream for what my career will be."

Marcella advises laying down your ground rules up front and making sure they are adhered to; otherwise, time and money are wasted. She also recommends creating the optimal working environment. "I am trying to make money. I got candles going. Candles are a requirement! I don't even want the artist in the room when I'm mixing until I'm done. I work in the dark and it throws off my vibe when people come in. The artists and crew get kicked out—and I let it be known," she asserts. "I do a lot of additional production on the mixing side to polish the record off. I add the sprinkles, as [my producer friends] Danjahandz and Timbaland call it, and polish the record off. I have to listen to the record over and over again, and I like quiet."

Rachel sets the stage for artists before they even get to the room. "Communicate what they might encounter before they get to the studio and give them food for thought. I have them bring in records they like to give perspective," she adds.

Rachel also warns engineers not to judge a checkbook by its cover. "Funny, the deeper the pocket, the more trouble you get from them financially," she notes. "You think they have resources. They end up having these budgetary issues with money running out or the project taking longer, so you end up waiting to get paid or getting less. And the ones with the least to spend are the ones who end up tipping me! Getting a deposit up front is always a good idea."

Studio Etiquette for Artists

Marcella understands that artists come in all types. But she also encourages artists recording an album "to know where you wanna go. Nelly [Furtado] is all about a vibe; she thinks like a producer. We did the songs on the *Loose* album—and they all made the album. We didn't do twenty songs to get them. If you're hoping for someone to give you the idea, it's not really you; it's the rare breed [of artist] that can take another idea and own it."

Rachel supports this and takes it a step farther. Engineers need for artists to keep it real with them as they record. "Say what you mean, not what you think I want to hear," she says. "Be straight up with me so I can deliver the sound for you."

The sad part is that not all artists are capable of articulating a vision . . . because there isn't one. Marcella's experience has shown her two types of artists: "the artist's artist and the artist. The artist's artist understands what being an artist is as an entity; the art of refreshing a sound, knowing how to present oneself. Then there are the people who just get by, which is so unfortunate. They come to the studio and they don't really know what to do. They just sit there and try to figure it out along the way, can barely write down a verse. Also in the 'artist' category are the ones who have writers come in and write for them. That makes my job easier, but it's torture when the ones who want to be artist's artists aren't there yet," Marcella says, sighing. Determine which type of artist you are and either improve upon it or accept it. Either way, be professional.

Marcella points to Britney Spears as a great example of professionalism.

The tabloids give her hell, but she handles her business in the studio. She may not be a songwriter, but at least she plays her position of vocal performer full-out. Marcella recorded several songs for her album *Blackout*—and has no problem giving the embattled pop star her props. "We worked with her for a year. She's one of the most hardworking artists I've ever worked with. We even worked with her at home after she had her second child. She has input on her vocals and keeps going until she gets it right. She doesn't bullshit. She stays in the booth until it's done. We'd be in the studio all night with Britney, and the next day the 'news' would say she did [some crazy thing] the night before. We knew she was with us!"

Marcella gets that artists need to create their own bubble to achieve a comfort level in the studio, but there is a line. And artists need to be respectful of the fact that engineers are artists, too. "If they need to have girls sit around and look pretty and that helps, do it. Just don't bring talkative girls. That is annoying."

Rachel echoes this sentiment, asking for basic integrity, especially if it's something the artist volunteers to do. "Don't be the irresponsible artist," she intones. "I may be a woman, but I'm not your mama. If you're sending me lyrics sheets or say you're going to call me, do it."

Finally, Rachel recommends that artists come with an "open mind. I'm not saying forfeit your vision or accept things you're not happy with. Just be open to the flow of the creative process," she says. "The ones who get the most out of the [recording] experience."

Marcella's last piece of golden advice applies to engineers and artists alike: Show some self-respect. Marcella had to get physical in a completely different way with one producer whom she wishes to remain nameless, since she almost "whooped him" (as she put it). Ladies, the double standard that sexism imposes means that one woman's sexual conduct has a ripple effect on our collective perception as women. This construct has a stranglehold on the vast majority of men who work in our business—men who see women in submissive, denigrating sexual positions as part of their work, from the strip clubs to the music videos. Most of our male counterparts see us as objects, even if we're fully clothed and determining the sound quality of their records. Marcella was on the receiving end of this rampant misogyny and can speak on its impact on her interactions with men on the job.

"Those are the women who mess it up for other women. They set an unfair standard for the women who want to do business for what the business is really about," she remarks emphatically, her voice taut with resignation. "On the one hand, it's their business . . . but I wish all women had self-respect in every moment of their lives, because I don't know when it's gonna get to a point where they stop. Girls might get what they want out of it, but at the very end, they've messed it up for anyone trying to get in the business with that same guy or his friend—because these guys think they can get it done sexually. I had a situation like that with a producer that tried to speak to me that way. I thought I was gonna get fired because of what happened next. He's a prominent producer, one who was always working—he was [basically] paying the light bill at the studio. I stood up for myself and almost beat him. I got really scared. The next day, I called the studio manager first thing in the morning and talked to him first. [The manager] told me I handled it right and wouldn't get in trouble because he [the producer] had a reputation for doing this to women. The word got around that I almost beat him up. That's why that was the only time that happened."

....

THE A&R SIDE

....

Nearly coming to blows to ward off inappropriate advances is foul, but sometimes you have to meet slime on its own level to get past it. Aside from women who occupy the studio setting as artists, which is the most common, and the fewer numbers of women engineers and producers, women A&R executives also bear the brunt of being heavily outnumbered by men as they work to get records made and albums completed. Perhaps the stress that comes along with this resistance is what has reduced the presence of women in A&R in the music industry overall. Who wants to go to work every day waiting for the other shoe of sexual harassment to drop, in a world that sees little problem with it? It's hard enough to deal with women who are threatened by you because you know what you're doing, look a certain way, or both.

Before establishing One Rockstar, LLC—her own management and A&R administration company—Leah Harmony contributed to the mercurial success of Edmonds Entertainment and E2 Management. Over the course of her three-year stint, Leah (pronounced like the Princess from *Star Wars*) executed A&R administration for soundtrack albums including *Save the Last Dance* and *Love Don't Cost a Thing*. She also created a system for scheduling and recording the company's staff producers. In addition to heading up operations alongside music supervisor executive Michael McQuarn, she acted as the in-house product manager for Jon B. and Third Storee when DreamWorks Records was dismantled, leaving both acts between distributors. As the ex-wife of platinum-selling rapper Numskull, one half of the Oakland-based duo the Luniz, Leah became an executive who also fought for artists. She understood how bad contracts affected families from personal experience. "I had no idea what I wanted to do when I was married," she recalls. "At that time, all I knew was music and how it made me feel. Reading his contracts made me an advocate for artists and got me interested in the business. Seeing all the stuff he was going through, I realized that my husband had to share five cents off of every album, *after* they recouped all the money it took to make the album. That's where I learned the industry."

Her commitment to artists and tireless work ethic established her as an A&R administrator who closed albums and song deals against all odds. The irony of Leah's situation was that while her efforts shone because of the small staff, she also found herself working far beyond her job description for a salary that did not match her level of responsibility. A&R admin is arguably the most underrated and yet most critical part of the music-making process. Songs and albums can be average, even sloppy. But the paperwork, clearances, and credits must be neither subpar nor incorrect. When they are, it causes a mess for all parties involved, especially music publishers, managers, and the record company. When she was assigned the "Wake Up Everybody" voter awareness project, she really saw just how much she was doing at once. Her description of that time in her career illuminates what A&R really is. It's more than chillin' in the studio, evaluating demos, and taking meetings at fly restaurants.

" 'Wake Up Everybody' was a milestone in my career," Leah reflects. "I had to record some of the artists in Miami, and some in New York, coordinating all the artists for the video we also shot. All the while I'm setting up co-writes [for songs], managing producers, selling and placing tracks on albums, and liaising between the lawyers, labels to negotiate the fees that go with each song placement—and I'm like, 'What's my title? Queen of the World?!' I was overworked and a bit frustrated—and there was only so far I could go inside the building where promotions were concerned. That doesn't work when you have two kids." Leah left Edmonds Entertainment to oversee project coordination for Kenny "Babyface" Edmonds, who knew and respected her work. She coordinated his recordings with Rascal Flatts, Sheryl Crow, and others. And while she had experienced a great deal of insecurity on the part of other African American women in the industry, she is quick to point out that she "never got that from Tracey [Edmonds]. Tracey taught me how to read contracts and speak the language." But the fact that Leah worked successfully with powerful men, and as a former model happened to be gorgeous, was always a problem for her female counterparts. "I have a certain poise and confidence that they take as a threat," Leah notes. She sounds off on the other kind of fallout that comes from the perception of women as sex objects: being wrongfully labeled as promiscuous when professional conduct and track record ought to be the sole criteria by which a woman is evaluated. "I had been through too much with my kids before 7 AM than to be worried about [insecure women]. Check the résumé! Why fuck all the men in the same building, then take home a teeny little check? My executive ability speaks for itself. It got to the point where when people couldn't prove I was fucking everyone, I ended up being gay," she explained with disgust. "I'd say, 'I'd rather be gay then be fucking you.'"

Leah wasn't the only one who had to put up with the fallout from not mixing business with pleasure. Before Tina Davis became Chris Brown's manager, and before Kyra Sedgwick had a hit show of the same name, Tina was known as "The Closer" in Def Jam's A&R department. Tina has tackled soundtracks full of collaborations and solo albums by artists as disparate as DMX and Ne-Yo. But for some, the work never seems to speak loud enough. "I always respected Dame [Dash]," says Tina. "He was [a] good businessman, but he seemed to hate me for some reason. We'd all be meeting about the Roc [Roc-A-Fella Records] and he'd say, 'What the fuck is *she* doing here'? I was actually checkin' for him, too, until the personality came out."

During potentially frustrating and humiliating moments like these that threatened to burn her out, Tina would remind herself of what's really important. "I pray and thank the Lord every day. I keep Him first and remind everyone that I'm just a vessel. Having that spiritual foundation allows you to be able to deal with people when they are not being godly."

Tina has the rare combination of being a brilliant identifier of talent and being an exacting, efficient administrator. She defines both the creative and back-end responsibilities this way: "Being a great A&R executive means being in the studio, making the records, creating the songs with the artists, and having relationships with producers. A&R is also knowing where music is going to be in the next six, seven months and knowing a star when you see one that's rough. I'd ask an artist to act out a song for me," she says with a grin. "And if they did it, I'd know. A&R administration is budgeting, credits, and sample clearance." She now uses her A&R acumen to conceptualize and close Chris Brown's albums, to the chagrin of those at his label who "fight me when I ask for A&R credit" as his manager.

The Publishing Side

Tina got her start in the business assisting veteran music publishing creative director LaRonda Sutton (no relation to Percy Sutton of Inner City Broadcasting), senior vice president of music development and production for Foxx King Music. LaRonda also began her career as an assistant to Club Nouveau founder Jay King. LaRonda had visions of being fabulous in the business, inspired by her aunt Margaret Bush Ware, who assisted Sammy Davis Jr. for decades. According to LaRonda, Aunt Margaret made the business look good! "She was so fabulous to me, big shades, stunning. I would visit her in LA, which was so *shiny* to me! The walls of her duplex were covered with photos of President Ford, Bill Cosby, Jesse Jackson, the Rat Pack. It was amazing," she enthuses.

LaRonda interned with Jay King the summer of her junior year in college in pursuit of fabulous, and worked it using her typing skills and photographic memory. "I went from an intern with no job description to his executive assistant, fielding calls, throwing parties, planning travel, coordinating on their behalf with Benny Medina, who was the head of A&R for their label, Warner Bros. Jay sent me to sit up under Karen Jones, Benny's assistant," LaRonda recalls. "She gave me the tutorial on being one. I was such a beast at my job, I knew every number in the Rolodex; Jay could call me anytime and be able to get a number." Well, LaRonda was so focused on "doing the glamorous stuff" that she "didn't really care about Jay King 4 Publishing." Unbeknowst to her, it was a foreshadowing of her move to EMI Music Publishing. "My job was to liaise between songwriters and the administrative side of our copyright administration department. The creative side is going to collect the songwriters' songs, but they're not keeping track of the incoming songs to fulfill the artists' commitments. I was the person that booked the studio for songwriters to come in; [I had to] estimate the budget for the session, keep track of the songs, deliver the data, and do charge-backs for the time used," says LaRonda. There was a bit of a learning curve for her, however, since she hadn't really worked on Jay King's publishing assets. It took driving to San Diego to meet Queen Latifah to show her the distinction between writers and performers. "After three days of working there, I saw Latifah's name on a sheet and thought she was a writer. I drive all the way down to San Diego to meet her after a show. I gave the guard my ID to get backstage. She lets me in. I introduce myself and leave, only to realize she was *sampling* one of our writers." Once LaRonda's supervisor left the company, she became the interim manager. "A year later I got promoted formally," she states. She clung to a pearl of wisdom from Jay King as she threw herself into music creative: "If the radio is on twenty-four hours, you're on twenty-four hours," she says quoting her mentor. "This has propelled me to where I am today." In fact, Tina told me that LaRonda had passed that pearl down to her, slightly tweaked to fit her position as an A&R representative. " 'The radio never turns off, so A&R can never turn off,' Tina says, repeating the mantra. "It was a gift and a curse; because I feel bad if I'm not working!"

LaRonda went on to have a string of hits as the architect of two publishing divisions over the next several years of her career. For Chrysalis, she signed thugged-out R&B singer Domino, whose gold-plus debut spawned the R&B/pop smash "Sweet Potatoe Pie." "That allowed me to sign many types of writers," LaRonda recalls. "I aquired Roy Ayers's catalog at the time. I signed Kipper Jones—he wrote 'I Wanna Be Down' and 'Brokenhearted' for Brandy; [soul singer-songwriter] Rahsaan Patterson; Mark Shelby of Black Note, who is such a gifted musician, he could write his ideas in musical notes. Now he's scoring and he's overseas, he's large. But I'm proudest of Outkast and Goodie Mob."

From there, she went to HitCo, where she signed Kevin "Shek'speare" Briggs (TLC's "No Scrubs," Destiny's Child's "Bills, Bills, Bills"), Rafael Brown ("In My Bed" by Dru Hill), and a young lady named Beyoncé who caught LaRonda's attention at a Houston step show. "I talked to Bey one-on-one and saw the most cool and amazing spirit from her; calm and at peace. I got the feeling that she knew she was here to be great at what she does. She told me she wanted to produce, loved to paint, wanted to play the guitar. I told her the next step was being a songwriter. I signed her."

So what is LaRonda signing these songwriters and recording artists *to*, exactly? A publishing agreement. This can involve an advance to help the writer buy studio equipment or demo work in the studio. But more important, it commits writers to a certain number of song placements within a time frame on commercial releases, either their own albums or those of other artists who perform their songs. The agreement may also include administration of the writers' songs for other uses across other media platforms or for use as samples. When the song accrues royalties from airplay and performance, the publisher repays itself the advance from those earnings and accounts for the writers' revenue, usually issuing residual royalty checks on a quarterly basis. The right publishing deals give artists some breathing room to live without having to pull a part-time job so they can write, demo, and ultimately place songs. They also serve as an important means of artist development and creative exploration for the writer-performer, leading to artist deals with labels for some. Finally, affiliating with a publisher avails a writer of collaborations with other artists on the roster, or established acts on other labels.

When LaRonda went on to become the VP of creative for Universal Music Publishing, she brought the roster together out of necessity for what she dubbed the Universal Writers' Block Party, inventing a music meeting she still convenes today through her company, ARTIST Exposure. "I started it because what I knew was if I put a bunch of people in the room, the business would take care of itself. When you're the only Black executive responsible for a roster of seventy-five writers who all want to be serviced, I didn't want to hear 'I'm not getting serviced,'" she explains. "They'd all be in the room with some food and drink. The A&R reps would pitch to my roster. I put lyric people with track people and get co-writes going. The writers got to see what their peers were doing, and work with them if they liked them. [Next came] meetings with A&R folks. They'd play songs. If the [A&R] rep liked it, I was golden!"

So if you're sitting at home writing songs or weaving together lyrics in your head or journal, what is someone like LaRonda looking for in a signing? She will tell you that the "future of the business is going from being producer-driven to being all about lyrics and melody. I don't care if you're new or super-duper. The talent is all equal; some have just been doing it longer," she notes. "I look for something that touches me or catches my ear and piques my intellect and you're creative with it. If you are a track writer, I am listening to the chords and want to know if you play instruments; I am looking for the variety in what you do."

Cheryl Potts, founder of Crystal Clear Music, on the other hand, is looking out for writers and producers on the back end. Her firm is dedicated to providing the services that ultimately ensure that artists' intellectual property is protected and profitable, including publishing administration, copyright registration, sample clearance, royalty accounting, and royalty collection. She channeled her passion for music into artist advocacy and a lucrative career. She left the technology field and enrolled in NABFEME's Mentoring Program; there, under the tutelage of a vice president from a performing rights society, Cheryl learned about the publishing business. She then met and studied copyright law under Lolly Gassaway at University of North Carolina–Chapel Hill, which prompted her to start a music publishing company. Two years into the endeavor, upon meeting an established gospel writer, she realized she was on the wrong end of the business.

Cheryl explains: "I realized he was talented and had been taken advantage of. He had some big songs and one where they had used it without his authorization. He approached me about helping him collect his royalties. So we entered into an agreement to do his administration and not share in his copyrights. The first things we did were to go after his royalties against a major label and another producer, overturn a copyright registration with his society, and secure past royalties and credits. And yes — it is labor-intensive," she admonishes. "You can't just jump in off the street and do [publishing administration]. But I loved it. It's so easy to put up a record-label sign once you file the paperwork as an LLC and buy your own CDs; you can be a label in no time. But there were so many issues with uses. People do not realize that it is against the law to put people's music on a disc and sell it. After we won, he was so excited. I realized this was where it's at.

"Three years ago," she continues, "I reorganized the company to focus on administration, because we found there were a lot of writers who needed our service." Writers weren't her only callers. Cheryl also acquired independent-label clients from her work going after royalties on behalf of existing clients. Upon discovering they were breaking laws, many of these small companies opted to retain her for future projects.

Cheryl has a few of her many tips for avoiding messy publishing battles that are helpful to artist and indie label alike:

1. "I would not recommend the poor man's copyright. Because when you have an infringement case, they will ask if the song is registered with the US Copyright Office. It doesn't mean you'll win, but going through the proper channels to claim it works to your advantage. Do not play it anywhere without [the song] being registered. I have yet to see the poor man's copyright hold up in court." (The "poor man's copyright" is the act of protecting intellectual property by sealing it in a marked, unopened envelope and mailing it to yourself.)

2. "If someone wants to use your music, write it down even if it's on a napkin: what they will pay you in royalties once a deal is in place, an agreement that says you are the true owner. Then have the other person sign. Even though that's your boy (or girl), get it in writing."

3. "Educate yourself on the business. I've done numerous conferences and panels and it's jam-packed about getting music played, but when it comes to handling your business, people are networking in the hall. Join organizations and seek out a mentor in the field, or take a job in publishing or at a label."

Cheryl recommends that writers and producers hold on to their copyrights for as long as they can, but she also recognizes that in order to amass experience, credits, and songs released to market, writers may need to give up something in the short term. It's an unfortunate chicken-and-egg scenario, but it isn't insurmountable. The key is securing credit for your contribution, then ensuring reversion of copyright (*reversion* refers to ownership rights coming back to the writer) once that short term is up.

"Record labels have to put up a lot of money to market you, from the payola to the videos," Cheryl notes. "Major publishers rarely sign an unknown, so you have to get [music] placed [first] to get them to approach you with a deal. You can't put a price on experience, and eventually it will help you get [songs] placed on your own. If I am an unknown performer and I don't have a label deal, I would sign a publishing deal initially. I may have to give up my portion until I become known, then come back and renegotiate once I'm proven," Cheryl explains. "And I will have a lawyer handle that for me to make sure I'm not locked up in that contract for life. Now, if the label comes to you *because you're known,* you have a better bargaining position and [chance at] keeping some of your publishing. Artists just have to do a lot of work to come to the table at that level."

Until you reach that level, here is Cheryl's crash course in Publishing 101 in a few different situations.

As a Sole Creator of a Song

"Upon creation, the US copyright law says the song is protected once it's put on a fixed format. You own 100 percent of the copyright. There is no split initially; you are the owner as writer and own the publishing. Fifty percent is the writer's share and 50 percent is considered the publishing share.

Although you created the song, it is not published yet. Once you start selling or distributing it, it then becomes published. That means when it starts playing on radio, TV, or in the marketplace, you can now register the song with the performing rights agency."

When Publishing with a Co-writer

"If you co-write the song, then the two people share the 50 percent of both writer's and publishing portions."

Pertaining to the Standard Major Publishing Deal

"If you as the writer sign to the standard publishing deal, the writer retains the writer's share. But the 50 percent of the publishing share is being assigned [by the writer] to the publishing company. The [publishing company] will become a claimant, not the song's author [empowered to exploit the music and collect royalties], unless it is a work for hire."

When You Enter into a Co-publishing Agreement

"What is common today is co-publishing. This is the writer still keeping their 50 percent, and also keeping 25 percent of the publishing, leaving the 25 percent for the publisher. Now this is a 75–25 split in favor of the writer. When a writer *assigns* their publishing to a company, the claimant will administer the licensing and uses. But then they will take a fee for doing that, usually 10 percent, which now shifts the split to 65–35. So the entity that wants to use the song will ask the publisher's [permission] for the use."

*

Traditionally, publishing companies will issue advances to writers or producers for the privilege of being assigned publishing rights. But writer, beware: The same stories you see in movies about recording stars getting advances and then blowing 'em on clothes and cars can happen to you. Be careful how you spend the money that your songs have yet to earn. "People enter into publishing deals because the [companies] are dangling [an average of] fifty thousand to a hundred thousand dollars before them for the publishing share," Cheryl points out. "They are not giving you the money just to be giving it to you." She laughs. "That money you get is an advance against future royalties. If your songs don't sell, they'll be out of that money. So while you're rolling around in your new Benz with your bling bling, understand that you won't get paid until the hundred thousand dollars is paid back to the publishing company."

Another important piece of the recoupment puzzle is the erroneous or inaccurate royalty statement, which can make a writer's journey out of debt to the publisher long and arduous. Think about securing an administrator who can check these statements for you if it's a task you'd prefer not to take on yourself. "A lot of the time, labels have a release date they are so busy trying to make that the paperwork doesn't get done," says Cheryl. This can lead to a messy paper trail, or the absence of one altogether, and complicate writers' ability to be credited for royalties they have earned.

"You'd be amazed how often royalty statements are wrong," notes Cheryl. "We analyze the statements to make sure they are accurate."

The complexity of publishing administration cannot be underscored. Even Ruthless Records CEO Tomica Woods-Wright, holder of more than 350 song copyrights, admits that initially she was "intimidated by it. It's too much paperwork—and then the terminology! I always dealt with it indirectly; I was always aware of the income stream, but was involved on a 'cc' basis." Tomica got her wake-up call on the need to get more familiar with her catalog when her longtime administrator Madeleine Smith was hospitalized.

"I realized that [if] God forbid something happened to her, I needed to know my catalog," stresses Tomica. "Most people would have two, three people to work on cleaning all these files up and out. I learned a lot from Madeleine. She gave me the one-on-one. There are classes one can take as well, but when you can apply logic to theory it all makes sense. I got it all explained to me." In the process of empowering herself with practical knowledge of publishing, she saved her company from paying additional fees as well. "I had brokers who were saying they could exploit [the catalog] for me at a 20 percent commission. The brokers would want me to educate them about the catalog, only to turn around and take 20 percent! I thought, *I could do that.* Another year of not having [the copyrights] exploited would not hurt, so I took that time to learn the catalog. Certain [transactions] got messed up. I would stop what I was doing to fix them. When I had to clean up paperwork that didn't get filed, sometimes the agreement wouldn't even be there. Organization is as important as the clerical and administrative skills—giving accurate information and keeping the time in mind. Spellcheck doesn't catch these mistakes," she says.

"First, I focused on Eric's [Ruthless founder and Tomica's late husband

Eazy-E] likeness and image being protected and exploited. Then I looked at the whole catalog and decided what was a priority," Tomica continues. Once her publishing "house" was in order, Tomica and Madeleine went to Midem—an annual global music market and conference—to get a closer look at the global publishing landscape. They also wanted to meet the licensors who would negotiate for rights to use her songs, which included hits and album cuts from Eazy-E, N.W.A., Michel'le, J.J. Fad (whose hit "Supersonic" was sampled by Fergie on "Fergalicious"), and Bone Thugs-N-Harmony. She learned even more from Midem. "Overseas it's a lot cleaner slate," Tomica continues. "There are mom-and-pop operations who are friendly and eager to work; you just have to be able to pitch the other songs in the catalog. They like new music because it's cheaper [to license], but the big labels usually limit their effort to the chart-topping hits and classics. As a result, the Bone Thugs-N-Harmony catalog and hundreds of other songs have yet to be exploited fully. The big corporations [outsource the smaller licensors] anyway, so I cut out the middleman," Tomica says with a grin.

Tomica echoes Cheryl's sentiment about the ease with which publishing agreements and credits fall though the cracks. The lesson for any writer, composer, or producer here is to be vigilant in registering your songs; retain and document proof of credit wherever possible. Keeping your own records is just great offense in a game fraught with sloppy execution. "Publishing executives tend not to [experience turnover]," notes Tomica. "The people at labels, on the other hand, make it tough. Some A&R administration folks don't even know the basics of crediting the sampled writers! Sometimes we may not have agreements in place until a year after the record is released. I even have to argue about monies owed because they'd omit my sampled writers."

....

BARRIERS TO THE MUSIC-MAKING PROCESS
....

Variety in what the music industry releases is sorely needed in today's downward-spiraling market. Unfortunately, in times of hardship creativity at the major-label level takes a backseat to whatever sells records, downloads singles, or moves ringtones. Being creatively flat in a down market will not generate more sales for the industry overall. Music sells when music is exciting, refreshing, and bold; relevant to people where they are, while calling them into another way of being. Music moves units when the music itself is moving. The dip in creativity and risk taking is a barrier to the music-making process. When combined with the desperate need to increase revenue and the false perception that technological advances ensure quality music made at warp speed, it can literally spell disaster. Marcella elaborates on the myth of technology speeding the album creation process, and the danger of cutting corners by confusing talent contest winners with recording artists.

"Times have changed. The misconception now is how quickly [albums] can get done. Honestly, an album can get done in two weeks, but that's not always best," she asserts. "Let us record and let us live with it for a second. We may need to make changes. *Then* let us mix. Labels think that with lower budgets and faster machines, [music] should have a time stamp on it. What's a waste of time is when the artist doesn't come, and they expect the producer to just make beats. A lot of the time it's not the artist's fault; it's the label trying to be cheap. The artist and producer need to *interact*. That's what's missing, and part of why records aren't selling. And for new artists, that's a killer. The producers don't even know who they are; their personality, how they grew up . . . and when [producers] turn in beats, the label says, 'That's not what we were looking for.' That messes up the flow and the energy. What's the rush? If we do an album in two weeks, and it's not good, you need to go back in.

"Labels want to make money but they don't want to put the push behind it," Marcella continues. "And when it doesn't sell, we all fail. There was an album we worked on that had to be done by Thanksgiving, and out by Christmas. She was a brand-new artist and she'd never worked in a studio in her life, and as a result it went very badly. People go on these shows and they win or they don't, but just because they can sing doesn't make them artists. Labels need to go back to developing them instead of expecting producers to just give up hot tracks. That's a piece of the pie, but the artist needs to be developed. And figure out how to do it so it isn't as expensive. These acts have potential, but they can't just be thrown out here. You have to crawl before you walk."

The urban music business, in its pathetic need for publicity no matter the cost, has relinquished the power to influence customers over to media, wresting it from consumers. In today's market, particularly for contemporary R&B and hip-hop, artists can barely coexist in the landscape without being pitted against or compared with one another. The 50 Cent–Kanye West chart bout is a prime example. Def Jam and Interscope pooled their marketing resources to maximize media exposure for both and eke out more mileage for their dollars, but at what cost? Kanye winds up looking like even more of an egomaniac; 50 comes off like he's bullying the nerdy kid in the hall only to fall short in the after-school fight. The reality is that in this sales climate, 50's debut numbers were very impressive at 691,000, yet the perception is that he "lost" to Kanye's 957,000. In fact, both are compelling figures in the format. You don't see Keith Urban and Kenny Chesney thuggin' it out for the top slot. Had one album been released the week before or after, I submit they could have each debuted at number one.

Tina has an excellent point about how the industry gets in its own way yet again once music of quality finally sees the light of day. "I attribute the business's ills to the fact that they pit artists against each other. Mario. Chris. Usher. Ne-Yo. They are all incredible; why can't they all be on the radio and live in their own lane? We had Marvin [Gaye] *and* Teddy [Pendergrass]; Babyface and Luther were able sell a ton of records and coexist at the same time. They each could have sung the other's songs, but it didn't mean they were the same person.

"Ne-Yo will never do what Chris does on stage. Chris will never write like Ne-Yo does. Mario can sing circles around them all—but it's about 'Oh, he's killin' so-and-so.' If the world was allowed to buy it all, they would. But when you make consumers have to choose, it works against the business. It doesn't make sense to ask who they like better; music is based on emotion and how it makes them feel."

The music industry has also lost control of dissemination. With single and ringtone sales dominating the virtual retail space, the album is bordering on becoming an afterthought, since it can now be compartmentalized at the insistence of online retailers. The result? A&R with iTunes and Verizon in mind instead of the people who push the buttons, and a one-season crop of one-hit wonders year after year. After more than a decade in A&R for Def Jam, Columbia, and Island, Tina can see the shift, and it's not pretty.

"In 2007, it was all one-hit wonders. Sean Kingston, Lil Mama, Soulja Boy. But will they be here in another five years? The key is to make a full album of great music," Tina emphasizes. "Then we can rebuild the record buyers' trust and get them to buy full albums. Overall, labels are not putting great product out right now. We're not signing great talent, so we have no classic artists. We can finally say Timberlake, Usher, Beyoncé . . . but are they *really*? Stevie Wonder is timeless. Patti LaBelle had eight albums before she became a classic artist, and she was in two groups before that."

Bassist, performer, bandleader, and producer Meshell Ndegeocello is among this generation's classic, timeless artists. In 1994, she was in a unique position as the first artist signed to Maverick, co-founded by Madonna, an artist who appreciates reinvention and originality. And even though she enjoyed a measure of creative freedom denied to most new artists, she has come to a stark realization that serves as sage insight for all artists as they write, rhyme, play, and sing. "I have discovered that [the industry] is a hustle, and just a hustle. You really have to discover why you play music, why you create, and why you have to. Or the hustle will get the best of you fast." Meshell's art affirms that she has arrived at her own reasons. She has resolved to remain musically ambitious and never be out-hustled, because "sometimes you get hired and sometimes you don't. Some people like you and some of them won't. Dues enough for one may fall short for someone else. I don't consider myself above anything."

From this humility and love of craft comes a repertoire that spans genres, sounds, styles, and sensibilities. Meshell has touched soul, hip-hop, rock, jazz, blues, funk, ska, dub, pop, dance, even electronica, leaving them all better off for her contribution. Commitment to expression for expression's sake over the whims of the marketplace is what music is about. Not so, however, for the music *business*. "I never made anything that satisfies one group for long; it's never Black enough, or female enough, or urban enough, or singer-songwriter-y enough. I do all those things," says Meshell. "There's no box for that. Plus, labels think that's bad for business. The appreciation for a well-rounded, curious artist has waned, and to defy a category really means you don't repeat a formula again and again." The big four record companies are overdue for a refresher course in music appreciation.

SUMMARY OF SECRETS REVEALED

WHAT YOU THOUGHT YOU KNEW:

Music goes from the artist's mouth and instruments to the microphone to the radio and TV.

WHAT YOU NEED TO KNOW:

Music is a labor-intensive, painstaking process that involves recording, mixing, mastering—all ideally *after* artists are sufficiently developed to be not only confident in their vision but also respectful of the artistry of the engineer, producer, and A&R executive in helping achieve that vision.

WHAT YOU THOUGHT YOU KNEW:

Engineers are the dudes behind the board, and they pretty much do one thing: work the machines.

WHAT YOU NEED TO KNOW:

There are many types of engineers. I merely touch on three main distinctions here: audio recording engineer, music mix engineer, and film sound engineer (Leslie Ann Jones appears in chapter 8). There are also dialogue and special sound effects engineers. Each specialty requires a different touch and temperament, and offers a different pay scale. The most valuable engineers are those with acumen in more than one area. Every engineer I spoke to can both record and mix.

WHAT YOU THOUGHT YOU KNEW:

Publishing is just about books and magazines.

WHAT YOU NEED TO KNOW:

Publishing also includes intellectual property in the form of songs, lyrics and recorded music. And once you create something from which publishing can be derived, it's yours until you sign, sell, or give it away. If you write lyrics or music, being educated about this intricate process is vital, and can save you time, money, and stress.

WHAT YOU THOUGHT YOU KNEW:

All I need to bring to the studio is my talent.

WHAT YOU NEED TO KNOW:

Whether you come to the studio as recording artist, songwriter, engineer, mixer, or producer, you need to bring much more. First and foremost, bring your A-game. A collaborative work environment is best served by a collaborative spirit. Anything else can cause tension in the studio. Think of it as a womb, where the sounds of music and entire multimedia projects are born. If you were pregnant, you wouldn't want anything happening in there that shouldn't be happening in there. You want a healthy child and a smooth pain-free delivery. Strive for this in the studio as well. Respect the other artists you are working with. Respect the process.

CHAPTER 6

Read the Label

··

Gwendolyn Quinn ✳ Jackie Rhinehart ✳ Jasmine Vega ✳
Kim Ward, Esq. ✳ Louise West, Esq.✳ Quincy Jackson ✳
Shanti Das ✳ Tracii McGregor ✳ Wendi Cartwright

··

*The biggest myth I've discovered is that the industry is not
suited for women, when in fact women are handling our
business,* and *his business.*

—Kim Ward, Esq.

Here's what this chapter is not about: the actual mechanics of how labels work. There are many books that cover the textbook aspect of the record label's traditional revenue model: issuing an advance against sales to an artist in exchange for marketing and promoting the album(s) and/or engaging in publishing agreements to bolster that artist's income, et cetera. More important, the subject would be almost a waste of ink in this volume because the model is presently undergoing a seismic shift.

Record companies have been hemorrhaging money in the face of digital downloading, piracy, the exodus (or layoffs) of experienced visionary executive talent, and the near elimination of both artist development and creative quality control. The scramble to recover money from any and every source that began in earnest in 2001 (following the double whammy of Napster and 9/11) is now a mad dash to cash in on legal downloading, mobile products like ringtones, and corporate cost sharing through brand partnerships. One conversation now in full swing is the return of domestic labels to a 360-degree deal structure, where the artist signs to the label for distribution, merchandising, management, and touring. Another involves the defection of iconic artists away from major labels, the most public of which was Prince's emancipation from Warner Bros., and the most recent being Madonna's business-to-business multiplatform deal with Live Nation (ironically she, too, left the Warner system). Radiohead executed a revolutionary sliding-scale online sale of its album *In Rainbows* without the label's initial participation. Even Lil' Kim parted ways from Atlantic and opted to release her post-prison comeback album independently. Jay-Z re-upped with Live Nation to the tune of $150 million for a comprehensive recording, touring, and branding agreement that includes a new music imprint, Roc Nation. Young Hov's deal is not your average 360-degree situation, however. His Live Nation deal is actually a partnership in which he is both shareholder and artist. According to Billboard.com's May 2, 2008, article,

> The company [Live Nation] yesterday (May 1) filed a Form-8K with the SEC which states that the artist is getting 775,434 Live Nation shares, plus an option on an additional 500,000 with the exercise price of $13.73. The shares go to Marcy Media, the company affiliated with Jay-Z (born Shawn Carter), in connection with the formation of Roc Nation LLC, a joint entertainment venture between Live Nation and Jay-Z. The roughly $150 million pact includes Roc Nation, as well as the rapper's own recordings and tours for the next 10 years. Live Nation will reportedly contribute $5 million each year in overhead for five years and offer $25 million to finance Jay-Z's external acquisitions and investments, plus $10 million per album for a minimum of three albums within the deal's term. Jay-Z will also receive another $20 million for other rights including publishing and licensing.[1]

To add insult to injury, in addition to touring companies becoming record labels, traditional record labels now must compete with mobile service providers getting into the music business. Timbaland has agreed to produce a mobile "album" for Verizon Entertainment, which will offer it exclusively to its network of customers. And even Starbucks has entered the record biz with stockholder Kenny G's latest release, a departure from his twenty-year career with Arista. This model effectively cuts out *two* middlemen: the record company and the retailer. Suffice it to say that whatever I might write here about label structure would be obsolete by press time. That is a testament to the unprecedented volatility of record companies in the twenty-first century.

What this chapter *is* about is the *unspoken* structure of labels: the unwritten rules as they relate to the career woman. You'll hear from women who have worked for or currently hold down positions at labels, be they a one-woman show for their own independent label or executives in business affairs, marketing, and media relations. All of them let their hair down and kick off their shoes for a candid conversation about what really goes down at a label, what the survival tactics are, and what insights they've gained. Many are former employees and thus able to break a silence of sorts about double standards and unsavory practices. They have so graciously agreed to pass all this on to the next generation of working women. This chapter also features two entertainment attorneys, the venerable and wise Louise West, and the young and talented Kim Ward. They get down to business on the legal side of doing business with labels, vital information for every artist. Finally comes my set of general guidelines as to whether, when, and how to take legal action as an employee: The Ten Severance Commandments. As layoffs and mergers continue, this section will be invaluable for executives looking to make the strongest exit possible, especially those who get pink-slipped without a contract.

Each of the women featured in this chapter shared relevant comments on multiple topics, so it will feel very much like a roundtable discussion as you read. The esteemed collective includes the aforementioned entertainment attorneys West and Ward, along with an independent-label GM and co-owner (McGregor), a business affairs and licensing executive (Cartwright), two former major-label publicists (Vega and Quinn), and three vice presidents of marketing and product management (Das, Jackson, and Rhinehart). Among the eight of them, these women have a hundred years of industry experience. Gather 'round.

....

LEARN THE ENVIRONMENT
....

Labels can have a number of looks these days, but they generally break down into four types: the major, the major indie, the small indie (with or without traditional major distribution), and the digital label. It is important to know the culture of whatever label you work for or are signed to. This will help you navigate the political territory you will inevitably find yourself traversing. Further, understanding your surroundings will help you manage your own expectations of what you can do from inside the label, and what you think the label ought to be doing for you. "You can learn a lot about a company by the executives in place," says Wendi Cartwright. "Are they play-hard, work-hard [types], or do they lead by yelling and intimidation? I definitely had to clean up a lot of shit or go in and straighten out problems time and again. And these were messes that guys would make. They'd just watch the piles grow and grow."

Examples of major labels include parent companies like Sony BMG, Warner Music Group, and Universal Music Group. Major indies are companies like Virgin Records, Sub Pop, Hear Music, and Koch Entertainment; small indies exist in the hundreds and include Disturbing tha Peace (Ludacris), ATO (founded by Dave Matthews and Michael McDonald), So So Def (founded by Jermaine Dupri), and Hiero Imperium (Domino and the Hieroglyphics crew). Digital labels like ARTISTdirect and LifeNotes Music are cropping up like crazy. Even T-Pain has his own digital label, Nappy Boy.

Be advised: The bigger the company, the more corporate it is in culture. Don't let the loose dress code fool you: Protocol and politics remain the order of the day. Though you'll see people in jeans and people in suits on the same floor, how you look in a meeting of any kind is crucial, and should be appropriate to your position and the meeting at hand. If it's the interview, make a powerful impression, just as veteran media specialist Gwendolyn Quinn did when she interviewed for her national publicity director position with Arista Records. Gwen remembers her supervisor-to-be confiding in her afterward about her look, saying she "knew I was perfect for the job because of my one-of-a-kind coat from Germany and a big weave with my hair all out," she says with a laugh. Publicists are walking billboards and should have as much star power as their clients; they just shouldn't outshine them.

Attorney Kim Ward believes that the entertainment business is one of the few corporate environments where women can have "personality, style, and flair" in the law field. Kim also raises an important point about the label environment extending far beyond the elevator and the office. You must be prepared to stand on your own in these extracurricular zones—social settings outside the parameters of a traditional work environment. I have yet to see the bar, lounge, or nightspot with an HR or benefits department, but Kim says, "Go places your prospective clients are likely to go, including certain clubs." She winks, leaving out the strip clubs. Some female promotions representatives go to strip clubs anyway, because that's where the records are being played and being reacted to.

Marketing maven Shanti Das was among the handful of executives who built LaFace Records from the ground up, working in promotions and eventually marketing for multiplatinum megastars from Outkast and Toni Braxton to TLC and Usher. She now oversees marketing and artist development in her position of executive vice president at Universal Motown, where she guides the careers of Chamillionaire, India.Arie, and Erykah Badu. Shanti knows how to blow up records, artists, and brands. She sees outside work and networking as the part of the business that offers such a unique opportunity. Because music is a thread in the fabric of people's lives, working at a label by definition means getting out there and experiencing lifestyles when and where they are happening. "It's about getting to know the product; being in the clubs and seeing what your competition is doing, where people are hanging out, what they think is cool," says Shanti. "I read people's expressions. I close my eyes and fall into the song. I get to know as many people as possible. If you're on the wall, you're not 'out at the club.'" Be you artist or executive, the key is to remain focused and calm about the things you may witness or experience and the people you'll be hangin' out with. When you move in circles as an artist's representative, you also have to remember that you represent yourself and the company as well, which we will explore in depth in the conduct section.

Quincy Jackson, VP of marketing for Columbia Records and product manager for John Legend, Mary Mary, Yolanda Adams, and the Destiny's Child franchise of Beyoncé, Kelly Rowland, and Michelle Williams, encourages women not to let the relaxed dress code lull you into thinking your game can slip. As she asserts, there are things men can get away with in this business that women simply cannot. "Being less detailed is one of them," she says with a smile. "Having less information to back up what they are saying; meanwhile I have to have footnotes for everything I say! Men can also be unreachable. They tend to get an on-off switch, and women don't."

Wendi Cartwright, former business affairs and licensing executive for major indie labels like Priority, Virgin, and Rhino, had a keen observation about always having to be on, especially once you become a mother. It's what actually helped her choose to exit the music end of the business in favor of acting and lifestyle modeling, which she discusses in detail in chapter 3.

"What caused me to want to leave the industry was how women are treated once you have children," Wendi notes. "Once you have a time commitment or choose to be with your baby instead of going to a party, women get passed over for promotions, talked about, or dismissed as not being serious. Once you become a mommy, you're not as available, be it sexually or time-wise. They make assumptions about women who work smart and as a result don't work long hours," Wendi maintains. "To men, that looks like lack of commitment, or like she may not be choosing to put her work first."

To maximize your time and juggle the demands of being an executive, especially one who manages staff, Shanti recommends using your team as your ministers of information at all times. This strategy allows her to manage her relationship with the label president and think big-picture. And while the pieces of an artist's marketing story come together, Shanti makes sure the progress reports and heads-ups keep flow to her from her staff. This, in part, is how she made the leap from being director of marketing with interns and eventually one assistant at LaFace (a major indie) to running the urban marketing department at Arista when LaFace was folded into its former parent. Shanti elaborates: "At Arista I had my first [full] staff. I became the head of urban marketing. I was focusing on urban projects, and still working Outkast, who had since come to cross many genres. [I was] having to do my work, *and* worry about what everyone below me was doing. I stopped going out as much; I was at the office till ten or eleven at night. My workload had tripled. I had to be super-organized," she recalls. "When L. A. [Reid, Arista chairman] would call me about an act that I wasn't directly responsible for, I had to figure out how to manage my day-to-day and know enough about the roster to be able to speak intelligently about anyone on it. I spent time finding the right assistant; that person had to keep me organized and sane. I was in more meetings and that took up more of my time," she adds.

So how do you attend back-to-back meetings with very little prep time in between, as well as keeping pace with the flow of each, without looking like you're bullshitting—even if you just might be? Even the most thorough executive gets thrown for a loop now and again. "If you know the major points, you can maneuver your way through a meeting," Shanti says. "It's very embarrassing to sit in a meeting and not know how to respond. Take notes in meetings. Know the major highlights: [airplay] spins, video play. Keep a calendar on hand and know where the artists are that day. I keep my book of calendars, one for each act. My staff does 'What's the 411' reports that include who our acts tour with, deals we've secured, et cetera. I keep the info readily available." Now, on the off chance that you're human and forget to have an answer handy—and that assistant you utilize so much is out sick that day—Shanti advises just keeping your word as you keep it real. "Say, 'I'm not sure, but I'll get right back to you on that'—and be confident in your response. Make them feel comfortable that you will get back to them."

Tracii McGregor is in the unique position of only having to answer to one other person across the proverbial boardroom table: her business partner and the label's franchise recording artist, Buju Banton. Gargamel Music operates with a core staff of two, she and Buju. And while Tracii, the general manager, enjoys more latitude than her major-label counterparts in calling shots, even her meetings can start to get a little crazy after a few conversations, because the stakes are so high for each of them. Tracii has to figure out when she was talking to the reggae icon or the expanding business owner. "With Buju, I am to the point where I know when the artist is speaking versus the business partner. I have to remind him sometimes why he's doing a ton of interviews—because he said he wanted to do it," she explains with incredulity. "I remind him that now it's about him being a CEO as well."

Indies offer artists and executives the agility and support to be creative in generating whatever it is: sales, buzz, awareness, tour receipts, endorsements. They can also elicit a more liberated sound from signed artists depending on where they are in their lives, whereas at the major level, the obsession with profitable multiformat hits has taken priority over solid albums.

"It's just tougher to market [now]; you start losing the passion," Shanti notes. "To the artists' defense, the labels have fewer dollars from a T&E [travel and expenses] standpoint." Shanti laments that the trimming of budgets directly impacts her product management staff's grasp of the markets they are working. Which has the ripple effect of (1) creating mistrust and lack of confidence in the staff on the part of artists; (2) encouraging sedentary product marketers, impeding their on-the-job effectiveness, because the product managers need to see and experience the places where artists do well, how they connect with consumers, and exactly who those consumers are; (3) causing marketing misfires, because when the market is not fully understood and its current changes are not taken into account, the project suffers setbacks. These factors can add up to plant the seeds of division between an imprint and any major parent distributor. Shanti elaborates: "My staff doesn't benefit from their work the way I did; I can't [always] send my product managers to the hot radio show. That's learning the marketplace, from the hottest retailer, club, and show — and who the audience is. I wasn't constrained by being in the office. I knew Houston, the Bay, and Los Angeles [from touching each market]. And it was easier to work with the sales department to figure out what works and why, or why not."

All this diminished contact and interaction between label executives and the artists they represent can make the opportunities the artist and label do have together ring false or suspicious. Artists and their handlers figure you must want something by the time you actually come around to create some sort of bond. Shanti talks about the studio being a place where the groundwork was laid between executives and artists. She learned about the acts and their work ethics in that environment while at LaFace. However, major label specialization has all but eliminated this as a creative professional common ground from which hits and stars are made. "I wish certain executives understood the relationship between marketing and A&R. They go hand in hand. [Before,] there was never a time where I didn't go by the studio. I needed to know what artists were saying, what they were about, who they represent culturally, the struggles they've gone through. At the big labels you're distant from that part of the process," Shanti continues. "So artists don't know where you're coming from; it's the trust factor [that's missing]. At Universal, there are so many camps with established artists, building the relationships could be taken the wrong way; they think I want to be down with them. The artists may also feel like I'm here to take information back to the parent company."

Tracii asserts that the indies have the upper hand in this shifting landscape, and that wary artists got that way for a reason, usually from being underserved as part of an endless major-label roster. "It's about being resourceful, making sure your team is on point; that you're getting the most out of every deal. [We] don't give everything away to anyone. Everybody just wants control," insists Tracii. "Ask them, 'What do you plan to *do* with it?' I've had people talk about all types of shit they can make happen, and when I follow up, they were 'too busy to do it.' But I'll never be too busy for my own label; I guard it with my life and do deals that way — aggressively and thoroughly negotiated by knowledgeable participants in that part of the business." It may be a brutal grind of insane hours and persistence, but Tracii confirms that doing it independently carries its own sweet reward despite "not sleeping until August one year," which she disclosed as she shared her greatest moment of victory running Gargamel Music, the Reggae Label That Could.

"Getting my box of promos for that *Too Bad* CD was a proud moment for me. It [finally] was *tangible:* All our hard work was in this little package. Buju worked on that record for a long time; you gotta deal with artwork, designers, the credits, the publishing—it's a lot. Seeing my name under Buju's as co-executive-producer—then it was set in stone. It was like, *yes!* And when we got the Grammy nomination, that was huge—he's been nominated many times but *never on his own label*. It said, 'Buju Banton. Too Bad. Gargamel Music.' That was big. And I am the one calling the specialty shows and reggae stations, but at some point it started to happen on its own. When [the music] is hot, people want to put it in their mix. I got a call from *Billboard* in January of 2007 and they told me his single 'Driver A' was the second highest debut of the week on their R&B hip-hop charts. I also got a call from Rodney Morandi and DJ Enuff at HOT 97. They were like, 'We're adding the record.' That let me know the music was out there and it [felt] amazing!"

....

KNOW HOW TO CONDUCT YOURSELF
....

By virtue of the fact that you are a woman who has the chutzpah to be in this game so very crowded with men, you become attractive to them. You will get hit on. And when your work demands that you spend what would normally be your personal time socializing for work purposes, it's all about your ability to keep the peace and, as Shanti offers, "keep it light." "Women spend so much time working, it is inevitable that you'll date inside the industry. However, a double standard applies to women when we do. Men experience [virtually] no consequence for doing the same," she says. "I've been approached by artists since I started in the business. I don't want to be nasty or offensive [to them], but I'm not here for that. If you give them no rhythm, they won't come back twice and play themselves."

Quincy agrees. "The work shows [you best], not the gift of gab and being social. That works for a while, but it will also get you laid off." She adds,

"If you have talent, know what you're doing, and you're confident—not cocky—about your talent, you don't pay attention to the odds and percentages of success. Your talent becomes a certain non-negotiable truth. That allows me to be fine in the room—and whatever other people's issues may be are on them."

Tracii: "I've always been a straight-up kind of girl. I command and demand respect, but I also give it. I do what's necessary to get the job done in a timely fashion. I never missed a deadline at *The Source*," she recalls, where she worked for eight years and eventually became the VP of content and communications. "I carry myself and dress in a particular way, one that sets the tone for where men can go with me. And I've got a smart mouth. I'll let you have it in a minute if necessary, respectfully of course, but I will. I'm so cool but I will flip it in a minute! And I am up front with people about that."

Gwendolyn relays a story of how her attitude upon securing her first label job resulted in her getting an unexpected attitude adjustment. A former hairstylist who had trained with Vidal Sassoon, Gwen got started in the business by assisting and touring the world with R&B/dance icon Gloria Gaynor, going on to assist the world's first Black supermodel, Beverly Johnson. Gwen had worked the scene and brushed elbows with everyone from Andy Warhol to Halston. When Vidal would come to the salon where she apprenticed, guess who was assigned to wash his hair? Gwendolyn. "He said I had a nice touch," she beamed. I can't front; after a jet-setting career like hers, I might come in to my publicity coordinator gig with a bit of a chip on my shoulder, too! Gwen recalls her Mercury Records experience, which was a new world in another part of a glamorous business.

"I did tour press for Vanessa Williams and Third World. We had a very active roster and I did a lot, but I had a really bad attitude. I wasn't respecting my boss like I should have. I didn't think I'd get fired—but I did. I became the Queen of Temp Agencies; it was depressing."

After getting this lesson, Gwendolyn went on to have a tremendously successful career in public relations, first as the in-house PR executive for Flavor Unit Management, then holding senior positions in publicity with Arista, Island, and Capitol Records, where she got her first real taste of being laid off, this time through no fault of her own. Ironically, though she had left Flavor Unit for the label gig, it was Shakim Compere, her former boss, who tipped her to the layoffs. Gwendolyn explains: "Shakim wouldn't talk to me [after I left Flavor Unit]. He was so mad! A year later he called me and said, 'I called to tell you they're gonna fire you.' Then he said, 'Okay, I'll talk to you later.' And from that point, it all went downhill," Gwendolyn recounts. "You start coming to work stressed. I was responsible for male R&B group Portrait, gospel legends Bebe and Cece Winans, and jazz pianist Rachelle Farrell. A month or so after Shakim's call, the ax got lowered. They let us go the Friday before the Grammys. I called Cece, because she was nominated *and* performing. It was big year for her," says Gwendolyn, who now would not be by her side during the telecast. Hell, it was big year for her as Cece's publicist as well! Of course, Gwen was glued to her TV set. "Wednesday comes around. Grammy night. I'm trippin'. I don't know what will happen next," she continues about both the awards show and her career. "Cece won her award and made her acceptance speech. My name was the *only* one she mentioned by first and last names. My phone started blowin' up like a switchboard! Black artists would [often] leave Black publicists once they felt they had arrived, but Cece was loyal. Jackie [Rhinehart, Gwendolyn's friend and mentor] called me from the lobby [of the awards show venue] with Hiram Hicks [then head of Black music for Island Records]. He wanted to see me that Friday, and I had a job at Island Records the following week."

If there was a number one rule that I could point to after speaking to so many women about their careers, it would be No Crying at Work. It may have worked for Hillary going into the New Hampshire primary in January 2007, but it was not the deciding factor in the Democratic nomination. Some would even argue that it worked against her to show emotion. If "there's no crying in baseball," there's definitely no crying in presidential politics. It didn't win President Carter any cool points. The same goes for the entertainment world. Unless you're Halle Berry accepting the Best Actress Oscar on the heels of a century of Black actresses who were overlooked and underestimated, sniveling by and large is unacceptable.

I was putting together a very frustrating Gavin Seminar showcase at a club called The Townsend in San Francisco. I can't even recall whose showcase it was since it was so long ago, but something pissed me off to the point of me shedding tears. I wasn't in Halle Mode, and the club was pretty dark, but my crying spell was enough of an emotional demonstration to prompt my dear friend and one of my industry Big Brothers, J. C. Ricks, to pull me into the cut for a pep talk. He understood where I was coming from and could see why my crying was justifiable, but he was resolute in his counsel. He said, "T, no matter what is going on, don't ever let anyone see you cry. They don't deserve to see that. There's nothing wrong with it, but do it privately." I went to an all-female high school and undergraduate school—environments where women were in the majority. So I was unaware how crying was perceived in the work world, until I did it. While it's something that all humans do, when women do it, it can be perceived as an inability to control their emotions, whereas when men cry—which is very infrequently because as boys, men are socialized to believe that crying is girlish—it tends to be seen as some noble display of sensitivity first, then as quintessential bitch move second.

As a female, you will be judged negatively for your tears, period. No matter why they fall. Shanti was counseled much as I was when she let the tears flow during a moment of anger at LaFace. It stuck with her as she matriculated in the business. "Someone told me that men and women ironically will see it as a sign of weakness," she says. "Sometimes women get too emotional, myself included. We tend to let others see us sweat. In certain situations, women would play their cards better if we'd just held on to them. [Emotion carries] a huge double standard. Men are aggressive; 'He's crazy, that's just how he is.' Women look hysterical and can't handle it. And then they start reevaluating our positions at the company. It goes on a checklist men have for us. I have to wait for my angel on my shoulder to tell me not to react a certain way. I take time to think before I react because I don't want to respond too emotionally. We'll have to deal with that until the end of time." Shanti sighs, shaking her head.

Quincy's on the same page, but she has one exception. "Let's be human. If a loved one passes and you're at the office, have a heart and cry," she offers. "Business should never make you cry. Part of being a businesswoman is being able to maintain your composure under pressure. If you have to duck away in a bathroom stall, do it, but no public crying. It's a surefire way to lose respect."

Which brings me to the whole use-of-feminine-wiles conversation. Women got it tough up in here! No crying, you've gotta dress a certain way to keep men at arm's length and to be taken seriously, all while you walk the tightrope of being social but not being *too social* outside the office. Careful, pretty soon you'll start morphing into Gidget!

So where is the line? Do we get to be women in the boardroom? How much femininity is too much? Is there such a thing?

Jasmine Vega is a pioneering Latina in the world of music and media relations, especially hip-hop and R&B. She cut her teeth doing promotions for a club DJ, the now world-renowned house legend Marques Wyatt in Los Angeles. She moved on to a gig as the publicist for Delicious Vinyl, a small but mighty indie that realized success with acts as diverse as the Brand New Heavies, Masta Ace, Inc., and the Pharcyde. Before joining Virgin Records, she served as the publicist for Ice Cube, Master P, and a scrappy entrepreneur with a single called "Dead Presidents" named Jay-Z at Priority Records. As she neared the twenty-year mark in her field, she felt part of herself slipping away . . . the female part. Jasmine explains. "When you're a woman and you speak your mind . . . no matter how hard you work, you're still going to be looked at as a woman. Not as a peer, not as one of them. It's a boys' club most definitely. What I found is that as I climbed the ladder, I started to lose a bit of my femininity—or at least I felt like it—to fit in, because you have to. You gotta get your job done and not be so girly, you have to roll with it, work those hours, do more than the man next to you . . . I mean if I would've done some unethical things, I would've climbed the ladder faster, but my integrity was more important to me as a woman, especially a Latin woman. And back in the day there were hardly any Latin women in hip-hop publicity."

Former Universal Music Group VP of marketing Jackie Rhinehart tells a completely different story. She came into the business designing personalized T-shirts for one of the raunchiest singers in R&B, Rick James and the Stone City Band (read: she's been in the game a long time). She did such a great job, it impressed Ann Maven, who at the time was Rick's product manager at Motown. Jackie literally went from working as the director of the governor's mansion under Dick Riley of South Carolina to overseeing Rick James's merchandising. In addition to being beautiful and self-confident, she was (and still is) all woman with no apology. "Even though he wanted me, when I told Rick to back up, he did," Jackie recalls. Wanting women is what Rick James was known for, along with just about every other straight member of the male species in the record business. Jackie, however, was not only unfazed; she was flattered—and her philosophy is to use this tendency men have to her advantage. "I believe that even if they want to have sex with you, that's not such a bad thing," she explains referring to men she'd encounter at radio stations and on the road. "They saw that when they wanted to screw me, fuck me, or whatever—I could get past that and get to work. When you get past it, they do, too. They *all* should want to fuck us! They're supposed to! It's not money, it's not politics—it's who controls the pussy that controls the world. So as a woman, you should be happy pussy makes the world go 'round—because you've got it! Mentally, I have the fortitude to push past those things and carry through with what I want to. I *am* a sex object, *just not yours*," Jackie affirms. "You have to take your values with you and remain who you are. If you don't you'll be consumed."

....

DO THE WORK

....

Jackie is also big on getting the work done, no matter how female you choose to be in the workplace. In her mind, this applies to everyone, no matter how high up the organizational flow chart. "That sense of entitlement is a dangerous muthafuckin' thang! I've seen it work against a lot of senior executives; some would be long gone from their posts at labels and still expect to be treated like they are rollin' at the office! I had a staff of thirteen women at Universal as the senior VP of marketing. I felt everybody on my team should be as competent as me, if not more so," Jackie says, noting that many of her staffers had earned master's degrees. "Never will I ask you to do what I won't work as hard for. I always felt like when it was time to bust ass and clear a table at the governor's mansion, I'd do it right along with the maids and butlers."

Quincy says that there's one misconception about working at labels that still gets on her nerves: "that it's just a fun job. It is, but I also deal with seven-figure budgets, analyze data, do market research, and conduct real business daily. It's not just going to see them on tour. I am constantly mediating," says Quincy about her role as a brand guardian. "Make no mistake. I work for the label, but in working for the label that means I must provide a profitable release for the label and still guard the musicians' artistry. Their job happens wherever they are. I get to go home at night. I am the reality check for the label that this is a person with a life whose hands, voice, and body are how they make their living, whereas I make mine with my mind. I make sure we can make money *and* maintain the integrity of the artist. So I think of solutions to create a win-win when I'm fighting for my artists. I have to consider both sides. The moves I make have to be win-win so everyone's happy. And everyone [may not be] happy, but everyone respects the position I was in; if a deal can't be struck it's probably not a good match, and maybe it's for another artist or another time."

Sometimes doing the work ahead to achieve that win-win Quincy speaks about means getting educated or reeducated on the task before you. Tracii went back to basics when she became co-owner of Gargamel, so that any deals she made would be done with understanding and precision. "I've made a lot of transitions over the course of my career, and all of them have happened pretty naturally. Where I felt I had the biggest learning curve was running this label. I didn't want to assume [I could do it] because I had worked in the business for so many years, even with overseeing the *Source* record label at one point. The first thing I did was buy all the books. I took myself back to school on the business of music. And while you're in the midst of reading, it makes you hypersensitive—which can be good and bad. Sometimes that makes you immobile. But I felt that was better than making a move and not being able to see what was ahead of me, or seeing the consequences of making the move." Tracii spent over a year researching and taking meetings before securing distribution for the label, which wasn't all about traditional retail sales—or letting a parent company handle digital distribution.

"A lot of folks would get P&D [production and distribution] with marketing deals, where the major was controlling the way you market and promote the record, and we never wanted to do that. We wanted to do it all from soup to nuts. One of the first things we did was lock in our own iTunes deal *before* we had any distribution. I found a direct iTunes contact and I set up the label with them first," Tracii notes. She then set about the business of ramping up a bona fide PR campaign, drawing on skills she had honed as a writer, editor, and media strategist in the absence of a budget to outsource PR. "Starting out, the only tools I had were my writing skills and my e-mail lists," she recounts. "Having worked in the biz for so long, I knew that if people don't know, you might as well be invisible. So it was about creating a new awareness of Buju, deflecting the outdated and obscure press about him, and hitting people over the head with the truth from his perspective. It wasn't something I could hand off to someone else."

Jasmine shared a great example of executing effective PR against the odds when she was the VP of media relations for the urban division of Virgin Records, which she was appointed to start and run. One of her greatest PR challenges happened to be one of her most rewarding as well: that of working with soul crooner and multi-instrumentalist D'Angelo. She had to get as creative with her media tactics as he was at making music.

"I think when they're a true artist, they only know art, they only work with that side of the brain. When you're trying to bring business into it, you have to know how to walk that line to get them enticed, to get them to do what you need them to do and handle the business at hand. I was finding ways that made him excited to be involved more on the business end," Jasmine muses, citing one tactic she employed. "He'd say, 'I have to stay in the studio.' So, understanding that, I'd make journalists come to the studio and tailor it to D'Angelo instead of doing roundtables, which I've done before with Ice Cube. It makes the experience more exciting, makes it more intimate. D'Angelo is not one to say *I'm going to do fifty interviews for you*," Jasmine adds, laughing. "It was more like *I'm gonna do five, so make it happen*. It's difficult working with artists like that, but you're doing it because you truly believe in him; you want him to be as big as he possibly can because people need to know about artists like him." Still, Jasmine had to turn five interviews into fifty without D'Angelo exerting any extra effort past five.

"When I found out the new album was called *Voodoo*, I said, 'Perfect' . . . there was a big voodoo convention in New Orleans. I sent out the media, we did a voodoo tour, we went to the graveyard, a voodoo ceremony, and did the whole French Quarter, ending the day with a D'Angelo performance. That was the ultimate. It gave me everything I needed to happen [media-wise]; everybody was like 'We'll give you whatever you need!' That was mainstream press, urban press, street press, he got everything."

UTILIZE THE LAW (AND RETAIN A LEGAL PROFESSIONAL WHO UNDERSTANDS IT WHEN NECESSARY)

I interviewed two attorneys who specialize in entertainment law to illuminate some dos and don'ts for artists, as well as shedding some light on the career itself for women with an interest in the intersections of music, media, law, and intellectual property. Louise West has been practicing for more than forty years, representing Donald Byrd, Timbaland, Missy Elliott, and countless others. She also worked in the US Copyright Office as a copyright examiner while in law school. She contends, "The people who want to learn, want to struggle, and actually learn the business are the ones who win. The ones who leave it all in [a lawyer's hands] and don't want to know the business scare me," she warns. "I don't have clients like that."

Many attorneys like to keep clients in the dark about the inner workings of the law so they can keep clocking those billable hours. Undoubtedly, West is such a proponent of education for her clients because she became an attorney after working as a professor in the jazz studies department of Howard University. One year, her students included "Angela Winbush, Richard Smallwood, Tawaka Age, and Shelton Beckton," she says. "They were a group called Hot Tea. Interestingly, Angela went on to work with Stevie Wonder, Shelton is a Broadway performer, Richard is a renowned gospel artist, Tawaka went on to work with Luther Vandross for most of his career and was principal songwriter with Mtume. They all said I should hear them sing. I kept putting them off until they made me come hear them one day. I couldn't believe what I was hearing. I felt they needed to meet some people who could get them a record deal," she recalls. And that is how she began networking with A&R men and producers to broker deals. She hasn't stopped yet.

"What sets me apart, especially with young clients just starting out, is that I encourage them to have a business plan in mind for setting up long-term goals for publishing and where they want to be in five to ten years. I also recommend books and go over chapters with them. Timbaland is one of my most serious students; he actually read the books and asked the tough questions. Missy as well; she was serious, grappling with the technical aspects."

Just as important as a working knowledge of the law is a curiosity about where the business is headed. Louise cites this as the toughest part of the game for her, even after all her decades of practice. I asked her what the future looked like from her vantage point. "Figuring out how to expand as a business and dealing with the constant state of flux that it's in, means I have to know what the trends are," she notes. She sees the return of the comprehensive 360-degree deals on the horizon but has yet to work on one. She is acutely aware of the digital labels and the independents' rise as well. "Digital labels will substantially change the landscape. Artists can sell their own record directly to the public, so there will be a lot more of that. However, there will still be room for majors because it will be hard for artists to brand themselves."

Kim Ward cites her role as one of "advocate for those who are unable to represent themselves. I saw many artists were being taken advantage of because they were not aware of what rights they could retain, so others were profiting off of their rights." Kim believes a blend of formal educational training and hands-on learning serves the client best. "It's not enough to say you're an entertainment attorney," she admonishes. "You have to practice it every day, or you will miss something that is beneficial to your client. As the digital age grows, the business model for the industry changes, so learn it and know it."

Kim breaks down her day-to-day responsibilities: "Just because the word *entertainment* is incorporated in it, there is nothing entertaining about the scope of the [attorney's] role. Unless you like litigation, draft agreements that work to prevent lawsuits; it's primarily transactional work. If you don't like dealing with intangible rights and licensing, this is not the field for you," she offers. "It's drafting and negotiating accounting provisions, publishing interests, royalty rates, all of which take a thorough knowledge of record and production companies as well. Choose which clients and issues you want to take on, because you may be fighting against a colleague you may need down the line for a client who's going nowhere, but has caused problems everywhere. Law school does not teach you this." Kim also debunks a myth to which many artists subscribe: that contracts are all the same and have to be accepted at face value. "Although there are industry-standard terms, no standard applies to everyone. But know that it costs money to be in business. Anybody that is serious about their business will be represented by an attorney. Stop trying to do your own contracts and making matters worse," she insists. "And please don't attach an attorney's name to any documents you have created."

....

THE GOOD FIGHT
....

Wendi believes the biggest mistake women make in this business may be one that holds true for us and business in general: "Selling themselves short and not fighting for what they want; not as in being underhanded, but as in standing up for themselves and saying why they deserve it. The outcome should not have to do with whether you get the promotion or not. [It's] more about standing up for you in a professional, adult way." In defense of women who remain silent, there is not a lot of support or positive reinforcement out there for knowing your value and advocating for its recognition, whether it's for the raise and title bump we seek or to report misconduct on the part of a colleague. Even Wendi has to acknowledge the double standard she saw playing itself out in corporate label settings.

"Fortunately for women, the laws are such nowadays that we're supported more. However, I have seen over the years that when there's sexual harassment, men are slapped on the hand and told to go away for a bit, but they still have their careers and the chance to work and feed their families. I don't see the same for women," Wendi observes. "It's far harder for women who speak out, especially when you're in promotion, publicity, or A&R. If you're in accounting, you're a goddess and no one will give you problems; business affairs had a different feel. But my friends in those artistic areas had a hard go of it," Wendi reflects.

And women in entertainment are still having a hard go of it. The most widely publicized lawsuit filed by a woman in recent history was that of Lisa Cortes, who in chapter 9 of this book talks about the emotional impact of her suing PolyGram Records for racial and gender discrimination throughout her tenure as CEO of her imprint, Loose Cannon Records. Even then, the news reports on the suit came and went as quickly as it was announced. She settled for undisclosed terms that she does not discuss for legal reasons.

What is known is that Alain Levy, the head of PolyGram at the time of Lisa's settlement, moved to EMI after his tenure there. His reward for EMI's lack of profitability? A seven-figure bonus. According to *The Birmingham Post*:

> The former boss of EMI's music division quit the troubled group with a £3.7 million pay-off, it has been revealed. EMI's annual report yesterday revealed that Alain Levy was handed the multi-million pound cash windfall on top of his £912,000 salary after he was ousted in January amid plummeting sales and a profits warning. Mr. Levy, who had been chairman and chief executive of EMI Music since October 2001, was handed a £1.1 million bonus and £2.6 million severance package plus pension payments and company benefits for a year after leaving the group, as part of a contractual agreement."[2]

The article goes on to reveal that Levy "also received 20 million share options under the group's long-term incentive plan, however, the drop in value of EMI's share price has left most of the options worthless." Aww, that's too bad. Good thing he's got the other 3.7 million pounds to help him ride out his severance. Meanwhile Lisa Cortes, an accomplished and capable executive and the only African American label president in the company's history, had her life turned upside down on his watch.

And sexual harassment goes on, rarely reaching the light of the media's flashbulbs. Suits that are brought are settled with mutually agreed-upon gag orders sealing the details from discovery, masking the outcomes. The ring of silence has penetrated other fields as well. Investment banking is paying a pretty penny for harassment claims. In 2004, investment banking giant Morgan Stanley paid fifty-four million dollars to settle various discrimination claims made by woman brokers, awarding twelve million of that to one woman, Allison Schieffelin, who sued after being denied a promotion.[3]

Anucha Browne Sanders, once a star athlete at Northwestern, had her four-year tenure as a marketing VP with the New York Knicks organization halted by being fired after complaining about on-the-job harassment. She alleged this to be retaliation and was ultimately rewarded with an $11.5 million settlement after going to a very widely publicized and damning trial for defendants Isiah Thomas and Madison Square Garden. As part of the settlement, Ms. Browne Sanders got her job back, too.

For those executives reading this who find themselves on the receiving end of any kind of discriminatory or unequal treatment, understand that it is very serious business, and that you have rights that not only protect you, but are worth fighting for. Because I am by no means a legal expert, I urge you to consult an attorney to learn all the options before you; and only then make the informed choice to bring suit or negotiate a severance. Should you go either route, here are what I call The Ten Severance Commandments—my set of guidelines for navigating some very intimidating and emotionally draining terrain. You owe it to yourself and those paralyzed by silence and fear to do what's best for yourself and your career.

The Ten Severance Commandments

1. Thou shalt remain spiritually grounded through prayer and gratitude.
2. Thou shalt not lose your cool with colleagues.
3. Thou shalt fight for your job as a matter of principle, even if you don't want it.
4. Thou shalt fully utilize your employee benefits in times of distress.
5. Thou shalt document meticulously and correspond respectfully.
6. Thou shalt not make your experience the subject of office gossip.
7. Thou shalt not antagonize human resources.
8. Thou shalt know and repeatedly express company procedure and your rights as an employee.

9. Thou shalt retain and be prepared to use a skilled attorney with a soft walk and a firm hand.

10. Thou shalt not reveal your attorney until absolutely necessary.

Commandment One: Thou shalt remain spiritually grounded through prayer and gratitude.

When you are faced with a situation that may involve a severance or resignation by agreement, your self-esteem *will* take a beating. Attacking your effectiveness and capability is the first line of offense for whoever wants you gone. That person may be threatened by your attributes, relationships, or executive prowess. If your bosses inherited you, they may have their own hire in mind for your job.

So often we as accomplished career women collapse what we do at work with who we are in the world. During a departmental battle, the uncertainty of your future in the company will bring out doubts and fears you never confronted. This is part "this job is the best thing that ever happened to me" Corporate Jedi Mind Trick, and part "what am I gonna do without this job" self-inflicted nonsense. Both will happen, and both will do their best to drive you completely crazy. If left to ravage your psyche unchecked, these thoughts will have the effect of actually weakening you at work, creating the opening for your termination on reasonable grounds as soon as you get caught slippin' into darkness.

All of this is why it is imperative to seek refuge in whatever Creator or belief system you subscribe to: for clarity and peace as you walk into the strike zone each day, relive and rethink each occurrence through documentation, and rely upon the select few people outside the office you talk with about the horrors you experience almost hourly, just when you thought the last one couldn't be topped. Have the conversations with that higher power when you need to give your spouse, mama, or best girlfriend a break from your play-by-play. Worst case? It's the end of this job and a stint with unemployment, not the end of your life! Read spiritual and uplifting materials. Recite and post affirmations. Listen to the messages Spirit sends you. Surrender to a power greater than yourself.

Commandment Two: Thou shalt not lose your cool with colleagues.

This one's a doozie. This commandment is two-pronged, relating to both the adversaries in your scenario and the people you like at work. Let's deal with the problem colleagues first.

I know there is nothing you'd enjoy more than going postal on the bootlickers who started this static with you. You have homies you could call who'd make sure the enemy felt pain sometime over the weekend and never saw it coming Friday afternoon. You want to come out the side of your neck and tell them how you feel, what they're full of, and where they can go. While it would be so gratifying to spit in Mister's water like Celie did in *The Color Purple,* you cannot and you must not. The last thing you need is to break the rules of company conduct. You also do not want to be perceived as the stereotypical bitch or hysterical whiner. So while you don't have to chat in the hallway with them or kill them with kindness, as the elders say, remain cordial when you can, especially in the presence of your department head. They know it's inauthentic and that you have no respect for them, but they will also know you understand how to play this game and intend to see it through to the end.

Don't give problem colleagues the satisfaction of ruffling you! If colleagues or superior-ranking executives are gunning for you, make them work hard to force you out by playing it cool. They will be gathering evidence, whether substantial or not, whether relevant or not. They will definitely cause undue stress, and could also compromise your physical and emotional health. These tactics usually add up to a hostile work environment for you. The term *hostile work environment* is the basis upon which you file your grievance and seek restitution. Before you can enter into combat, the hostile environment needs to have been fostered—just not by you.

What about the friendly colleagues? You used to share everything about your work and its politics with them. Now your situation has gone beyond the usual crap all employees endure, and while they sense or even ask point-blank if something's going on, you can no longer get into the detail to which they have become accustomed. When you are the target of a corporate assassination, your group dynamic will shift. This is in part because you've gotten quiet, in part because they know something's up but don't know what. Unfortunately, you can count on whatever you say now to get back to someone for whom your words were never intended. Speak with the intention of delivering a message to anyone who might catch one, or don't speak at all.

Whatever you choose, never speak about what you document or report to HR in group office settings. You weaken your position and lose integrity in the eyes of those you'll be negotiating with down the line. If you've got to say something to a trusted colleague or mentor, speak to that person off-site, via phone after work hours on noncorporate phone lines, and insist from the outset that your conversation remain confidential. In fact, ask them: "Can I count on you to keep this confidential?" Then take your chances and weigh the consequences. I recommend that you vent to family and not co-workers here, because you avoid dragging folks you care about at work into the fray.

Commandment Three: Thou shalt fight for your job, even if you don't want it.

Hel-loooo! It's the principle of the thing! You have worked hard to get where you are. You have definitely busted your ass to get the job done, to rescue clients, to shield the inept, to make your boss look good, and to make this company a ton of money whether you work in a revenue-generating profit center or not. Mergers and layoffs are one thing. In those scenarios you take the package and move on, some harm, no foul. You probably knew it was on the horizon anyway. But these commandments are for the times when your position might be eliminated not due to a merger, but for some other reason. Maybe your seniority has continually gone unacknowledged as your expertise continued to be called upon; your department head would (stupidly) rather roll the dice to push you out than promote you; your once junior colleague has been promoted above you and is now on a megalomaniacal power trip aiming straight for your job and your pockets. All of these are attacks on your track record, your career, and your American way of life! They mean *war*! All kidding aside, you didn't come this far to be sent packing when someone's beef is more personal than professional.

Commandment Four: Thou shalt fully utilize your employee benefits in times of distress.

You most likely were a diligent employee who worked so hard and rarely took advantage of all the benefits your employer extended to you. You enrolled in the 401(k), wore out that health insurance card, played hooky with a few sick days every year, and left it at that. Chances are that you might have been a "Lonely Only" in your department: a specialist who could rarely be away from the office lest you be asked to do some sort of task or answer a question for which only you had the answer.

Now that your enemies have revealed themselves, the rules of engagement have changed. Now the benefits you shelved like those tomes of in-network doctors will need to be dusted off, examined, and utilized to, well, your *benefit*. These are weapons in your arsenal that can sustain you during the quest for clearing your name and keeping your job or restoring the integrity of your reputation in the interest of providing the strongest possible parachute.

Research your benefits package. There may be some hidden gems in there that can assist you in self-preservation during the battle or through the severance negotiation process. You may not realize it, but all the mental gymnastics you're performing while you continue to perform your job duties may be leaving you anxious, unwell, sleep-deprived, or demoralized, if not clinically depressed. Terrie Williams's book *Black Pain: It Just Looks Like We're Not Hurting* speaks to these symptoms. These occurrences simply need to be assessed by medical professionals with the right letters behind their name where applicable. These benefits were put in place as part of the system for your well-being. Use them! Employee wellness hotlines, complimentary counseling, the corporate gym (you've got pent-up aggression, and probably have gained or lost a few pounds in an unhealthy way; now's a good time to join, because this could go on for months), a personal leave of absence, Family Medical Leave Act (thanks, President Clinton!), extended paid sick days—take advantage of whatever may be available to you through your plan. You can only use them before you actually leave the job. Now is not the time to be shy about doing so.

Commandment Five: Thou shalt document meticulously and correspond respectfully.

Your files should read like the perfect recipe for your ideal outcome. You need to list what happens as it happens, with dates, times, and specific details. Include when you receive correspondence from people involved with the situation. Print out any e-mails relating to the issue, and keep copies at the office and at home. A great backup system that works quickly in the moment is to forward company e-mails to your personal e-mail address, then print and store them at home; I mean, all the documenting can become time consuming and you are still doing a day job! I recommend backing up your time line documents at home as well via e-mail attachment. While you may not want to wait until you get home to enter new information, you need to have your data there in the event you take an extended vacation or leave of absence—or if you take the day off to meet with a lawyer and need to bring the facts along. Finally, communicate via your personal e-mail with attorneys, employees of the EEOC, or anyone else you may be in touch with about your situation. Those company e-mails may come back to haunt you if the company opts to retrieve them. Just because you deleted an e-mail from your hard drive doesn't mean it's gone.

Chances are you won't ever need to present or use much of what you gather, but you'll be surprised at what the smoking gun could be, so keep everything until the matter is completely resolved, down to the final severance agreement!

Commandment Six: Thou shalt not make your experience the subject of office gossip.

It weakens your position. It gives someone other than you the power to spin the events of your life, wresting those same events from your control. You also wind up looking like the Boy Who Cried Wolf, telling all the wrong things to the wrong folks at the wrong time. Then you place yourself in the role of having to do damage control on rumors that started with your inappropriate or perhaps hyperemotional disclosure, expending precious energy needed for the issue at hand. It is bad personal PR and a bad look all the way around. I know things can get to be too much sometimes, but unload it outside the office. See Commandment Two for more on the subject.

Commandment Seven: Thou shalt not antagonize human resources.

While they ultimately represent the interests of the corporation, they are accountable to you as well as a member of the company's community. Let them account. Listen. If people actually used HR representatives fully, these executives would never even have a chance to use the restroom. Unfortunately, discrimination, bias, prejudgment, stereotyping, impropriety, and intolerance are the order of the day in America. While diversity is what makes our nation great, our citizens deal with it like that bull in the china shop, doing the kind of damage that jump-starts class-action suits. By extension, subtle manifestations of this insensitivity run rampant in the workplace. Thing is, we as dutiful employees are conditioned not to make waves. We as people who may be female, of color, differently abled, gay and lesbian, or of non-Christian spiritual belief often blame ourselves when we are harassed,

READ THE LABEL 145

abused, or thrust into a hostile work environment. We are unaware of our rights and privileges, or intimidated by the system, afraid of putting our livelihood in jeopardy. Bills are real, and this we know for sure. However, the reality of the situation is that your livelihood is officially in jeopardy already; might as well stand up for yourself. For those of us who just don't have the fight in us, take heart. It is okay to just resign. But once you commit to the stand, let the people of human resources do what their department is supposed to do. They are there to keep the company out of court, and they have every reason to do this. It's what they get paid for—why not let them advocate on your behalf in the process?

Human resources can do more than you may realize, so take an informational with them when all the drama starts. This will give you some familiarity with your rep before things reach a boiling point. It also helps your case as you document your efforts to report activity or work with the company. HR can interview people informally and privately if you find yourself in a my-word-against-theirs character assassination. And you never know what's in co-workers' files; your follow-through may be the straw that earns them their walking papers, eliminating them from your work life altogether. Present HR with your experiences, your documentation, and your track record, even written testimony from those you work with. Then give them time to assess the situation. At worst, it may have the effect of calling in a watchdog and cooling the situation off from the outside. At best, it gives you a stronger negotiating position and, oddly enough, paints you like a team player from a macro standpoint. You may look like a sore loser or a snitch to some associates, but to the HR department, you look like someone who takes her career and reputation seriously enough to work it out internally and discreetly.

Commandment Eight: Thou shalt know and repeatedly express company procedure and your rights as an employee.

The rules by which all employees must abide are available to us through the intranet in corporations. If it's not online, you can access it through your HR rep. Knowing company policy and procedure helps you in all your interactions. By knowing them, you are aware of how far you can bend rules without breaking them. Additionally, when you communicate your knowledge of procedure in meetings or correspondence with anyone—your boss, your adversary, the department head, HR—you send the message that you are the wrong one to fuck with without uttering a single expletive.

Commandment Nine: Thou shalt retain and be prepared to use a skilled attorney with a soft walk and a firm hand.

It is imperative that you work with a labor lawyer. I know, your uncle and sister-in-law are lawyers and they'll hook you up pro bono or at a reduced rate. Don't do it unless either of them specializes in employment law! O. J. did not retain Judge Judy for his double murder trial—he got the best in the business for that kind of law, including the late, great Mr. Johnnie Cochran. Had he chosen anyone else, he would have been rolling the dice with the results. While you aren't looking at spending the rest of your life behind bars or worse, you *are* fighting for your livelihood, your rights, and your good name. Are those anything to roll the dice with? The best thing friend-lawyers can do is *refer you to a great labor attorney,* period. In fact, canvass your personal community for at least five solid referrals and have an informational conversation with them. This talk should be more about them than about your issue. You simply need to assess their temperament and determine if your personalities clash. Weigh your options, then select one. Even if you have to pay for a few quarter hours to narrow it down, it's money well spent.

Now that you've added a brilliant legal mind to your team, you will feel a sense of dread at first, then relief that you have an expert on board. Don't turn your lawyer into a shoulder to cry on; your spouse's or cousin's shoulder comes free of charge. That of your attorney has a price tag attached. Keep your calls and meetings strictly business. Use an attorney like a coach during your interactions with people in your work setting, *without* involving one directly. Lawyers can guide you on your correspondence and the order of your steps. They can show you land mines because they see them daily in their work and have a deep well of experience from which to draw. Keep yours in your hip pocket, revealing them at the right moment for the negotiation phase, and save yourself some billable hours. The right moment varies for every client, but it's usually that point when HR fails to recognize how dire the situation is, becomes less responsive, or closes the case without sufficient resolution while the problem persists or worsens for you at work. Make sure the lawyer you choose is not abrasive, antagonistic, or prone to overreacting; at the same time, you need someone with chutzpah who is not intimidated by the size or brawn of your employer. You'll rely heavily upon the soft walk and firm hand for the moment you invoke the last commandment.

Commandment Ten: Thou shalt not reveal your attorney until absolutely necessary.

Once revealed, attorneys cannot be hidden. An attorney's presence takes your interaction with HR out of the confidential interoffice realm, and moves HR out of the comfort zone. This is known as the point of no return. This is the next level of being in it for the long haul: hearings, proceedings, settlement talks, a potentially grueling trial, and fees on top of fees. If you intend to go all the way, introducing an attorney formally by copying him or her on documents, or informally by alluding to him or her with veiled threats of consulting one, are two ways to throw the gauntlet. Just know that you're officially leaving the green zone, and will be treated very differently by all parties going forward. I can't believe I'm actually quoting Dubya here, but once your lawyer's in the picture, the philosophy now becomes: "If you're not with us, you're against us."

SUMMARY OF SECRETS REVEALED

WHAT YOU THOUGHT YOU KNEW:

The best friends I will ever have are the ones I make at work.

WHAT YOU NEED TO KNOW:

Maybe, but that's a rare long shot. Don't look to the workplace to source your friendships. If it happens, consider it icing on the cake, but by and large this is a risky enterprise, because people tend to be opportunistic, superficial, and transient. Quincy adds, "I hoped that I would gain some friends while working in this career, even when friendship comes a distant second in this business. I thought I had formed a working friendship with colleagues and realized that in no way was friendship there. Because I thought there was, I got incredibly burned. I opened myself up in a way that left me vulnerable in the workplace."

WHAT YOU THOUGHT YOU KNEW:

No means no forever. That door will never open to me again.

Don't let defeat stop you from going for the *yes* after the *no*. It may simply be obstructed, waiting to have you clear the path to yes.

Shanti shared a story that lives as a prime example of how we as women can let *no* from a powerful man stop us in our careers. Over the course of her tenure at LaFace, she had built a solid relationship with Chaka Zulu and Chris Lova Lova, who were the music director and an on-air personality for HOT 97 in Atlanta. She entered into a deal with them to sign Chris to her production company, contingent upon her company securing distribution through LaFace. Shanti was confident in Chris's sound as an artist; he already had a song reacting in the city. And he had an airplay platform, all the makings of a surefire deal, right? Not exactly. . .

Shanti describes what happened next between her and Antonio "L. A." Reid—the *La* of LaFace Records: "L. A. and I have laughed and joked about this story now, but back in '97–'98 I expressed to L. A. my desire to have a production situation. He told me to find my artist and come back to him. I had a contract between me and Chris, who had other label interests, but because he saw my passion and my track record, he said 'Let's blow up together.' I had my big meeting and played his demo. For whatever reason, L. A. didn't hear it. Now, I didn't have the hustle I have now, and I took no for an answer. L. A. believed in me as an executive, because he gave me my shot—but as an A&R source, he didn't think I was capable. I was so crushed. I fought until people liked that 'country shit' when they would talk badly about Outkast, but I didn't have the fight in me to go back to L. A. I don't know why."

The *Chris* in Shanti's story is Chris "Ludacris" Bridges, who eventually did get a deal. It just ended up being with Disturbing Tha Peace, distributed by Def Jam. Shanti heard something, and it turned out to be multiplatinum album success. Could she have kept shopping? Sure; Chaka and Luda did. Could she have approached L. A. again? Sure; his telling her no wasn't the end of their business relationship by any means. What Shanti experienced was most likely a combination of exhaustion, anger, and self-doubt after rejection, which combined to deplete her of the resolve to keep the deal alive, even if it wasn't with L. A. at LaFace. Fight that fatigue when you feel it coming on and pursue a *yes* after the *no*.

WHAT YOU THOUGHT YOU KNEW:

I can flirt, date, and sleep around in the industry without consequence.

WHAT YOU NEED TO KNOW:

Be careful. This is a delicate dance that requires knowing when to wield the power of the P. The double standard that sullies reputations and undermines credibility is alive and well here. Men can do this with relative impunity. The simple, sad truth is that women cannot. Men hit on women. It's just what they do. It's a game to them. Flirt and have fun when advances are made, but unless you are fully prepared to absorb the on-the-job fallout, decline gracefully to quell the resentment men can feel upon being rejected. Be selective about who gets the goodies, and who knows about it. And when it comes to artists and co-workers, try not to freak where you eat.

WHAT YOU THOUGHT YOU KNEW:

What do I know about starting or running my own label?

WHAT YOU NEED TO KNOW:

If you've ever multitasked or hired someone to provide a service for you, chances are you have skills that are useful for going the indie route. The key is to acknowledge what you don't know and ask the right professionals the tough questions. Use your network for strong referrals. Get educated through conferences and workshops offered by professional organizations and read, read, read. No need to reinvent the wheel, but you want to be up on the latest tricks of the indie label trade. And take heart: There is no better time than now to be independent.

WHAT YOU THOUGHT YOU KNEW:

As a woman attorney in entertainment, my services will be less in demand.

WHAT YOU NEED TO KNOW:

According to Kim, men like women to handle their legal business. She speaks from experience. "Because women take care of business, a great number of men have expressed their wish to be represented by a female attorney in this particular industry. Some men still need to feel that mother's protection, care, and concern for their interests," she notes.

WHAT YOU THOUGHT YOU KNEW:

I feel like I'm being discriminated against, or like my work environment is becoming hostile for me. But I'm afraid I won't have a leg to stand on. Besides, I need my job.

WHAT YOU NEED TO KNOW:

Even if you're afraid to speak out, there's no harm in checking out your suspicions. Document the occurrences meticulously on your personal computer or even in the memo section of your personal cell until you can get the info down at home. Read up on the company procedures and see if they've been broken by your colleague; remember that the company is usually not the enemy, and it doesn't want to get sued any more than you want to sue it, but know you have rights that are protected and enforced by law. Trust me, you need your integrity and your sanity more than you need that job. In times like these, colleagues play games to keep you off kilter, all part of maintaining that hostile work environment. This constitutes harassment as well as the more overt behaviors like derogatory name-calling and inappropriate contact. This is the time to lean on friends, family, and an experienced labor lawyer for good counsel. That initial consultation is money well spent.

WHAT YOU THOUGHT YOU KNEW:

I'm up the creek with no paddle since there's no HR department where I work.

WHAT YOU NEED TO KNOW:

Okay. Your workplace is too small or simply does not have a human resources department. Or maybe it's a department of one, or a part-time bookkeeper-organizer. If the conflict is between you and a co-worker, document in detail and discuss in private with your supervisor or the company's owner to seek resolution. If the issue is between you and the supervisor or owner, the writing may be on the wall. In small-company settings, if you have conflict with the company owner, you will have to determine whether the interaction is abusive or constitutes harassment. Depending upon the severity of the conflict, it may be wise to seek legal counsel or file a complaint with the EEOC while you're still employed. Though it is wrong, unprofessional, and often illegal, some bosses love to make their employees' work and personal lives miserable as a means of exerting control. Don't look for those types to fire you. Doing that would spoil their fun. You may need to cut your losses and start a job search. Include organizations that provide advocacy and protective procedures for employees on your list.

WHAT YOU THOUGHT YOU KNEW:

Tears are expected from women. Shedding a few is no big deal.

WHAT YOU NEED TO KNOW:

Big girls don't cry, and neither do businesswomen. "If you feel it happening, remove yourself from the meeting—and do so emotionlessly," says Shanti. "Bring Visine to the office."

CHAPTER 7

So You Wanna Be a Supastar?

....

Angie Aguirre ✳ Christine Yasunaga ✳ Dyana Williams ✳
Shanti Das ✳ Tina Davis ✳ Yvette Noel-Schure

....

So many people want to be in front and be in the spotlight.
Who will the audience be when we all become celebrities?

—Yvette Noel-Schure, celebrity publicist

Entertainment is about shine. Radiating everything desirable; manifesting the impossible, and by so doing, making possibility *itself* a tangible thing for those of us looking on in awe. Stardom speaks to the gifts that go unopened within the majority of us for fear of our own greatness; it addresses our ignorance of our own power. Most people work for a living doing something other than that about which they are most passionate. Entertainment provides people with an escape hatch from their station, their situation, their struggle. It gives everyday people an opportunity to reflect brilliance, even if it is not their own; to shine.

Then there are those people the rest of us are watching: the stars themselves. Those who are driven to shine. Those who dream of nothing else. Who move through the world knowing they have gifts to give and it's just a matter of time before those gifts are bestowed upon their throng, be it thousands, millions, or—in the case of a rare few—billions of onlookers. They may not be book-smart or drop-dead gorgeous; they may even possess something most view as a handicap. Then again, they might be the total package of looks, ability, intelligence, charisma and savoir faire. All that matters is what they repeat to themselves and just about anyone else who will listen. Prince Rogers Nelson, one of their very own, articulated it best: "Baby, I'm a *star*!"

These days, the readiness with which people can be seen throws a bit of a monkey wrench into the whole "star" thing. Between hundreds of cable channels, the Internet, satellite radio, blogs and the mini screens of mobile phones and MP3 players, it seems easier than ever to become a star. Here is where I am compelled to make a distinction. The pervasiveness of media and the immediacy of images has generated lots of celebrity, but not much stardom. Reality show cast members are celebrities. The Jacksons are stars. The cast-off from *America's Next Top Model* may be a celebrity because you saw her on TV and can recognize her face. The contestants from that series who are straight-up stars can be counted on one hand. And I'm being generous. The real star of that show is Miss Tyra Banks, and she chooses to widen her spotlight so we can see the other players in *her* production.

These people are reasonably recognizable, not famous. They are visible, not dazzling. Compared with the icons and legends, such as the late Eartha Kitt, who clawed and bled to be adored by the masses when it was exponentially more difficult to be seen, heard, or experienced, celebrities are flat, dull, lackluster. They clean up all right, but even the Elephant Man wore a suit. You have to be a star to shiiiiiinnnnne. I'm not on some ol' "back in the day" nostalgia when I talk about a time when it was tough to get your shine on as a star. Sure, some of you reading remember a time when the people on the record jacket weren't even the people you were listening to. More recently, before the advent of the music video, you'd listen to your favorite artists and only see them on album covers or at their live concert. I don't even mean that far back. I am talking pre-millennium, pre-Internet — in-every-household-and-handheld. 2Pac is a pre-Internet icon. Yes, the Internet existed, but he didn't need it to shine. He had toured the world with Digital Underground before he even had his own record deal. He recorded like crazy before he went to jail, and recorded like even more of a madman once he came out. You think he's had a ton of posthumous releases? We have only heard a fraction of his catalog. Tupac Shakur put in work, and that's why he sells more records than most living emcees! And yet he's just one example.

Rehab, half-hour nose jobs, broads without drawls on, red carpets at the airline boarding gate, tabloids, blogs. It's so easy to be famous, celebrity is damn near played out. Can the bullshit celebs please sit down? Will the real stars please stand up?

I am a champion of stars, not celebrities. And the good news is that those of us who fuel the industry machine as executives and support staff while knowing we are stars *also* know better than to be on camera or on stage. We understand the power we generate when we shine our light behind or alongside the entertainers. I applaud brilliance and reject buffoonery. Public Enemy Flavor Flav? Brilliant. *Flavor of Love* Flavor Flav? You know what time it is boyeeeeeee. We are going to get into what it takes to be the Real Deal, a star in your own right. And while we can't all be the North Star or the Big Dipper, there's enough room in the galaxy for all the stars. It's time to get into what it takes to shine, no matter where you want to be in this business. This chapter will take an in-depth look at stardom center stage and behind the curtain. Be you supastar or supastar-maker, this chapter is for you.

....
STAR QUALITY
....

Yvette Noel-Schure, executive vice president of media for Columbia Records, contends that a key distinction between celebrities and stars is quality. Think about it: No one says *celebrity quality*. I asked Yvette, whose roster includes a high ratio of stars who've crossed over into the super and megastar categories (read: Beyoncé, Mariah Carey, Wyclef Jean, John Legend, and Lauryn Hill, to name a few), how she tells a celebrity from a star. "Celebrities are a dime a dozen. A star is something much more special," she intones. "Unfortunately, we are now in a world of Web sites and weekly magazines. Everyone has a camera in their phone and anyone can be famous. We have a tabloid media culture now, so making the distinction has become harder. With reality TV stars on covers as much as actors and musicians who've learned their craft, it's sort of muddy. The tabloid person is a celebrity. The star is someone you don't see often in magazines. They only do large features or covers—and you only see them when they are promoting a project."

The alluring and mesmerizing chanteuse Sade comes to mind for me here. She releases an album when she feels like it, when it's time. Sade has no problem going for eight years without releasing new music. I was among those feenin' for new music between *Love Deluxe* and *Lovers Rock*. She actually lets you miss her, making you play your Sade favorites while you pine for her return, imagine that. So naturally, when she resurfaces for the public's attention, media outlets flock to cover her—and even then, she is highly selective as to where and with whom she will interview or appear. While Beyoncé releases music with greater frequency and dances along the line of being overexposed at times, she is known for her discretion in interviews and is a fierce guardian of her private life, relationships, and family. Stars understand the power of the press, but also recognize that their relationship with media is one that can and must be managed. Having seen her artists work so hard to achieve stardom, Yvette takes maintaining their public image with great seriousness.

"If people who look up to Beyoncé could freeze-frame her, they'd see a girl who bruised her leg to get the step right, who was supposed to be on vacation but went back to the studio, who got no sleep but called the morning show. She'll give fifty interviews for a film and treat interview number fifty like interview number one." And Yvette's not just saying that because she's her publicist. I witnessed Bey's tireless, gracious work ethic firsthand as her advertising writer.

But as her publicist, Yvette's role is part protective mother figure, part media management strategist. "Part of the job is that people feel entitled to know everything about you. If they hurt you personally or attack your family, you do have to respond, but you don't have to go along with the media if you don't want," she explains. "The amazing Oprah, who everyone loves, ignores them. When she's ready to interview, she does it with a top-notch journalist and usually for an amazing cause or project. The problem with a lot of the young so-called celebrities is that these tabloids have become a drug of sorts for them. It's the constant clapping they need to hear, and when it dies down they put themselves in the middle of it. They often have lives that the tabloids want to get a piece of. How they handle it makes the difference."

Artists, before you can look at handling stardom, you need to handle the business of being an artist. The days of being that recording artist or actor who just wants to do her art and leave the business up to someone else are over. You will need a team. You won't need a legal or an accounting degree (they never hurt, but that's not the position you signed up to play); but you need to know everything your team is doing on your behalf. Equally important: You will need to determine how much of a team you need for each stage of your career. And if you like the idea of having more than one stage in your career, you'll need to devise . . . (gasp!) a plan. I know this isn't as fun as imagining the feeling of wet concrete between your fingers when you immortalize yourself on the Hollywood Walk of Fame, but you have to start somewhere once you're clear about the dream of being a star. Will Smith said it best to Yvette Noel-Schure: "He said to me, 'I have to think of this as a nine-to-five.' Because then, you know you're gonna get up and get your butt to work and work hard because you're being watched."

I am going to leave the creative aspect of this goal-setting process alone for a while so we can look at what managers have to say about the business attributes artists need to not only succeed — but also sustain a career in entertainment. I am confident that if you're an artist reading this, you are pretty sure what kind of artist you are: actor, music producer, songwriter, comedian, dancer, rapper, singer, spoken word poet, or something we have yet to see in the business. Hold that thought. I mean, hold on to that dream; it's time to put your dream first.

Artist Manager Angie Aguirre is a founding partner of Skor Entertainment, the management firm that represented veteran envelope-pushing hip-hop artist Pharoahe Monch. You'll learn about how she came to this place in her career later in the chapter. Over the course of her career as a manager, she has represented and worked on deals for Outkast, Blu Cantrell, Macy Gray, Zap Mama, and others. So she has seen the full range of an artist's trajectory, and worked for artists who've sold a little on one hand, or a lot on the other. She's also seen what happens when an artist who sold a lot on one album sold very little on the next.

Angie has some pointers for when to involve a manager. She asserts that the best time to bring one on is as early as possible, certainly before the signing of a recording deal or a publishing deal. "Ideally, I want to be there before they sign any legal documents. Artists feel represented when a manager can be there for them during that part." She also recommends that if artists "can hold on to masters and publishing, they should do so for as long as possible." If this is not feasible, be smart about the degree to which you sell off any portions of your publishing and master rights to ensure your compensation as the creator of the intellectual property; it may be preferable to license your publishing instead of selling it.

Angie also has a note for you managers out there about being on board with an artist from a position of strength *and* benefit. You may well choose to work with artists after they've cut a deal. And if they cut a bad one, you'll inherit the mess it makes for you both without being compensated for securing the deal itself, no matter what you're able to do to clean it up. Angie's advice? If you come into the picture after an artist signs with a production or record company, be in on securing the publishing deal whenever possible. "Publishing deals [often] last longer than label situations, and they renew a decade at a time. Managers can get paid a percentage of that deal ongoingly."

Artists, it is important to recognize the mutual relationship that management represents. You may have it in your mind that you're all that with a soda on the side, but managers are choosing artists in the same way you are evaluating managers. Management is a delicate dance of hand-holding, pit-bull protection, shrewd deal making, education, and psychology that is a lot of work. Managers worth their percentages pour more into growing your life than they do into theirs; their passion is seeing your dream come to reality through strategy and execution. It's a job you don't want them taking lightly. Their commitment and excitement must be present right alongside keen business acumen. And where Angie's concerned, she has to like you, too. "I want to be able to picture having a personal relationship with [clients] even though it's business," she says. "I want to feel like we could be friends if we weren't in the industry. That's important to me. You speak so often on their behalf. Covering for an asshole can be done, but life is too short!" Who wants to keep having to speak for an asshole, anyway? After a while your breath's gonna stink, you'll feel like shit far too often, and nobody will enjoy doing business with you. There's no percentage good enough to love waking up to do *that* job. Which is why the best managers choose their clients wisely.

Tina Davis, the CEO of the Tina Davis Company, wound up making her choice to manage Chris Brown after being fired as his soon-to-be A&R representative. Follow me on this: After working with Lyor Cohen and Kevin Liles as part of the Def Jam Dream Team since 1990—interrupted by a brief stint at Columbia—Tina's last six months as VP of A&R for Island Def Jam happened to be L. A. Reid's first six months on the job as its newly appointed president.

After stints at Def Jam, Columbia, and by this time Island Def Jam, Tina has developed such an incredible ear for hits and an eye for superstar talent that artists she had fought to sign while in her post at one label would end up being turned down by her bosses, only to get signed and blow up somewhere else. Instead of letting this frustrate her, ever confident, ever faithful, Tina just played it cool, continuing to grow her relationships with top brass. Tina put it to me like this: "I know records, stars, and hits. And the reason is because of God and my faith."

She cites some examples of missed opportunities at Def Jam before L. A.

Reid arrived. "I brought them TI. They didn't think he was star. I brought Kanye to them *before* he wanted to sign to Roc-A-Fella. They told me to hire him as an A&R guy instead." She laughs with fresh, audible disbelief. "Kevin and Lyor would hardly ever sign anyone I brought them, so I would just hold artists and not even send myself through those changes."

Well, as irony would have it, Kevin and Lyor ended up going over to run things at Warner/Atlantic, where TI happened to be king of the urban roster. Meanwhile, Tina was at the new Island Def Jam, but as part of the old regime. Imagine the pressure of inheriting a new boss—and not just Any Ol' New Boss, but Antonio "L. A." Reid, the man whose name is the first half of LaFace Records—with six months left on your contract. Not a lot of time to find a new gig. Now imagine Tina delivering the multiplatinum signing who just happens to also make a mint in publishing as a hit songwriter for everyone who matters in R&B and pop. You're imagining the part where Tina signs Ne-Yo to Island Def Jam. *Cha-ching!* L. A. renews her contract. "So I bring in Chris Brown," says Tina, recalling his first performance for L. A. and key staff members. "I took him to L. A.'s office. I gave him some tea. I said, 'Talk only to the ladies and act like you're in your bathroom singing to yourself.' He was blowin'. And L. A. was like, 'Don't let him out of this building!'" The label wanted Chris so badly, execs revealed Tina's future at Island Def Jam to Chris and his mother before informing Tina herself.

"They loved him, but they told Chris they were about to fire me," Tina explains. "That was cool, though, because now I had a contract that I could get paid out on." New wrinkle: If Chris signed to Island, Tina wouldn't be there to oversee the A&R and production of the album. And since Chris had yet to sign, she could not enact the key-man clause in her contract and bring him with her to another label that might hire her. "All I could do is tell Chris and his mom where I stood," she says. Tina was relieved of duty, as is the tradition when a new president comes in—and that goes for all of Corporate America, not just record labels. Fortunately, she was the only one at the label who answered Chris's mother's questions satisfactorily. "One of them was whether Chris needed to give up his publishing to close a record deal," says Tina. "When I told her no, I became her new best friend! That's when I asked her to consider me to work with them in whatever way they wanted. Chris told his mom he wanted me to manage him." That's how Tina went from being Chris Brown's soon-to-be A&R to becoming his manager. She backed up her passion for Chris's success with action. She took it personally.

"I bought him books, outfits, and paid some of the family's bills. The kids in his hometown started messing with him for having new clothes. So I moved him into my house. He left Virginia and he came to New York to stay with me for five months. I would teach him about the business; he watched movies and read about the great singers. That was the best thing I ever did."

She shopped Chris to four other labels, including Atlantic. Kevin and Lyor looked out for Tina, offering Chris a deal that eclipsed the one L. A. had on the table. But with a budget for schooling and better overall terms, Jive ultimately won the bidding war. Tina's commitment has evolved into a business partnership with Chris. Not only does she manage all aspects of his career, but they founded a label imprint as co-owners. Tina put in the time and effort before there was a deal, so Chris felt confident with the Tina Davis Company as his one-stop management firm. The company earns a percentage on all deals cut for Chris Brown. "He agreed to do it because he knows I have his best interests at heart," says Tina. "Agents for film or TV get their portion, too. If I wasn't involved, I wouldn't read scripts or negotiate terms, but I do. I cut out everything he doesn't need to deal with, which allowed me to tie his album, movie, and tour in with Christmas." And that's exactly what happened: His sophomore CD *Exclusive* was released in November 2007, followed by the release of the number two box-office hit film *This Christmas* during the same month, a film in which he performed not one but two songs. Tina tied that one up with a big red bow, but has no ego about her skills. After dealing with her fair share of managers from the A&R point of view, she's learned from their mistakes and their hubris. "Managers mess up by getting all these experiences and accolades. They don't realize that they need to be grateful as well and share what they get with the artists. Artists share with the manager all the time. It's hard for artists to quantify e-mails and coordination; but they see that they showed up to perform. It helps because then, they don't feel they're giving all the time."

Now, a manager can only work that hard for someone who puts in the level of work that requires an equally intense commitment to manage it all. Angie and Tina have seen this commitment from Pharoahe Monch and Chris Brown, respectively. Here's what artists need to know to be great at being stars.

Dyana (*dee-anna*) Williams is a thirty-five-year veteran of the entertainment and media industries. She was instrumental in the creation of the legislation that instituted June as Black Music Month in America. Dyana co-founded the International Association of African American Music (IAAAM). She started her journey as a radio personality who became an artist development and media coach after years of success on the air and on camera in Philadelphia, New York, and Washington, DC. In the 1990s, she reinvented herself as a media coach and artist developer, providing the services that labels began to outsource to independent consultants. Dyana is the guiding hand for artists as they wake up to the cold reality of their schedules once they are in the promotion phase of their projects. If stardom is what you really want, Dyana says, "You must be prepared in your personal *and* professional life for *all* the demands of being an artist: getting up at 5 AM to do makeup, wardrobe, and hair, press, phone interviews, doing drops for radio stations, going to sound check [to rehearse], doing a show, hitting the hotel, and getting up the next day to do it all over again." This can be overwhelming for what the business calls "baby acts." If you manage to make an impact with your project, you'll get a shot at another one. With experience comes the knowledge of what to expect, and ideally some wisdom about how to work intelligently so you preserve your health and your instrument. However, even seasoned artists have situations they need counsel on, especially where media is concerned. Dyana is the type of specialist label clients call in for expertise on media opportunities that need to be handled with kid gloves. She shared a few with me that were solid examples of how to create star quality by leveraging media outlets, causing that quality to expand using a non-negotiable ingredient: charisma.

Dyana was hired to coach Lil' Kim for one interview and one only: *The Howard Stern Show.* "She'd had an incident with him when he said something disparaging about Biggie," Dyana recalls. "She was ready to whoop his butt!" Howard Stern's was too big an audience for the label to ignore, so Dyana and Kim strategized how to turn what was sure to be a tense meeting with Stern into a win for Kim. The strategy was to ooze femininity, kindness, and, most of all, deference. Dyana recounted the interview, still wowed by how well it went. "She told him *he* paved the way for women like her to be able to talk about sexually charged topics! By the end, Kim had Stern eating out of her hand. We had a successful interview; we won! Kim came out of the green room and high-fived me. The more committed the artist is to doing their homework, the better."

Doing homework not only applies to knowing your interviewer; it applies to knowing yourself as well. Dyana's role is one of navigator as artists take stock and look inside themselves to discover what they want to achieve, whether the goal is short- or long-term. She gives each artist-client an individual workbook to keep notes and refer to often, particularly after Dyana has moved on to her next artist in need of her Seven Step Influence System. "My clients walk out confident, empowered, and capable of doing it without me," she remarks.

"To this day when I see Bow Wow, he's nurturing and generous with spirit. I worked with him when he was very resistant to coaching—until I sat him down and showed him all his clips where he repeatedly said, 'Nah mean nahm sayin.' And the moment where we ran into each other at an event and he said, 'I remembered what you taught me,' then said he had a new artist of his own for me to work with—that was worth any paycheck!"

Dyana has some great advice for how to set goals for the creative part of your career. As I promised earlier in the chapter, here it is. "With Ne-Yo, I did [an exercise I call] Sky's the Limit, asking him, 'What are the goals for the album's performance? What [do you] want to get from the experience?' Some struggle with the answers, or they say 'I'd like to go platinum at least'—and I say *no:* You need to think the maximum. Diamond-plus! Everything he put on the list, he has achieved: huge solo album, songwriting for other artists. You have to language it. Life without direction is a problem," admonishes Dyana.

Yvette watched John Legend support himself in the real world while he worked his plan to become a recording artist. "He just applies the principles of success—hard work, passion, and persistence—to music," she says. "John would have been an amazingly successful doctor, lawyer, and restauranteur if that's what he wanted. He kept a job at a financial company while he waited for the music to break. A lot of people don't have a plan B."

Dyana's aforementioned schedule of preparation, appearances, and performances holds true for stage and screen artists as well. And most of it happens before you get your big break, so suit up for a long haul. Christine Yasunaga is fifth-generation Japanese, born in Hawaii. She began ballet at age three to correct a misaligned hip and never looked back. She attended UCLA as a dance major, where under the tutelage of Ron Brown she fell in love with modern dance.

She went on to become a principal dancer in the original Broadway cast of *The Lion King,* but only after years of auditioning while struggling to make ends meet. "I struggled teaching a million dance classes after school. Once you get into the real world, it hits hard," she reflects with a sigh. "I was auditioning like crazy for Hollywood jobs. I was making it to the very end, but not booking—because I was short and Asian. If an ethnic dancer was hired, they'd hire *one* [person of color] across all the ethnic groups. That was very challenging and disappointing." She was also experiencing a fair amount of shade from other dancers of color who would hoard audition information just to better their odds.

Christine knew that she was in her prime as a dancer, and that while she was a member of the Lula Washington Dance Theater in Los Angeles, Hollywood wasn't ready for her. It was time for her to go where the action was. "I wanted to pursue modern concert dance, and LA was not the place for that. At twenty-three, I thought I was so ready and in such good shape," she recalls. "I felt I was too young to be teaching. So I just up and moved to New York."

Christine took a huge professional leap of faith in order to further her creative goal. As she worked her way toward a slot in a concert dance company, she hit an unexpected roadblock: training requirements. "They required that I train for two years before I joined the company, and I didn't have that kind of time." This curveball taught her a profound lesson about what it takes to make it as a dancer in the Big Apple: audition or die. "I found out about *Backstage* magazine from people I met in classes. I auditioned for everything I could. Two months later, I booked as a dancer for Radio City Music Hall's spring show. That's where I learned about the business; about what to do—and what not to do." There, she was taken under the wing of Broadway veteran Mamie Duncan-Gibbs, who would gig at Radio City between Broadway productions. "Mamie said I should do musical theater. She helped me get voice lessons, get my résumé' together, and encouraged me to sing even though I never sang a note." The spring show led to Christine joining the performers' union Actors' Equity. Having her Equity card made her eligible for many more auditions. "The more I sang in front of people, the better I got," she says. "I went on auditions for things even if I knew I didn't want the job, just to get seen and network with other dancers. I even volunteered to dance for choreographers auditioning their numbers in front of directors."

By the time she auditioned for the Broadway production of *The King & I*, Christine was a regular on the circuit. She auditioned several times and was denied several times before securing a small role. When she auditioned for *The Lion King*, she found herself standing before the same casting director from *The King & I*. Christine learned another important thing about the business: It's not only a small world, but an even smaller industry.

"The casting director saw me do the choreography for *The Lion King*, and he said I would be great in the show. Garth Fagan's choreography for *The Lion King* fit my modern background and felt so good it was a natural fit. I was in *The Lion King* for four years."

The potential for artists to roller-coaster along their journey is high, whether their measure of profitability is CDs sold and ringtones downloaded or touring or box-office receipts, even commercial residuals. In order to survive as you make your way to stardom, you'll need a saving and investing ethic as tireless as the work ethic that got you your first deal or paying show. Dyana has seen her fair share of famous, broke-ass artists. She's got real-world tips for what to do with your advance or big paycheck, starting with: "Be prudent. Keep your credit clean and maintain a decent FICO score. Get in the game and own some property." That can be real estate, but it can also look like objects that appreciate in value over time. "I started buying art twenty years ago," says Dyana. "I would sacrifice buying Prada shoes to buy art. Instead, I was making payments on my Romare Bearden, Jacob Lawrence, and Elizabeth Catlett paintings. One Bearden has quadrupled in value. I would never sell it unless I was in a pinch, but even then I'd make my money back and then some."

In addition to getting certified as a Pilates trainer and keeping an office job as a clerical worker for her cab money, Christine went another route: saving and investing in the market. "I saved a lot of my money while I was on Broadway. When an old boyfriend of mine saw I had thirty thousand dollars in my account, he told me what an IRA was and encouraged me to visit Charles Schwab." Her investing strategy has served her well long after her retirement from dance. She now invests in herself as the creator and executive producer of *Destination Groove,* a dance competition show airing in Hawaii that she created to discover new dance talent on the island. All equally sound advice for survival as an executive, where the security blanket of a full-time job with benefits just keeps shrinking, right along with the talent pool.

....

THE DEATH OF PROFESSIONAL DEVELOPMENT
....

Development—be it artistic or professional—is in shorter supply with each fiscal year. On the artistic side, it shows up as the near erasure of artist development budgets; for budding executive talent, it looks like the erosion of structured internship programs that have become revolving doors for gofers instead of a training ground for the next generation of star makers who will sustain the business.

Dyana is the architect of many media personas we see from some of the biggest stars in music, from Usher to Rihanna. However, at one point, she was just starting out as a media performer herself. In pursuing her own career, Dyana's approach to the business was simple: In the absence of internships, she created what she now calls "résumé building opportunities." Her clarity and determination to take initiative helped her get in the door in the late 1970s, when it was commonplace for women to be relegated to Girl Friday status. "I was working with professionals and in proximity to them such that they would become my colleagues. I was at City College, and WRVR was the premier twenty-four-hour straight-ahead jazz station in New York at the time. I called [on-air personality] Van Jay McDuffie and said 'I'd like to come see you do your thing.' I told him I wasn't getting coffee or being his flunky. He made my first audition tape [aircheck] that I sent to most of the Black radio stations. I got a call from Bob 'Nighthawk' Terry and moved to DC to work at WHUR. I was making six thousand dollars a year. I lived in the YWCA, I didn't know anyone, but I was so thrilled, I would have given them the money!"

While Dyana made a way out of no way and turned a cold call into her first radio aircheck, artist manager Angie Aguirre got her industry experience from an internship that not only provided a stipend, but also earned her college credit. To be clear, you can find internships all over, but I can't help but wonder if the decrease in viable programs with mentor support, stipends, or school credit and access to the hiring pipeline upon completion of said program has adversely affected the executive star quality inside music labels.

Angie is a Latina born to Nicaraguan and Mexican American parents. She grew up listening to Roger & Zapp in Southern California. No wonder she ended up in the Black music division of Dallas's BMG distribution office while she attended Southern Methodist University. Her entry into one of the world's largest distributors of music was critical to the winding path her executive career has taken. How does "the only Latina walking into the meeting" as a college promotions rep end up managing multiplatinum Grammy winner Outkast? For Angie — as for many of us hungry to be in the business — it starts with a real internship program. And it even starts out that way for people who don't know they want to be in it, but find out they love it once they get bit by the industry bug. That's how it happened for me.

I majored in international relations with an ethnic studies minor at Mills College, a women's liberal arts school smack in the middle of East Oakland. It was 1988 when I arrived, and Too $hort was still slangin' tapes (yes, you read right—as in cassette tapes) hand-to-hand though he had signed to Jive Records and released his major-label debut *Life Is . . . Too $hort* that same year. In Oakland, music surrounds you. The city's independent spirit paired with a commitment to musicianship is pure magic. It was that magic—and my need for a job that paid me at least eight bucks an hour—that led me to the campus career center at Mills.

There was a listing from a company named DeLeon Artists seeking an intern who could also do light office management and handle phones. It was an internship that paid! I applied and met with the woman who ran the office, Demetrius "Cricket" Evans. We clicked immediately. I know she was impressed that someone who was only eighteen knew who the firm's clients were so well, to the point of naming songs and albums they'd recorded. All my vacuuming to Willie Colon and washing dishes to Etta James was finally about to pay off! It didn't hurt that my parents went to Lincoln University with DeLeon's biggest client, Gil Scott-Heron; I knew his catalog inside out. Looking back, I think she needed another sista in the office. She was in there with the Latino owner, Lupe DeLeon, and the Jewish head agent, Bruce Solar. Talk about a small company! This was three people in a one-bedroom bunga-low tucked away in Piedmont, a granola mix of millionaires and Birkenstock rockers who seceded from Too $hort's City of Dope by securing their own zip code. But the homies cruised it anyway. Piedmont was still Oakland, nobody was fooled. I walked out of the interview with a job and a twenty-hour-a-week schedule, working for icons of soul, jazz, and Latin music.

Angie started out in RCA's radio promotion department, earning a fabu-lous fifty dollars a week. She got the tip from a fellow student who was a radio intern. She took an interview with then radio promotion co-national Taryn Brown, who needed to break a couple of unknown hip-hop acts, Wu-Tang Clan and Mobb Deep. They were also responsible for a trio of street girls with a sweet sound called SWV—Sisters with Voices. Angie remembers her early days as a college radio rep: "I called college and community stations and tried to get airplay for them all, along with Chantay Savage. I was *so* amped about SWV. I told Taryn we had to go to their show. They were playing with Shai and Silk. We hit a diner after the show and SWV was *in the restaurant*. I went up and said, 'I really enjoyed your show.' And it wasn't even a year later that I was working their follow-up album, *New Beginning,* at the college level. Plus: RCA had just signed the 'Coca-Cola kid' . . . Tyrese." Angie had only been on college radio duty for a few months, but she applied for the college marketing rep (CMR) job when it opened up anyway. "I applied, didn't get it—and I hate to say it, but I felt like my not being Black played a part. Everyone in Black music was Black then. I felt people questioning, *Why you?* I had some anger, but I just ended up saying, 'I'm gonna prove it to you.' I made a mental note and moved on. That actually enabled me to foster some relationships. I was heavily involved in the BMG distribution office, and the folks at the Arista, Jive, and Loud Records offices in Dallas were watching me. The second time I applied for the job, I got it."

It was her understanding of the BMG system that led her to move to New York, working for Arista proper. Her colleague Jason "JC" Ricks was the head of crossover promotion there. He eventually recommended her to Blue Williams, who managed Outkast. Blue needed an assistant. Angie knew everyone that worked Outkast at LaFace because she worked for BMG, LaFace's distributor. In this case, it was who *and* what she knew that got Angie the gig. "My first assignment was to set up Outkast as the opener for the Lauryn Hill tour. As Blue's assistant, I was making between thirty-five and forty-five thousand a year. Outkast earned five thousand dollars a show on tour with Lauryn, and by the time I left, at the top of their Grammy-winning *Speakerboxx/The Love Below* double solo album project, I saw offers for them at a million dollars per show." Angie parted ways amicably from Family Tree Entertainment and went on to create her own management firm, Skor Management. She now leverages everything she learned working with 'Kast on behalf of her clients.

Just like Angie, Dyana was also being watched, but by radio promotion veteran turned president of Perspective Records, Sharon Heyward. She recalled exactly how it happened. "Sharon took me to lunch and she said, 'You should be a coach. You have an ease with artists, you get them, and they get you.' I had been co-managing Gary Taylor with Sheila Eldridge. He actually wrote 'Good Love' for Anita Baker, among other songs. So I started doing research and went back to school. I combined the practical theory about communication with all the experience I had interviewing everyone from Miles Davis to whoever was current on the radio when I was on. I was hired to work with Angie Stone's group Vertical Hold, and my phone hasn't stopped ringing since! I coached Jimmy Jam and Terry Lewis. Karen Taylor

Bass hired me to coach D'Angelo. I developed more insights with each client, and tailored the coaching to the person."

....

BE AT THE DOOR WHEN OPPORTUNITY KNOCKS

....

Some executive talent, like superstar entertainment talent, is hiding in plain sight just waiting to be noticed and given an opportunity.

Tina Davis, the woman who's usually standing behind Chris Brown as he accepts BET Awards, is a great example of this. She had moved to Los Angeles from Sacramento, where she had trained in classical piano for eight years as a child and seen her father jam in the family's garage with Sly Stone and band members from Con Funk Shun. She hung out in the studio with her cousin Earl (known to the rest of us as E-40) as a teenager. She saw Krush Groove when she was thirteen. That's when it hit her.

"At that moment, I decided I wanted to work for Russell Simmons," she recalls fondly. "I told him that when I met him. Aside from managing Chris [Brown], Russell has been influential in every business choice I've made." After getting her start as the assistant to LaRonda Sutton at Chrysalis Records, she got in the door of the House That Russell Built. It was 1994. At the time, street promoter turned A&R executive Paul Stewart was running the A&R department of Def Jam West. He offered Tina a job as an A&R administration coordinator. A&R coordination is a meticulous, painstaking job that involves tracking and maintaining all the paperwork associated with a recorded work, from sample clearance and publishing information to liner notes and credits. Tina was making about twenty-five grand a year.

Stewart had signed R&B singer Montell Jordan to his PMP imprint, but the album was on hold. Unbeknownst to Tina, Def Jam label head Lyor Cohen and Paul Stewart were no longer seeing eye-to-eye. Tina recounts the story of getting a call out of the blue from the New York office. "Lyor asked me to find and pack everything and relocate the LA office. In the midst of that, I found a dusty CD with 'This Is How We Do it' written on it." She took a listen and her mind immediately went to work. She heard a hit. "I told Lyor, 'We have to put this out. It's easy to clear the sample. We own the master [recording rights to Slick Rick's 'A Children's Story']." Lyor agreed. "This Is How We Do It" was released and went platinum. With one song, two stars were born: Montell Jordan and Tina Davis. "After Montell blew up, Lyor sent Chris Lighty to meet me," she continues. "He was running the [entire label's]

A&R department at the time. I was running the LA office, still doing A&R administration, and had begun to A&R Def Jam's soundtracks. I worked on *Rush Hour, Nutty Professor,* and did the administration for *Belly.*" All the while, her salary had yet to change. She was offered thirty-six thousand dollars a year to take a position in New York. She declined. Lighty upped the salary to eighty thousand. That was more like it, but Tina didn't want to move. "I said, just give me the eighty thousand and I'll do everything from LA. I ended up coming to New York every two weeks." Tina was the best administrator on the label's staff; she was their album closer. Her travel schedule was brutal. However, crossing coasts every month brought her closer to Russell, with whom she pleaded her case. She also had an ace up her sleeve: a job offer from MCA as director of A&R at $150,000 a year.

According to Tina, Russell had one thing to say. "Russell said, 'Next time you come, bring the MCA contract and ask Lyor what he's gonna do,'" she explained. "Lyor gave me $175,000 and the senior VP of A&R position, where I remained for six years." By simply being the best at what she did and knowing what she would not accept, she turned a competitive offer into a top brass position paying well over twice the initial salary offered to her. Like their on-camera counterparts, executive stars are also coveted and, to be retained, must be compensated well.

When my opportunity for a national media position presented itself, I was just minding my own business putting together hip-hop panels on campus for Mills's African American student organization, Black Women's Collective (BWC). But true to the notion that your work is always being watched, there was someone in the audience who saw me moderating the panel and thought I'd be a good candidate for the job he was about to vacate.

Kelly Woo was the rap editor for the *Gavin Report,* an industry trade magazine of charts, features, and reviews whose positioning line was "The Most Trusted Name in Radio." And it actually was, because the magazine only reviewed music its editors liked, whether their labels advertised in the magazine or not. *Gavin* editors were in service to radio programmers first and, by extension, the record-label promotion executives who vied for those stations' airtime. *Gavin* also held the most informative and well-attended music industry seminars of the 1980s and '90s called the Gavin Seminar. Because of the affinity Kelly had won from stations and artists alike, he was well liked and known for being able to tell radio about a hot act first—what's known as breaking an artist. Among other artists, he did this particularly for Wu-Tang Clan. His prescience was rewarded with a shout-out at the close of "Wu-Tang Clan Ain't Nuttin' to Fuck Wit" from The RZA himself. The position of rap editor was one that came with a lot of pressure and a great deal of power for a journalist to whom more than three hundred stations reported their weekly playlists.

And yet while I was moderating my panel on Black men, stereotypes, and hip-hop, I had no real idea what *Gavin* was, and certainly had no clue Kelly Woo was in the audience of an event I'd conceived and helped the BWC execute. Until, of course, the panel ended and he approached me with a proposition. "I'm leaving *Gavin* to take a job in LA with Priority Records in one week," he enthused. "Would you be interested in interviewing for my job?" Kelly told me he'd seen my clips in Bay Area free papers like *Klub* and *Grits-N-Gravy* magazines; he thought I could handle the writing part. He was nominating two other candidates to replace him. All I would need to do is learn how the chart system worked. He offered to teach me the system if I'd consider interviewing with the CEO. At this point, I was working with Bruce Solar as office and contracts manager for his own agency, Absolute Artists. Trouble was, it was only part-time. I was fresh out of college and as much as I loved Bruce, I was in *serious* need of a full-time job. And this was a job where I'd get paid to write about hip-hop music? *Hell yeah,* I was thinking! "How soon can you teach me the chart system?" I asked in the most even tone I could muster. Within forty-eight hours, my interview was scheduled and I was learning how to do Kelly's job after I locked up at Absolute Artists. Bruce, being the mentor and fair boss he was, supported me 100 percent.

I sat next to Kelly while he showed me the ropes of the *Gavin* rap chart for a full week and the weekend. For a moment, I wondered who the other two candidates were—and if Kelly was showing them the ropes, where was he finding the time? During that week, I interviewed with *Gavin* CEO David Dalton, head of sales Bob Galliani, and editorial director Ben Fong-Torres. Though I had no formal editorial experience, they could see from my clips that I was a good writer, and I assured them that I knew my hip-hop from top to bottom (not that they could have cross-checked me; I knew more about rap music than the three of them combined). I left the interview knowing I had done my best, charged with anticipation, and praying the job was mine. At the end of Kelly's final week, I got the call—and got the job. Shortly thereafter, I found out from Kelly via phone that I was the only candidate who had taken the time to acquire a full working knowledge of the chart system. And with the magazine's weekly deadline looming, Ben could teach me how to be an editor on the job, but there could be no rap column without radio charts. My first day as *Gavin's* first (and only) Black female rap editor was December 1, 1993, three days before my twenty-second birthday. My journey to executive superstardom began.

SUMMARY OF SECRETS REVEALED

WHAT YOU THOUGHT YOU KNEW:

Being a star means being an egomaniac who thinks my shit doesn't stink.

WHAT YOU NEED TO KNOW:

You need the confidence about your talent that comes from a healthy ego, but being confident is not the same as being arrogant. Stars don't always mistreat people. The brightest stars are usually clear that they are merely a vessel through which God or however they call Spirit shines. This understanding inevitably guides their being, making for humble and gracious souls. And then there are the people who are just plain ingrates and, as a result, end up being nasty to people, from their entourages to their fans. Usually this has to do with their view of themselves and their view of the world. I'm no shrink, but if you walk through life thinking it owes you something, it's probably because you were denied something along the way, be it love, money, home training, or education. That attitude takes away from every star's luster, so take a look at yourself and deal with whatever internal stuff may be blocking your shine. It will ultimately help you be comfortable in your own skin . . . one of the main attributes that makes stars attractive in the first place. You'll be better equipped to handle the demands of stardom as well.

WHAT YOU THOUGHT YOU KNEW:

Being on TV, in tabloids, or on the Internet means I'm a star.

WHAT YOU NEED TO KNOW:

Being on TV, in tabloids, and on the Internet means you're on TV, in tabloids, or on the Internet. Being seen is not the same as shining.

WHAT YOU THOUGHT YOU KNEW:

All stars have to do to blow up is show up.

WHAT YOU NEED TO KNOW:

Yes, but not as in show up on the red carpet. Stars work to bring out their shine and train hard to make it last; they just make it *look* easy. That's what distinguishes them from the temporary celebrity caught on camera. So if you wanna be a star, show up to rehearsal, to practice, to vocal coaching, to acting class, to the gym, to media training. Recognize that while you may be talented, you may also need work. Seek out and embrace your professional development! If there are holes in your star game, do what it takes to fill them. If the holes are too big to sew up, accept that and play to your strengths. Respecting the team that makes you the star you are is also a huge part of showing up. Take care of your people and they will take care of you. Honor them. Compensate them. If they're working with you, they are stars, too.

CHAPTER 8

The Art and Nuance of Production for Script, Stage, and Screen

....

Abra Potkin ✳ Alexa Pagonas ✳ Erika Conner ✳
Keesha Rai Levy✳ Lana Garland ✳ Leslie Ann Jones ✳
Nana Brew-Hammond ✳ Nayo Wallace ✳ Nomi Roher ✳
Marjorie Clarke ✳ Monique Martin ✳ Mo'Nique ✳
Robyn Lattaker-Johnson ✳ Rose Caraet

....

The last man standing is the woman who knows
everything.

—ALEXA PAGONAS

So much of the way women maneuver through the entertainment business is about touch; it's all in the approach. This chapter explores a variety of women's approaches in the area of production across multiple areas. Each woman featured here took her own individual approach to education—both formal and hands-on. Each determined what her career passions were and took on their relentless pursuit. Each gained profound insights and uncovered some secrets vital to success—however she defined it for herself.

As a music and lifestyle writer who wound up in production for advertising, radio, and television, what I glean from my own experience and the ones intertwined with mine in these pages is that ultimately, a woman's career is a production all its own, constantly being designed, refined, reinvented. We've already taken a close look at production from a musical perspective. So let's uncover some secrets and smooth the path for anyone connected to or directly involved with the art of nonmusic production, namely for stage and screen.

Production is defined by Dictionary.com in a number of ways. For our purposes, these serve best:

- The act of producing, creation, manufacture.
- A product.
- The creation of value; a work of literature or art.
- The act of presenting for display, presentation, or exhibition.
- The organization and presentation of dramatic entertainment.

As I indicated in chapter 5, the simplest meaning of *production* is the one that is most often overlooked: the execution of an idea or vision. Unfortunately, executing, ideating, and being visionary are attributes ascribed more often to men than women in present-day society. We are usually over in the "looking good" and "*re*-producing" columns on the Societal To-Do List. The irony is that as the world's reproducers, we broke the mold on production. And as such, it is the opinion of several producers who spoke with me that there is a distinct woman's approach or touch to production. Women's work as producers in entertainment is broad, vast, and overshadowed by the perception that men are somehow better at it by virtue of their biology. Count that fallacy among many smoke-and-mirrors tactics has propped up for us to accept as reality. Let's look at what's true about production from some lesser-heard points of view.

....

WHAT SEPARATES GOOD FROM GREAT

....

The best producer is a talented multitasker. By *talented,* I mean someone who can work on more than one task at a time while giving each the total attention and focus required. The best producer is at once present in the moment, and omnipresent to the final objective. I'm not mad at the textbook definition of a producer, but it's always better to hear it from the people who embody the definition. Erika Conner, producer of multiplatinum Grammy winners Outkast's cinematic debut *Idlewild,* gives the role a feminine incarnation right off the bat. "The producer is the mother of the project, but you never want to be babysitting on set," she says emphatically. "The producer is a director—the director of the project's crew; you have to know which people to bring in on a project." In Erika's view, "vision" and "an internal instinct" are must-haves for anyone who strives to be a great producer.

Broadway stage manager tuned theater producer Monique Martin believes this so strongly, she named her company Intuition Entertainment. As the stage manager for *Sarafina* and the tour marketer for the Tony-winning smash *Bring in 'da Noise, Bring in 'da Funk,* she saw how important that often intangible form of intelligence was to production. It became startlingly apparent once she put up her own show, *Soul Erotica,* a theatrical exploration of sex, spirit, and sensuality through music, spoken word, and performance. "Intuition is an untapped resource. Men tend to rely on facts and logic, but there is a Buddhist quote that says, 'The heart is wiser than the intellect.' Yet because of the dominant patriarchal society we live in, we [as women] don't want to admit this in a business meeting; that something is telling [us] to use a certain font or color, for example, when we are made to use the language of measure and fact." The same intuition that was guiding her creativity as a producer was also sending her signals about how to conduct business. However, it took Monique growing in her career to start listening to her gut, especially where business partnerships were concerned. "I've gone into partnerships with people who were unsavory, or had more potential than productivity, then moved forward in the interest of being 'friends' with grave repercussions," she recalls. "The idea that you have to be friends or have a relationship beyond the deal in order to be successful on a project is the cherry on top; I've come to know it's not a requirement. As women, we often want friendships, but men don't have that illusion. They can get to the meat of the deal quicker."

Once the deal is struck, the great producer is also comfortable calling shots, especially the tough ones. A win-win is always preferred, but in the interests of the final objective, some people may not get their way, and may get their feelings hurt instead. The producers worth their salt avoid these outcomes whenever possible, and confront them with firm, graceful resolve whenever impossible. Says Marjorie Clarke, senior producer for Uniworld Group, "To get a great product you have to be prepared to spend the money, be prepared to make the hard decisions, and mediate every situation. Understanding all the elements of the job and what it takes to get each job done from that of production assistants and drivers to craft services" eases this mediation process every time. "But sometimes, the universe lines up where you want it to, and when everything comes together, it's wonderful," she continues. "The cinematographer and director are working it out; the set looks great. The weather's perfect for you. That's the rush you get when you love production. That's why you don't sleep for three days to get it done."

Award-winning television news and documentary producer Abra Potkin, now vice president of development for Paramount Television, emphasizes that the great producers remember the human element and bring that to the business of getting even the toughest stories told. "I had to sit in prison with a molester," she recalls. "And I really cared about what he had to say. I had an opportunity to understand something better, as ugly as it was. Great producers care about people; they have a *need* to want to know," she notes. "Listening is vital. You can't fake being interested. You have to be 100 percent curious."

For Mo'Nique, the comedienne turned actor-producer of *Flavor of Love Girls: Charm School starring Mo'Nique* and *Mo'Nique's FAT Chance,* there's no faking the pitch, either. Producers have stories they want told, and often need buy-in from a network or studio to bring their vision to the marketplace. All the skills mentioned to this point have no opportunity to be utilized without someone, usually the producer, making the pitch. Mo'Nique is razor-sharp in her technique, which is equal parts no-nonsense strategy and heartfelt passion. I asked her how she knows she'll be taken seriously in pitch meetings.

"You're taken seriously when they take the meeting. And if I can't meet with the decision maker, I don't take the meeting. I don't want to meet with someone who has to get back to me with an answer." And once the meeting is under way, Mo'Nique speaks from the heart. "If it's not true to me, I can't sell it," she says. "My husband and I sold and produced a one-hour special called *Touched.* (It's about molestation; the devastation and the triumph.) I was a victim of molestation—and I say *was* because I am no longer. Not only did it affect me, it affected whole families. And in our community we don't talk about it. By the grace of God, the projects that have been true to me have been able to get sold."

But what happens once the concept is bought and is now in more hands than just those of the producer? This can pose a dilemma, especially for first-time producers who are confronted with the need to maintain control of the production process. Erika is quick to debunk the "it's who you know" myth in this scenario. "Who you know don't help you out; they might have been up for the same project. It's what you know—and how you maneuver." She recommends working for a production company as a first-timer, as opposed to working for a major studio. She calls the studio producer jobs "toilet bowl positions." It may sound snobbish, but all jobs aren't good jobs. "I never worked at a studio because you have to work on whatever they are putting out that month. It takes a year to understand the position—and another year to develop something," Erika explains. "If you're not meeting your quota, you get flushed out." In the production company setting, the network or studio is a third party to the production for broadcast and/or distribution. In Erika's view, you have time and security on your side as a production company staffer. "You get a salary as an executive, but you also get your producer fee, title credit, and benefits. As an independent, you hustle your next gig while one gets lined up."

When you are the on-air talent taking on the role of producer or show creator—as is the case for Mo'Nique—you may not have to hustle as hard for the job. You may have even pitched and won the job. But be prepared for your colleagues on set to be slow in making the adjustment that you have. Though you are the reason the job is even happening, some may continue to treat you like "talent." For talent, the expectation is usually that you show up, shut up, and get to work. Talent is rarely in the position to call the shots that producers are. Mo'Nique elaborates on an experience with a co-producer on a location shoot. "Going from talent to producer was challenging for me on *FAT Chance*," she says. "When we went to Paris, the people we worked with were only talking to my co-producers, never to me. Then I looked on the call sheet, and saw that my name was not only tenth on the list, but it had no title! So I had to have *that* conversation."

It went like this:

Mo'Nique: "'What y'all are used to is Black talent just being talent. But here I am the creator, the executive producer, *and* the talent. So stop playing with me and play fair.' From that moment we had no more problems. We meet with everybody at once, up front, so no one is more important than anyone else—from janitor to executive producer." And just as Erika suggests that a great producer is the mother of a project and must know who to involve in it, Mo'Nique refuses to settle for mothering a project halfway. If a production is a producer's household, so to speak, the house will have to run Mama's way. Mo'Nique sees silence as a woman's gravest mistake, in production and in the business overall. "Oftentimes we don't stand for what we know is right, and in our silence, we let it be known that it's okay. And because we are silent, it will be repeated. For me as Black talent, it shows up as being the creator, the executive producer, and the host—but then I walk onto a set and no one looks like me. I get to the hair and makeup room and there are no Black hair or makeup people, but half the cast is Black! And no one says anything. With every production I do, there's gotta be people of color. There are no ifs, ands, or buts. Otherwise, it's okay to walk away. If it costs you your integrity, it ain't good money."

A producer's integrity need not always show up as walking away from a job, however; it should also be about how you walk into the job. Erika was the first African American female hired in development at Mosaic Media Group. "Production is about forecasting, and I had this inner strength; I got a movie made in a year and it happened because I was strategic, savvy, and hungry." For Erika, she walked into *Idlewild* with a vision that was not only crystal clear, but shared equally with director Bryan Barber and the principal actors, André "3000" Benjamin and Antwan "Big Boi" Patton of Outkast. Erika created an ally by including Bryan Barber as part of the pitch for the film, knowing that he wanted to transition from directing videos. She also wanted the creative energy that Barber had established with Outkast by lensing many of their videos to be present for their foray into the medium. "I tracked [Barber] down; we were both underdogs and I had a home for [*Idlewild*] at Mosaic. I pitch the movie to [Mosaic's Allen Shapiro and Chuck Roven]. They look at me like I'm crazy! They thought Bryan was wrong as director. I had pitched it all over town. Everyone wants to be in the Outkast business, but no one wanted to finance a Black period piece featuring rappers. In my eyes, Outkast were not just rappers, they were crossover artists." She has a point there; Outkast is the only rap duo to have achieved diamond certification by the Recording Industry Association of America, by selling over ten million copies of *Speakerboxx/The Love Below*. The only other rapper to have done this is Hammer, and he's as crossover as they come. "I just knew the 1930s musical would work," Erika says.

In hindsight, *Idlewild's* reviews were mixed, but it has become a cult classic. It has been hailed for its inventiveness and bold blend of the 1930s period and new-millennium hip-hop. Teresa Wiltz of *The Washington Post* wrote, "For all its shortcomings, *Idlewild* also has something that few films can pull off: Moments of such pure cinematic fabulousness, breathtaking dance sequences and idiosyncratic flourishes that we are more than willing to forgive it for all its sins."[1] Further, *Idlewild's* marketing was dwarfed by the mega-budget push for *Dreamgirls*, released the same year. It was nominated for five 2007 Black Reel Awards, including Best Director, Best Original Soundtrack, and Best Score. At the end of the day, Erika was proud of her first full feature. "*Idlewild* definitely got swamped by *Dreamgirls*, and the *Idlewild* album date kept changing. We got nominated for a cinematography Oscar. It wasn't a numbers game for me. I'm happy that we did something that was out of the box."

But hindsight is 20/20 and we're nowhere near a complete film yet. After eight months of shopping to studios, Erika thought outside the box and called

HBO development. As it turned out, HBO Films president Colin Calendar was a fan of Erika's concept, but by now Outkast was recording *Speakerboxx/The Love Below* and had grown weary of flying out for film meetings that bore no fruit. Of course, the one time Erika needed Outkast, she had serious interest at the greenlighting level. This is the nature of the beast called production. The big break rarely comes at you in plain sight. While her bosses were still unsure about the project, Erika took the meeting without its stars. Calendar went for the pitch because he wanted to return HBO to making original movies and breaking new actor talent with smaller budgets. *Idlewild* got sold.

Then, the real mothering began, and, as Erika puts it, "You marry yourself to an idea and nurture it." This started with building trust between herself as producer and Barber as director. "I created a bond with Bryan to keep his vision clear. I also wanted him to see me as someone other than a suit." Next, she involved the Outkast members and their manager Blue Williams very closely and took the punches for them when they could not be in meetings about the film. This turned out to be hugely beneficial down the line, when the budget went from less than five million dollars to twenty-nine million—beyond what anyone thought it would cost.

To complicate matters further, Outkast scooped the Grammy for Album of the Year with *Speakerboxx/The Love Below,* confirming for Mosaic what Erika knew all along, that this brave new movie had an audience. "Once Outkast blew up and won the Grammy, Roven gave me the ultimatum that if I go on the *Idlewild* set, I better be looking for my next project," Erika reflects. "I told him that I was only doing what his wife (then associate producer) Lynda Obst did with *Flashdance*—and he had to respect that. Some say that I was a genius for getting them to buy in at that level. Others would say that they'd never hire me as a producer. All I knew was it was going to be a cult classic." Apparently, so did Cicely Tyson, who shared her hard-earned insight with the young producer one day on set. " 'You won't make any money from it, but this film is God working, honey! You make me proud to hold up the torch for something,' " Erika says, repeating Ms. Tyson's pearl of wisdom.

And yet the pitch is just the start of a production. Sometimes the pitch starts with a script and not just a concept, as was the case with *Idlewild*. And getting your script read—at least by someone who can actually greenlight it or move it along the assembly line from acquisitions into pre-production—really is as hard as they make it out to be in the movies. Do not let the odds discourage you from submitting it, though. The experience for former Sony Pictures

Classics acquisitions executive Nana Brew-Hammond was one of wading though a lot of crap on paper. Your script may be the one that cuts through the clutter. She started as one of three interns in the acquisitions department. And don't sleep on the title. She had more power than you'd normally associate with an intern. "I was reading scripts and making decisions about a bunch of films. I thought there were all these stories that were not being told because of racism inside studios," Nana reflects. "But there is actually a dearth of viable scripts about people of color. What was coming through were stories about a rapper hooking up with some Black American Princess . . . the stories and characters were both stereotypical and shallow."

DePasse Entertainment VP of development Rose Caraet is at the center of situations where a viable script does get the attention of a production company willing to develop it. She believes that "being a writer at heart" is an attribute that takes a producer from good to great. She admires Suzanne DePasse particularly for being a producer who began as a writer, and as a result can "not only critique a script, but can come up with solutions for it immediately," Rose marvels. "There's a lot of giving notes just to give them in order to justify their job somehow. I have tremendous respect for writers who face a blank page, so I show a lot of deference."

Would that all of Hollywood showed the same deference! Writers are the backbone of the entertainment industry. Songs, plays, late-night talk shows, series, awards specials, films, commercials, promos, trailers, and increasingly reality—all of it has to be written. As the writer's strike of 2007 demonstrated, production in film and television slowed to a trickle. And the Writers Guild of America was goin' hard on scabs this time around. Crossing the line as a WGA member meant your pass was revoked. Taking a writing gig without union membership meant you'd never be eligible.

Daily variety shows and late-night television suffered most. While I'm not in the WGA since I have yet to write a screenplay, as a voice actor and member of SAG and AFTRA, I feel where the WGA is coming from. If the project can't happen without the words on the page that serve as its map—yet I as the "mapmaker" can only be compensated once, while studios and networks get paid every time somebody buys or uses my map on a new media platform—well, all of a sudden I could see not being too psyched about mapping out road trip after road trip. And while there are other mapmakers out there, recognizing your value as an expert at times requires drawing the line in the proverbial sand. From on-demand viewing to downloading of films and programs, the digital age has ushered in multiple platforms that are providing real revenue for content owners, and the content creators simply want to share in the exponential profits generated by what they contribute. It comes down to knowing your value and being prepared to ensure that that value is respected.

Writing is one of those capabilities easily dismissed as simple enough for most people to do. Just because writing is taught in school doesn't mean everyone can be proficient at creative writing. Further, the writing that entertainment demands is pressurized and unforgiving. In addition to being able to breathe life into characters and situations, you've got to get it done repeatedly in the case of daily and weekly shows; for film, you've got to keep the story breathing for the life of its arc. I mean honestly, if it was that easy, there'd be more people signing up for the sweet torture screenwriters and copywriters endure, even with the pay being far from great.

Having associate-produced (*Unchained Memories: Readings from the Slave Narratives* for HBO), adapted a screenplay for a Walter Mosley production for film, and served as creative director for BET, Lana Garland, screenwriter, promo writer, and marketing writer, knows this all too well. The day the 2008 Golden Globes That Wasn't aired in the form of a press conference, crippled by the WGA strike, I asked her to illuminate for the rest of us what the writer's process looks like. Perhaps this will help shed light on why the WGA has put its collective foot down on the issue of residual payments to writers when their work is sold across new media platforms, among other issues. On this night, the estimated eighty-million-dollar loss to the city of Los Angeles from the cancellation of the awards show had yet to bring the two sides to the table. We both wondered how many shows would not go on in the wake of the stalemate. Then, both the fiftieth anniversary of the Grammys and the eightieth Academy Awards dodged the bullet of the same fate, all over sharing some Residual Pie. Ultimately only the 2008 Golden Globes suffered, proving that this strike hit the powers that be in the pockets. "Finally, we writers will be realized for [the] rock stars that we are," cheers Lana. And equally as important, for the profit centers and stakeholders writers are as well. To some degree, I can't help but believe studios and producers think this writing thing isn't as powerful as the WGA asserts. Well, maybe more studio and production heads should try banging out some award-winning scripts, screenplays, or novels. It's a lot easier to give notes on a script than to generate one.

Lana starts by clearing up a dangerous misconception about writing as an art form versus writing as literacy. "On the one hand, [just about] everyone can write, but not everyone wants to do the things you have to go through internally to do it. At some point in the process, you find out whether you are an idea generator or a person willing to go through the process of writing, rewriting, and rewriting. Rewriting is so greatly misunderstood. And that is 75 percent of it; getting the idea down the first time is just the first step," she explains. "True writers are people who can get their head around rewriting something they spent months on."

Writing for entertainment requires character research, a vast vocabulary, and a discerning eye and ear for words, wordplay, and diction, down to how they will sound coming from a character's mouth. Lana goes on to say that it helps when you can not only design your character, but also develop him or her to the point that you can interview that person—yes, the one you made up. "It's great to get to know your character on such a deep level; once you get to know your characters, the story starts to write itself. It's a bit schizophrenic; you might even start to have traits of the character. Actors get techniques on how to deal with that, but writers don't," she laments. It also requires an athletic level of mental discipline where the craft is concerned. Writers have to show up at the laptop screen or the page on a daily basis to keep the writing, composition, and creative muscles fit. Lana draws upon Mosley's example. "Walter Mosley is creating that space to do it every day. I know where he is at 5 AM: He's either writing or scratching his butt thinking about writing. For some reason the Muses want to wake me up at that time, too."

Lana also made sure to keep her writing skills sharp by writing, producing, and directing her own films, even as she held down a job. "I borrowed three thousand dollars from my 401(k) to do the film; when it's something you love, you're gonna do it anyway." Screening her own short titled *Rapture* during lunch for the HBO staff made her a candidate for a promotion when the company reorganized; she went from interdepartmental assistant to writer-producer for creative services.

....

HOW A PITCH BECOMES A SHOW
....

Former BET senior vice president of development Robyn Lattaker-Johnson has worked in film production as an assistant to director Rusty Cundieff, served as second assistant director on many films and music videos, and "snuck in the back door of development" after her production post at the

Sci-Fi Channel turned into that of D-girl for the cabler during the infancy of the reality genre. Yes, a sister developed shows like *Scare Tactics* and *Ghost Hunters* for the Sci-Fi Channel! In her post at BET, she turned around original programming at a breakneck pace, having launched twenty-seven series in three years. But Robyn and her team weren't rubbing the genie's magic lamp; if they were, they'd have run out of wishes three shows into her tenure. There is a time line for the development of programming—and there is no getting around the time that must be spent to ready a show for production.

Now president of Dubose Entertainment, she breaks it down this way: "The incubation period for shows will vary, but someone always pitches it. If it gets greenlit, the business affairs people negotiate a deal with the producer, who is [usually] not in-house. Then we'd pre-produce and develop the show. This could mean developing it on paper. It could also mean casting for a host, or set design getting approved before we pre-produced for the pilot. There isn't a rulebook for development; it depends on the show's elements—but all that would take six months or so.

"At BET, we crammed the process because we needed material to get on-air quickly," Robyn continues. "The hardest part was always getting the legal stuff on paper and making the deal. Then me and my team got our hands on the project to mold, finesse, and massage it. *Hell Date* was a good example; we shot the pilot in January, had a locked cut by February, focus-tested it, then shot eight episodes a week until we had sixty-five episodes, with six weeks to turn around *one episode*. We were shooting twelve hours [of footage per day on several cameras] and the editors have to get that down to twenty minutes. It takes three, four weeks to get a cut that editors want to show the network. Once we see it, give notes, then approve it, they go back and finish the episode [with graphics, sound design, mixing, et cetera]. And my job was to make sure all the players understand this time frame."

But before you get to any of that, if you are looking to hit the target when you submit a script, your first order of business is the protection of your intellectual property, even if it's just an outline of the concept and characters. Protect your fictional script or idea by registering the work with the Writers Guild of America and put the registration number it gives you on its cover page. Lana offers two tips and a caveat: "Being an associate [WGA] member lessens the copyright fee. You can do the poor man's copyright, but it serves [as] a first line of defense to protect an idea. It won't have as much merit as the traditional routes of protection." Now the caveat. When it comes to the US Copyright Office, "writers can only copyright the show once produced. If you have an idea for a TV show, you can register it [with the WGA] but you can't copyright it; you can't copyright an idea."

Next, do as much as possible to make the script as tight as possible. Join a writers' group. Take a screenwriting or creative writing course so you can experience being formally critiqued. Or if you can commit on a more intensive basis, apply for a screenwriting and development program, like the Sundance Screenwriters and Filmmakers' Laboratories. Once you feel it's ready, you can submit the script from a number of angles: to the manager of an actor you'd like to have read it; to the agent of a producer you might want on board to get it made; directly to an acquisitions rep like Nana, at a film studio like Sony Pictures Classics; or to the development executive of an independent production company like a DePasse or a Mosaic. Finally, you can research producers who have worked on films you respect and seek them out individually if they are freelancers. Start your search for them on the Internet, then move on to trade magazines to track them down.

Another kind of pitch that happens is a strong edit of the project already cut—completely in the absence of a script. Here is a prime example of how the editor takes on the role of a producer by shaping the storyline with editing skills.

With more than a decade of experience editing a variety of work from documentary series and films to television news, music videos, and commercials, Keesha Rai Levy exemplifies the editor who cuts like a producer, with the big picture in mind, committed to telling a compelling story, be it for ten seconds or fifteen minutes. She reinvented herself as an editor after working in marketing for music labels, literally going from an eighty-thousand-a-year salary and bicoastal lifestyle to offering her editing services for free to build a reel after taking a two-week trade school crash course. While she credits Connecticut College with giving her "well-roundedness and an understanding of deadlines and obligations," her liberal arts degree did not furnish her with the editing skill. Additionally, once you learn the mechanics of editing, it's all about learning by doing, first as an apprentice or an assistant editor before moving on to a lead editor position. Ironically, Keesha Rai's biggest and costliest teaching moment came from editing the *Hard Knock Life* documentary feature. It was her personal School of Hard Knocks education on the downside of being in on the ground floor of a project.

"I got fucked on the *Backstage: Hard Knock Life Tour* job. The project had two editors before me. When I took it over, it was the most unorganized, most ridiculous thing ever. There were eighty hours of footage from over three months of touring. No logs," she remembers, still incredulous at the idea. Logs are the notations made on tapes of footage in written form that delineate what happens on the tapes. To be clear, filmmakers don't always log tapes, but will usually give some notes or a skeletal direction with which to edit. This can be a general map that notes pivotal moments, or a description of what occurs down to the frame, which is a fraction of a second in visual time. Eighty hours of unlogged footage meant Keesha had no choice but to actually view all the tapes instead of being able to go to the moments she needed as she edited the film.

"I sat there and watched it all," she continues. "I shaped an unbelievable documentary for Damon [Dash] by myself with no direction and no assistant editor, which took more than four months. I gave all that footage a story line. My cut got him the deal with Miramax. That's the power of an editor. Chris Fiore was hired to direct, and Chris wanted to make me the *assistant* editor. I was like, 'Fuck you! I lived this project for months and that's what you come with?' I walked because that was ridiculous. No one knew that project like me—and they wanted to pay me less. I never got my credit. I had to do a lot of healing from that. I learned that I didn't want to be in the ghetto urban documentary world. I also learned long form was not for me unless I was saving the world, because it takes too much of your soul and your life."

With that experience long behind her, she has since become production director, BET Creative Services, where she oversees production of promos for the network's biggest series, including *American Gangster* and *College Hill*.

Keesha Rai's cautionary tale has multiple lessons. As a filmmaker or producer, your understanding of how you can ease the work of your editor begins with logging footage. Many editors refuse to begin work without all the elements in their possession, including logged tapes, approved script, and source music. Some editors are technicians who specialize in sticking to the script, so it bodes well to have your shit together. As an editor, negotiate for credit in writing as part of your compensation; even if you're not the only editor on the project, your contribution to the work informs the final product.

As a woman changing careers, learn from Keesha Rai's educated leap of faith. She was still a marketing executive when she took her editing course. She used the last two years of her tenure inside the record company to create allies and build relationships in production whenever she could: by attending video shoots for her assigned artists, sitting in on the edit sessions for the music videos, and meeting video directors and editors along the way. When the time came to get her own hands-on experience as an editor, she had contacts she could call to secure work. She worked for free, but only for a few months—then she started freelancing for a fee. Before taking a full-time position at a network, however, she had edited music videos like Jennifer Lopez's duet with Marc Anthony, "No Me Dejes," hard news for CBS, the MTV reality series *Making the Band,* and the HBO documentary *Pimps Up, Hoes Down.* She gained valuable experience and credits. She also discerned what kind of editor she was, choosing to concentrate on short-form editing. "You gotta be humble. Do as many jobs as possible and get as many experiences as you can—it will help you see what you don't want to do [for a living]. I was twenty-six years old on my second career and starting from scratch," says Keesha Rai. "I got my last MCA check the same day I got my first check from HBO. It's key for women to be strategic in the business. It's all chess, the players are the same; they just rotate."

In the worlds of film and television, there is more to production than scripting and cutting picture; sound plays an undeniable role in moving the story, if not its very telling—as the music of Outkast did beautifully in *Idlewild.* If all this insanity you've read about the hectic nature of production holds no appeal for you, but you love music and movies, you may want to consider contributing to the production process as a recording or scoring engineer, following the trail blazed by Leslie Ann Jones, a veteran music and film recording master who now serves as director of music recording and scoring for Skywalker Sound. Simply put, Leslie Ann Jones is badass. She has recorded and engineered everyone from Rosemary Clooney and Holly Near to Hammer, Con Funk Shun, and the Kronos Quartet. And that's just on the music side. She engineered Dianne Reeves, with whom she won a 2005 Grammy for their recording of *Good Night, And Good Luck,* and has recorded, engineered, or mixed film sound for *Zodiac* and *White Men Can't Jump,* among others. So I had to ask the expert: How does a girl figure out she's cut out for audio engineering?

"You must have a love of music," Leslie offers. "It may be the realization that you're not cut out to be a performer, but have a basic understanding of computers, or write music. The first thing you have to figure out is what you're going to be an engineer for." There are myriad careers in engineering for sound, a field in which specialties abound: recording, mixing, mastering, special effects, dialogue. Leslie started out playing guitar but wound up running a PA sound company. After doing her fair share of live sound, she found her calling. It doesn't hurt that she was surrounded by music from birth. Her father is legendary parodist and bandleader Spike Jones. Since it's the rare daughter who can claim a groundbreaking musician for a dad, Leslie recommends "seeking out a mentor and asking stupid questions, preferably not in front of clients," she says with a laugh. "Raise your hand and jump in, even if you don't think you know enough. It's the only way you'll be challenged and grow."

Leslie grew tremendously in her transition from music recording to film engineering. She talks about how she designed the next stage of her own professional production by seizing a career opportunity. "I was ready to leave Capitol after nine years, and was trying to figure out a way I could continue to engineer and mix records without working ninety-hour weeks. I decided the only way I could do that was to manage a studio and continue engineering part-time. It was then I read an interview with the then general manager of Skywalker, Gloria Borders. She was looking to hire someone with a film background to run the Scoring Stage and help it live up to its potential. I had been looking for a way to return to the Bay Area ever since I left for Capitol in 1987, but the opportunity never existed. I phoned, got an interview, and a few months later I was hired. I had never run a studio before, but after twenty-five-plus years I knew a thing or two about what worked and what didn't. Also, even though she wasn't initially looking for a mixer (most people don't do both jobs), that contributed greatly to me getting the job, along with the film music experience and contacts I gained from working at Capitol."

I asked Leslie if being female enters into the equation with her craft. "My musical sense, my sense of humor, and my technical competency are all very important to what I do. I do think gender plays a role," she explains. "I used to think I wanted to be agnostic about gender, because I was concerned about how people would react. I tried not to play my gender up or down. At some point, I realized my gender was a benefit because it was part of what I was bringing into the control room."

In her present dual role at Skywalker, even Leslie takes on the role of producer, guiding her staff and running the studio to ensure that clients receive the Skywalker experience. "Recording is a collaborative environment with many people to please. I feel lucky to contribute suggestions, and if they work, great. If not, we all move on. I don't work with many jerks; somebody comes in sometimes with a big ego, and you deal with it because one day, the project's gonna end." With all her credits and accolades, she remains humble. "I do what it takes to get the job done, and that's my staff's philosophy as well. Besides, even I can make a great cup of coffee!"

Television producer Nomi Roher asserts that "knowing how to rally a team and recognize the talent in others" is a big part of what makes her a great producer. It also contributes to a good reputation and longevity in an unstable field. "I know how to represent the team in such a way that no one feels threatened or unrecognized; I act as the face of the team [with the client], but don't take all the credit," she notes. Because she wants the team and the project to shine, she will always have a solid team willing to work with her. This is vital simply because there is no such thing as a Production of One. Even Prince, who writes, arranges, produces, and performs all his music, needs an engineer in the studio and a band on the road!

Now head of production for NYCTV, the network for the city of New York, including the mayor's channel, Nomi has experienced the distinction of being inside a corporate structure and having been an independent with her own company, ONTV Productions, for the last thirteen years. She breaks down the pros and cons of being her own boss. "The pros are being able to pick and choose your own jobs, and the people you get to work with. Knowing that all the work you do is for you and your team. Freedom and flexibility.

"But here's a pro that's also a con: the sense of responsibility and accountability for a project. At the end of the day when you run your project, you are entirely responsible for it. When it works you get the credit, and that's a great feeling of accomplishment. But if it doesn't work, you have to be strong enough to deal with the repercussions.

"The cons: Chasing your money. Deadbeat clients are just part of the business. Not having the machinery of a large company behind you [as a staff producer]. You don't get the built-in respect that comes automatically with a parent company. You have to work ten times harder as an independent to earn that same level of respect."

Once she began running a staff at NYCTV, Nomi had to redesign her way of doing business as an entrepreneur. Before she took the NYCTV position, she partnered with Claudine Atout, a former record-label marketing executive. This allowed her to focus on her new job and know that her company wouldn't suffer a loss of clients or business development. "Not everyone has the skill set to interface with labels and do all the hand-holding, damage control, and nurturing of relationships at the same time. Claudine's amazing at that. Initially, I wanted to partner with a man because I thought it would be useful to have a man in meetings and to stand up with that male presence that can change things. I was always looking for the right man to do this and never found him," Nomi says with a laugh.

....

RECOGNIZING AND NEUTRALIZING RESISTANCE

....

Nomi has found, however, that when it comes to resistance she has confronted as a producer, it has come more often from women, particularly on the client side. It may be the same multitasking, mothering thing about us women showing up as an exacting meticulous bedfellow with great expectations.

Nomi elaborates, "Surprisingly, men are less resistant. Women put you through more of a test than men do. Men are quick to let you in, but not so quick to let you join the boys' club. They'll test you out [as a business partner] but they don't often have the confidence in women to take them along with them all the way. Women put each other through hard tests because they've had to go through those same tests," she emphasizes. "The women need for you to earn your stripes with them. Totally different client dynamic; they expect greater service. Men communicate short and to the point; women have more demands." Nomi has even tailored her work style for women clients to neutralize any resistance early on in the working relationship. "I give women clients detailed synopses because that's what women understand. Men want you to get them to the end, or the point. You earn respect from a man by just getting it done. When you're dealing with women, you can earn more respect from them if they understand your process."

Keesha Rai is less diplomatic. Her view of the landscape reveals a harsh double standard in play for women in production roles where interacting with male counterparts is concerned. When it comes to men and women doing the same tasks in a professional setting, in her experience the men play the emotional card. "Men have us fooled into thinking we're the emotional ones. It's really them. Men can whoop and holler in the office. They can have tantrums and throw things. But when a woman fights for a point, she's overreacting. The 'period excuse' gets thrown out there on us. I've had to dumb myself down in situations; make the man feel like King Kong when I need to, pull back the bitch, and save that bite for another time."

Erika received some advice from a male mentor along a similar line. "Paul Hall told me, 'You know too much and they know you are sharp, so stay quiet.' I got offended, but realized he was speaking from the male point of view," she explains. "So I would downplay myself and just gather information because even at the top levels, women are always in the blind." Observing what Erika calls "the hidden politics of how-to" became a survival tactic she employed on the *Idlewild* project, keeping the larger objective of getting the movie made in mind.

The in-office injury inflicted by the emotional card is made all the more insulting by a male phenomenon Keesha Rai calls White Man's Confidence. Despite its name, this "sense of entitlement with or without credentials" can be worn by men of all backgrounds. Her experience is that women agonize over being qualified and doubt their abilities far more often than some of her male counterparts, who see no problem with being unqualified for a position in which they are placed. This works to the detriment of women in two ways. On the one hand, it creates defensiveness in these unqualified and therefore insecure men, prompting them to carry a deck of emotional cards around to play on women executives. On the other, it supports a cycle of incompetence in which men are allowed to fail, even fail miserably, and still get promoted. "Men are granted the opportunity to learn on the job, when women are expected to hit the ground running," Keesha Rai asserts. "They get a learning curve and a fuckup curve that women just don't get."

Given Mo'Nique's critically important comment about the damage silence can do, Nomi offers that a middle ground between flying off the handle and becoming voiceless has to be achieved. Her own approach is to kill 'em with kindness, even as she makes demands of her crew. "My director of photography calls it Magic Dust I sprinkle to get everyone to eat out of my hand," she says with a grin. "I spend my energy figuring out how to handle them instead of how to win them over. You can like someone and they'll still be sneaky and backstab you. You're not going to be liked by everyone. This was a hard thing for me to learn, and the sooner you come to terms with that, the better off you'll be in your career. They can say I'm a bitch or whatever, but I'm a perfectionist and the work speaks for itself. Go for being respected."

Now, that's all fine and dandy when you're in charge, but what about when you're not—and you really *are* in the process of learning? Mo'Nique says it's all in how you ask the question. "No question is a dumb question when it's your life," she offers in a serious tone. "They might say you're a troublemaker, but don't go in with boxing gloves, or raising your voice and kicking a desk. Just say, 'Excuse me, can you clarify that for me?'" Mo'Nique even makes her attorney break things down for her, taking nothing for granted. "I tell him to give it to me like I'm in the third grade. I didn't go to school for all that whereby and wherefore—I tell jokes." She laughs. "I tell women to *inspect* what they expect." Taking inventory of the outcome you want and working toward that outcome will have you asking the right questions when it is appropriate and most advantageous for you. Ideally, this clarity will help you gain power as you learn and keep you from being emotional unnecessarily. Emotional card neutralized!

....
PRODUCTION TIPS FOR TALENT
....

We've looked at what the production world looks like from the point of view of women in the wings, behind the camera, and at the control room console. But no production's getting done without actors, and the majority of them have managers or agents that act on their behalf to get them the job. Let's turn the lens onto some talent and a talent manager to see what they have to say about the invaluable roles they play, and how best to play them.

Mo'Nique had much to say about how her team keeps her grounded, and what makes a great entourage. Nayo Wallace is Black Hollywood royalty, but her roots did not smooth her path to stardom. The great-niece of Dorothy Dandridge speaks on the work and the fearlessness it takes to be ready for your big break. Nayo also gives up the goods on boundary setting with directors and agents. Kamilah Forbes, actor, founder of the Hip-Hop Theater Festival, and producer for HBO's *Def Poetry Jam*, offers some jewels on the lesson she learned about trading her art for money. Alexa Pagonas, senior talent manager with Michael Black Management, has represented Emmy, Oscar, and Tony Award–winning actors in addition to fight choreographers and models on productions ranging in budget from ten-million-dollar passion projects to two-hundred-million blockbusters.

"I went to Cass, a performing arts high school in Detroit, where I grew up. I took drama classes; it was awesome. I was being bad my senior year, so I ended up in public high school," explains Nayo with a grin. "No one I graduated with was acting. Then I went to community college, but I still didn't know what I wanted to do." With the Dandridge family legacy in entertainment as her birthright, you'd think Nayo Wallace knew she wanted to act from the moment she could speak. Well, she didn't, and she's conquered Broadway in *The Lion King* and plays a supporting female role in the Wachowski Brothers' cinematic version of *Speed Racer.* So if you're in the same place—in school without a clue of how you're gonna make your living—stop flogging yourself. It happens to a lot of us. Even if you don't figure it out, it will most likely choose you. You will be okay. But as Nayo found out once she relocated to Los Angeles, you've got to put in the grunt work to get the work you want.

"No one ever said, *Omigod, you're Dorothy Dandridge's great-niece! You should be in this movie. Just come on down and we'll fill out the paperwork.* For a long time, even though I'm proud to be part of the Dandridge family, I didn't put it out there. I wanted to rely on—and for people to see—my own talent," she emphasizes. Nayo's grind includes continual playhouse training and acting class work. And unlike collegiate or post-graduate programs, your coursework has no specific completion date.

"I've been studying at the Beverly Hills Playhouse going on eight years. Training and [formal] education are important, but I can't say one is more important than the other. You can study all you want. It's different when you get on set," Nayo warns. So often you'll hear about actors taking classes or studying one-on-one with an acting coach. Surely that cost can add up. Consider the playhouse to cut your teeth as an actor; it's a great model for working on set before you win that first film role.

Nayo elaborates, "The playhouse runs things like the industry. The thinking is, 'If you were shooting with DeNiro, would you miss it?' So you don't miss class [at the playhouse] for anything. You ask questions, get clear about things. My teacher Richard Lawson started an on-camera class where I learned about lighting, angles, and how the camera works, so it's a lot like being on set. But once you get there, the set's a whole different animal. And that's where the formal training comes in handy, because it allows you to learn about yourself and gain confidence by failing. You challenge yourself in terms of characters and where you're comfortable going with anger and intimacy. You become a more competent actor as a result." I know there are plenty of average actors out there, plus a gaggle of celebrities with questionable talent, if any. But let those people live on the C- and D-lists. The goal here is for your name never to occupy a line on those rosters. When it comes to production, no matter what level it's on or what the budget is, directors and producers want competent actors.

Similarly, actors who hone their craft to the degree Nayo describes expect a commensurate level of commitment from their representatives. Nayo believes she has found this in her agent and manager. "They are passionate about me. It's important for any actor that [your] agent believe in you. I am clear about what I can and can't do, and they know these things as well. They know where my strengths are. For example, me being able to sing is good to know. But just because I can sing does not mean I dance. I am a singer who moves," she says, giggling. "I can shake it, but don't put me in a Twyla Tharp show. If there's a part that calls for a hot, sexy, retarded tall girl who can do cartwheels, drools on herself, and is very Jim-Carrey-esque, they'd call me, tell me the perfect job for me came up, and send me to the audition!"

Which brings us to the question: What do these agents and managers do all day anyway? The picture painted that comes to mind for me is Jeremy Piven's character Ari in *Entourage,* part smarmy, part asshole, always out for the kill, and usually out of the office. Real-life talent rep Alexa Pagonas has her daily game plan down to a science. She believes that the game "is too competitive with people who want your spot" to stop paying dues.

Alexa breaks her job down like this: "A third of my day is trying to find new work for clients: nurturing existing relationships, reading what's out there in casting, making pitches [on clients' behalf], even helping people in the business get their projects off the ground to create work for your clients. Another third is spent looking over contracts and smoothing the way for clients who are already working. The last third is listening to what clients' needs and wants are for their careers and educating them about the business. [Overall] about 10 percent is spent seeing movies, visiting sets, having dinner meetings. I'm on the phone 90 percent of the time." She has refined the process over the last thirteen years, and her assistant helps her execute it with such efficiency that she takes a minimum of two hundred calls a day. "I have a five-page call sheet, a spreadsheet divided by clients and projects, then subdivided by what I need to do, and what I expect to happen with dates so I know how and when to follow up." She also makes time to take referrals for new clients, to keep current clients from being stolen or poached by other managers, and fights for her client's earnings when the need arises. Well, I for one am exhausted just listening to that rundown. We'll come back to Alexa's background when I examine the benefits of education for some of the women featured in this chapter more closely.

Mo'Nique had a pivotal moment with a manager who really gave her pause and changed the way she approached representation. "One manager and I didn't seem to agree on how we wanted to conduct business. He said, 'I'll give you some time to sleep on the decision you're making.' In that moment, I realized I would never give someone else the power to determine my destiny. Why am I paying these people 10 percent when I am doing the work and the calls are coming to me? Managers have gotten so cocky, and we as talent have gotten so afraid. It's unfortunate. I don't want it to seem like all managers are bad. There are some who've been with their clients from day one." Shout out to Derek Dudley (Common), Marcus King (Jamie Foxx), and Tina Davis (Chris Brown)! Still, there are a lot of shady managers out there, so stay sharp. "I'm a person who holds on to your word once you give it to me," says Mo'Nique. "I was never able to wrap my arms around 'Well, that's just the way they do it in Hollywood.' So now my team is my husband, Sidney Hicks, my attorney Ricky Anderson, executive assistant Joselyn Byrd, production assistant Mr. K., Henri on security, and Rhonda, my stylist and personal assistant. If you hire a manager and your career is going well, then after about a week they say 'I love you,' fire them immediately! Understand this is a business! When you start loving me, you start fuckin' up and takin' shit for granted. That's that Hollywood shit."

In addition to the common refrain that a manager is the actor's or performer's key to getting work, you've got the perception that there isn't a whole lot of work to be had. Nayo says that this can lead you to "sell yourself short" artistically. "As actors, scarcity has us think we have to be so grateful we got a job or even got sent out [on an audition], so we have to do whatever [managers or agents] want. No. You are an artist, so powerful you can change the world. It matters what you think and where you stand with a part and the choices you're cool with. Your voice as a professional is equally important." She underscores this with the story of her wardrobe and dialogue while working on *The Brothers*. Director Gary Hardwick offered Nayo a part that she did not audition for, that of a stripper, which happened to be a larger role. She objected to some crude language in one scene. "I wasn't gonna wait until I got on set and potentially have a problem. I asked my agent to put me in touch with Gary. We talked about it and I felt fine. Then I get to the set and I wasn't comfortable with the wardrobe," she recalls. The wardrobe stylist was on some ol' this-is-what-strippers-wear-and-you'll-like-it conversation. But because Nayo had spoken to Gary about the character, she was able to say as much very diplomatically to the wardrobe stylist. The director in turn offered her some wardrobe alternatives. Problem solved. "You don't talk shit in hair and makeup," Nayo intones. "That doesn't help anybody. Find an appropriate time to talk to someone who can do something about the problem in a way that's clean and not malicious."

Kamilah Forbes has asked and received, from securing money to establish the Hip-Hop Theater Festival and bring it to several major cities, to being commissioned to write a play and getting a fee plus a New York apartment as part of the deal. She urges women to speak up and ask for what they really want, because the truth is, "You can ask for anything," she remarks. And in the asking, you may discover that the people on the other side of the table with the purse strings don't even blink at your request, or they may counteroffer and still want you on board.

Kamilah has experienced this both as producer and as talent. "As women, there's a hesitation around that, particularly where upper management of TV and theater are concerned. The thought is that we are workers or facilitators as opposed to being in the driver's seat. Now my attitude is: I'll ask and see what I get. I still struggle with it and it's something I am trying to work though especially around money for my art, because I feel like I'd be doing this even if I wasn't being paid. So how and where I'm motivated plays a part. Mentorship is huge in knowing one's worth and figuring out what is viewed as an asset and what that asset is worth."

For Nayo, getting her value as an artist has been an ongoing process as well, one that became crystal clear upon cutting her shoulder-length hair at her teacher's recommendation. "I had been Weave Girl for I don't know how many years. And it was quite the transformation. When I first cut it, we shaved it real low. And I'm not much of a girly girl—that's probably why I wore weaves for so long. My hair got so damaged, he suggested I cut it off. I cried for a week, was traumatized, and then moved on. And I didn't tell my agent or manager, because I knew I could always throw on a wig. They were both like, 'Oh.'" And then the audition opportunity for *Speed Racer* came up. "The character breakdown as I remember was that she [Racer X's girlfriend] was superhot, sexy, and a scientist. I had been battling with my manager about what hot and sexy is — and that I was gonna just go with my hair. I said, 'I got that you're upset I cut it. And this is me and I know I can rock it out. If you can't represent me passionately with this hairdo, then let's be clear about that so I can pick someone else who can.' Agents sometimes feel like they're the boss of you. And you in turn lean on your agent because you don't know how much power you have. People aren't able to have those conversations because they don't realize their value."

Nayo won the hair battle. Fast-forward to the audition. Nayo recalls, "I went with no wig thinking, *I don't care—you can be sexy and bald!*" Warner Bros. head of casting Laura Kennedy and the film's directors were on the same wavelength, and Nayo got the part. "The Wachowskis are brilliant and so creative. They are like two people of one mind, giving, sensitive, clear, and direct. I'm glad they didn't put me in a wig. It's me and my natural hair in the movie."

....

EDUCATION IS RELATIVE
....

Nayo extols the benefits of school when it comes to acting. But she didn't attend a four-year college or major in theater. And yet she is a working actor who has focused on honing her craft with a mixture of stage work and class work. And then there's Alexa, who, like Nayo, also attended performing arts high school. For Alexa, however, San Francisco School of the Arts, though an enriching experience, just showed her she was not going to be an actor.

Alexa went on to Mills College, majoring in pre-law and economics with a minor in theater. Immediately after graduation, she earned her law degree at Hastings, reflecting that "law school was as patriarchal as you can get, and a great experience for learning the rules to the game." Instead of law-yering in court somewhere, Alexa's now using her understanding of the law to advocate for her clients; leveraging her understanding of how business works to "trace the money," as she puts it, generating more income for them and, in turn, for herself. "There are no rules to life, but there are tax codes, business structures, and legal relationships," says Alexa. "You have to learn them to affect change, be that around the dining table or someplace else." She also credits her all-women Mills education for giving her "perspective on how the world works and how it doesn't; and in particular the various ways women and women's issues fit into the workplace."

Both Abra and Nomi attended the Gallatin School at New York University, but Nomi attended as a graduate after majoring in TV, film, and business administration at Rutgers. Nomi built her own degree "and had a mentor, Barbara Abrush, for the entire program. I was already working, so I knew what I wanted. School not only helped to keep me grounded, but most of the people I work with today I met when we were all in school." Abra attended straight out of high school and benefited from Gallatin's mixture of classroom and external teaching via internships that were built into the curriculum. Simply put, she "*loved* it." And to think she was leaning toward staying local at Washington State, where she'd won a scholarship, to be closer to her high school boyfriend. Ironically, it was her parents who encouraged her not to play it safe when it came to college. "They were big on East Coast education," Abra recounts. "Had I not had parents who were on a mission to get me to NYU, I would not be where I am today."

Rose's parents were on a different mission altogether: to keep Rose away from the entertainment business. "I always knew I wanted to be in entertainment, but coming from a Filipino family, that was not an option," Rose states. "They wanted me to major in something where there is a job waiting for you afterward: accounting, engineering, law, or medicine." Raised in San Diego, she stayed local, attending San Diego State University as an accounting major. "The first class was a piece of cake, but they got harder, and I was too far into the major to change it. But I knew it wasn't me."

Still, Rose went on to Pepperdine Law. There she took entertainment law courses while satisfying her parents' wishes. Would she do it differently knowing what she does after a decade in development? "Knowing what I know now, would I go to law school? No. You can always hire a lawyer, but you have to be your own businessperson all the time. I would have gotten an MBA." Rose got a lot from the extension courses she took to learn more about development and production while she gained work experience, however. While employed at Universal Pictures as a legal assistant, she took advantage of continuing education, and studied script coverage, paid for by the company. By all means sop up all the free education you can.

Robyn took the road less traveled for her education in film; after graduating from the University of Washington in broadcast journalism, she got her MFA in film from the Art Center College of Design in Pasadena, California. By not going to film school as an undergrad, she got the coursework via a master's program. But when it came time to pay the bills, she wound up taking a receptionist gig at International Creative Management (ICM). And while she was bored to tears answering phones, she was paid better than some agent assistants, so it took a lot to accept the inevitable pay cut of being a production assistant on a film. That pay cut is more like a pay slash. So Robyn answered the phone and paid her bills, master's and all. "It was 'Good morning, ICM!' all day long. I sat there and wrote scripts on my laptop. I was losing my mind after four months, and started cold-faxing résumés. I went to an interview for an in-house PA and it was three hundred bucks less than what I was making. I asked if the director had a need for an assistant." That director was Rusty Cundieff, known for *Fear of a Black Hat* and directing episodes of *Chappelle's Show*. She was hired. Robyn was working on a real film set six months out of school. The lesson here? If you're gonna take a pay cut, why not make it work for you by asking for the job you really want?

On the other end of the spectrum, Marjorie contends that school knowledge is no match for what awaits you in the workplace. "School prepares you for a variety of things to use when you get to work, but for me it was theory with little application," she reflects. "There's nothing like what you get when you walk into the office with real shit going on." Marjorie's professional education was bolstered by an unlikely mentor named Henry G. Walter, chairman of International Flavors and Fragrances. She worked at IFF in her first job out of undergrad at Syracuse, as assistant director of advertising and public relations. Far-fetched as it seems, she cut her teeth in production doing research for him on the emerging Latin market for cosmetics. She was also a student of her best friend, the late Diane Nixon, assistant to Blue Note Label Group CEO Bruce Lundvall. "Even though she was his assistant, she had much more power than anybody knew," she muses. "Diane was the keeper of the gate and knew where *all* the bodies were buried. She taught me how not to wield the big stick: Because once people know you have it, you ain't gotta use it."

Remember Nana, the film acquisitions intern who ended up making notes on scripts that were ultimately greenlit? She never went to film school, proving that neither what you study nor whether you study formally at all will determine the work you get. She attended Vassar College and majored in Africana studies and political science. She had a "concentration in dissecting pop culture," specifically "the Black beauty ideal and the cues pop culture gives on what is beautiful." Her undergraduate thesis on this subject led her to "get into the business, to shape and shift that dialogue."

Monique Martin's education outside of school was the most impactful for her. After attending American Conservatory Theater in San Francisco and finding out that she didn't' "live and breathe being an actress" as she thought she would, she packed her bag and moved from San Francisco to New York. "I had tunnel vision," she says, laughing. "No bartending, no waiting tables or babysitting. The first work I started doing was props, and from there it was wardrobe, sound—anything that would get me a theater job. I respected the craft to the degree of not needing to be in it to be a celebrity. Once I learned all the jobs, I became a stage manager." Her assistant stage manager gig for *Sarafina* while it played at Lincoln Center turned into a long-term stint with the show. "When the show went to Broadway, the stage manager asked me to go with it," she recalls.

Erika's work experience was all the school she needed. She credits her "street sense, hustle and instinct, and not overthinking situations" for propelling her to success. She also laid the groundwork for her career as a producer by maximizing her assistant position. She worked with Keith Clinkscales at *VIBE,* breaking his revolving-door assistant habit. At the time, the magazine was developing its TV show, *Weekend VIBE.* She took the initiative and traveled with Keith for all the meetings and seminars so she could get the information firsthand, which helped them both. "Had I left it up to him, I wouldn't know about the business. It was a clever way for me to politic and meet the players." One of those players turned out to be director John Singleton, from whom she accepted a development job after cultivating her professional relationship with him over a two-year period with her in New York and Singleton out west. Her new job brought her to Los Angeles, into the thick of development and, ultimately, production. For label exec turned editor Keesha Rai and engineer turned studio head Leslie Ann Jones, it was getting the basics during technical school courses, then clocking thousands of real hours at the editing bay or in the control room that guided their careers. Both editing and engineering require a lot of apprenticeship, watching others work as you assist, and discerning what not to do along the way. But when you find yourself ready for a career change, don't be afraid to take a class and hit the books; it can only enhance you professionally.

When Leslie transitioned from engineering recorded music to films, she "realized there was a learning curve, a different language and technology to learn," she says. Leslie enrolled in a UCLA extension course taught by a sound editor. "I learned what happens in production when [film] is shot, what happens when sound design and score come into play. It gave me a knowledge base so I could communicate with the people I was dealing with."

While Connecticut College was good preparation, Keesha became a great editor from doing the work in studios, on sets for videos as a PA, assisting in the edit sessions, and eventually cutting videos of her own before joining the *Pimps Up, Hoes Down* team. In addition to her work on *Backstage: Hard Knock Life Tour,* she became a Web videographer, learning how to shoot as she edited content for 360.com, the precursor to BET.com. It was there that she learned the editor's secret weapon. "The Web forced me to become versed in every platform, every surface on which footage can be cut. I know how to edit using Avid, Final Cut Pro, Media 100, and good ol' tape-to-tape. I am also working in ProTools and learning aftereffects."

LET'S TALK TURKEY

Despite all the work it takes to become a credited entertainment writer, once you arrive, the gratification is not far behind. Lana Garland explains, "In marketing, promo, and ad writing (short form), you can 'be a writer' when your first promo airs. Segment producing has a bit longer arc to completion, but same deal. Once you get paid for writing a screenplay or series, you're official—and you're experienced." You've certainly done a lot to get to that point and believe me, it will feel like it took the longest to you.

Erika's got some real talk on how to live between projects, and how to remain solvent during unexpected events like a writer's strike. And you want to make money when the project makes money, especially if that's on what is called the back end in entertainment. "Sometimes you go through a major gap, so you have to manage your money right," she warns. "I stash cash to pay bills and be able to take a break. I have a financial planner who helps me do my taxes and helps me keep my money straight. I also had my lawyer negotiate my back-end percentage fees for DVD sales. I live on the residuals from the DVDs."

DePasse development VP Rose Caraet and Nana Brew-Hammond agree that knowing your worth is critical. The question is your reference point for competitive compensation. When I asked Rose what men hide most from women, she put it in a word: "Salaries. I believe there is a boys' club in every industry, including this one." Nana consults her female colleagues to crunch salary numbers for this very reason. "Don't hate on your friends," Nana says. "You need each other to bounce off ideas and talk salary range. No one else will tell you the real deal but your good girlfriend!"

For you audio engineers out there, Leslie Ann is that girlfriend. After a few decades in the game, she knows what the going rates are. And as more studios close their doors because so many are recording in home facilities, the last thing you want to do is sell yourself short.

Leslie Ann gets specific on the fee scale for the music recording side. "I would say as an assistant in a traditional studio, you'd make about fifteen, twenty bucks an hour. Once you start, if you have your own in-home studio, engineers can charge seventy-five dollars an hour because [the rate includes] them and their equipment. Some charge that at other peoples' studios. I tend to charge depending on what people can afford—which is not to say I have a sliding scale, but I can't always charge what I normally would to get the kind of clients I want. A lot of the top engineers charge by the mix, anywhere from fifteen to twenty-five hundred dollars a mix. Some get points [residual percentage points] on top of that if they're big enough; the record company thinks he or she knows what a hit is supposed to sound like—and these engineers command top dollar for what they're doing."

Monique breaks down the good news and the bad about stage management. "Stage managers earn between fifteen hundred and twenty-five hundred dollars weekly, or more if you are in demand or depending on the size of the show. You generally earn more on musicals than dramas." Now comes the bad news. You'll have a bit of chicken-and-egg drama of your own with getting to that earning level as a union stage manager. "You are required to join Actors' Equity if you are working on a union show. The Catch-22 is, you can't get a job in the union unless you are in the union but you can't get into the union unless you have a union job," she laments. "I was blessed to move with *Sarafina* from Lincoln Center as an off-Broadway run as a production assistant, and was promoted to assistant stage manager, which required me to join the union."

....

SUMMARY OF SECRETS REVEALED

WHAT YOU THOUGHT YOU KNEW:

Formal schooling is the ticket to not only getting a job but excelling at that job.

WHAT YOU NEED TO KNOW:

Formal schooling may be part of the ticket. What's certain is that nothing trains you for the job like the job itself, so intern, work for free for a while, assist someone at an entry-level or junior rate—get the job so you can get the on-the-job experience.

WHAT YOU THOUGHT YOU KNEW:

The title of producer means automatic respect.

WHAT YOU NEED TO KNOW:

Though the title sounds like it would be enough to keep folks from messing with, doubting, or sabotaging you, you will still have to command and maintain respect. Make sure you get it on paper in your contracts, in the credits, and on the production call sheets. Make sure your allies and enemies alike know that you are the plug, and without the plug there is no juice. Meetings and calls cannot happen without you, your attorney, or your trusted assistant. Period.

WHAT YOU THOUGHT YOU KNEW:

Doing the work will get me the credit.

WHAT YOU NEED TO KNOW:

Negotiate for your credit in writing up front.

It's called credit for a reason; it's currency in our business. Credit is worth fighting for, even if it's shared. I am music supervisor on the film *Anne B. Real* with Josselynne Herman-Saccio—but no one says, "You did half." We both gave 100 percent.

WHAT YOU THOUGHT YOU KNEW:

Speaking up for myself or speaking out guarantees I'll lose the part, the job, or the promotion.

WHAT YOU NEED TO KNOW:

By not speaking when something does not work for you, the one thing you're guaranteed to lose is your integrity. Speak softly if you must, speak professionally at all times, just speak up. Ask about the job even if you're not being interviewed for it, like Robyn did. Remind the production staff ever-so-diplomatically that you run the show, as Mo'Nique did. Follow Kamilah's lead and ask for the funding you really need instead of selling yourself and your project short. Ask questions. Speak your mind. The results you get may surprise you. And you'll respect yourself in the morning.

WHAT YOU THOUGHT YOU KNEW:

There is only one kind of producer: the one that makes the show happen.

WHAT YOU NEED TO KNOW:

There are many kinds of producers, all with specific skill sets. Before you become a producer, get to know the types there are and see which is the best fit for you, just as Abra did with news production. And once you delve into one area, there will be further distinctions between producer types. Following are a few basic examples of the producer roles that are available to you, as outlined by both Abra and Erika.

....

FROM ABRA ON TELEVISION PRODUCER ROLES
In the news and documentary space:

EXECUTIVE PRODUCER

These people oversee the production of the show from top to bottom, but are not necessarily involved in the field shooting. Their job is to know which stories have been initiated and how they'll work on-air.

SENIOR PRODUCER

Senior producers serve as liaisons between the executive producer and the producer, letting everyone know if a story is running into a snag and helping the producer to shape the segment. Senior producers are not usually in the field with the producer.

PRODUCER

Producers may wear the hats of writer, interviewer, or interview subject director at different points. They determine how much tape to shoot to meet the objective of the segment and tell the story.

ASSOCIATE PRODUCER OR ASSISTANT PRODUCER

These folks are helping the producer line up interviews, coordinate travel, set up meetings, and get and keep supplies—from tape for the camera to gaffer's tape. They can be on the ground with the producer or support from the office headquarters.

PRODUCTION ASSISTANT

This role is one of pure execution, from making sure the crew members have the supplies they need to getting releases signed from interviewees, and right down to making coffee runs. Not a small job by any means.

✻

In the programming and reality entertainment space:

SUPERVISING PRODUCER

Similar to senior producers on the news side, these executives will most likely also steer the post-production process to ensure the edit is set up, happening smoothly, and on time. They also make sure any outsourced companies or staff get paid.

FIELD PRODUCERS

These are the ones on the front line of the fieldwork and location shooting. They often fulfill the dual role of being line producers, overseeing the production budget and watching the costs. It falls on the field or line producer to make sure days don't run over and crews don't go into overtime.

....

FROM ERIKA ON FILM PRODUCER ROLES:

EXECUTIVE PRODUCER

An EP can be the representative from your production company if you are an employee, or the entity you go to for the equity partnership and/or for distribution. EPs are in charge of executing the finances of the company that cuts the checks and funds the production.

PRODUCER

Producers birth the project, providing it with the proper nourishment for the gestation period between getting greenlit and getting made. They hire grip, director, script supervisor, casting director, and often the other auxiliary producers.

CO-PRODUCER

Co-producers do the same job plus a bit more, because the producer needs eyes and ears on a project while working another one. Co-producers are often first-timers who are being mentored or apprenticing.

ASSOCIATE PRODUCER

Some say it's a null and void title. Still, associate producers are usually the assistants who make the calls and get information, secure talent or executive availability, and are on the set with producers to handle their day-to-day. It's a glorified assistant position. If they are smart, associates will run with it and bring ideas to the boss so they can get co-producer credit.

LINE PRODUCER

These folks budget your production. They map out how to spend the money and how much time it will take before you run out of money. They are cut-and-dried, and that's what you want. They're noncreative and all about the dollars. Their ass is on the line. They are hired to keep your producer and director in line. When the budget grows, line producers are the ones the studio calls back when producers request or need budget increases. They're also the ones to tell the producer if she or he will get the money.

*

If none of these roles appeal to you, there are myriad roles for you in the crew, as anyone who stuck around to read film credits knows. You can operate the camera or lighting. You can be a production and set designer. You can be an animator or graphics and effects producer. You can be a costumer or sound designer, stuntwoman, or fight choreographer. The list is too exhaustive for me to detail here, but know that there is a place for you on the set. You simply need to learn and be committed to the craft to assume it.

CHAPTER 9

President and CEO

....

Cathy Hughes ✳ Dawn Haynes ✳ Lisa Cortes ✳
Mona Scott-Young ✳ Sharon Heyward ✳
Tomica Woods-Wright ✳ Tyesh Harris ✳ Vanessa Gilbert

....

The Bible says that no weapon formed against me shall
prosper. It doesn't say those weapons won't be formed.

—TYESH HARRIS, CEO, PHOENIX
ENTERTAINMENT GROUP

What makes a great chief executive officer? The answers from the women listed above will surprise you. Meet a determined teenage mother. A money-loving hustler. An eccentric genius. A ruthless negotiator. A compassionate mentor. A gangsta rapper's unbreakable widow. A quiet master of relationships. And an untamed free spirit. Some were the Head Woman in Charge within organizations; others run their own companies today. They've all ascended, learned, grown, made their mark, made compromises, and taken losses. Most important, they've done it all on their own terms. In this chapter, eight presidents and CEOs uncover the myths that shroud the road to the top, share trials and triumphs, and reveal their strategies for clearing the hurdles they encounter. While these women operate at the highest executive levels, their insights provide inspiration at any altitude.

✳

The Fugees. Nas. Cypress Hill. Da Brat. Even Mariah Carey. Tyesh Harris is a big part of how and why you heard them on the radio. Now the CEO of Phoenix Entertainment Group and Odyssey Entertainment, she has a Midas touch with marketing and promotion that has benefited artists including Alicia Keys, Mario, and Cassidy. Tyesh also claimed her space on the Web via Hitbreakers.com and the The Leak Music, both aimed at exposing new music to tastemakers around the world while allowing them to connect with one another. Much like Nas, who autographed an album cover to Tyesh calling her "my second mother," she was an explosive child prodigy who brought freshness and credibility to Columbia Records. Beginning her tenure at the label as an intern at fifteen, she was the company's director of rap promotion by the age of nineteen. Tyesh was handpicked by Donnie Ienner and Tommy Mottola. She was CEO material from the start, but she was also playing with the big dogs at a very young age, which left very little room for error.

"When you're younger, you do things you wouldn't do once you get older," she says, chuckling. "I got away with a lot because I didn't know what I should or shouldn't be doing. But I tell folks who come to work for me that people will let you get away with things — as long as you're producing," Tyesh admonishes. "And to this day people still say 'Tyesh from Columbia Records' because I busted my ass, never wanting to disappoint the label. Ate, slept, and drank it, delivering time and time again without any other thought but to give 200 percent. I wanted Columbia to win."

And win Columbia did. The label moved more than a hundred million units in Black music product while Tyesh was in command. And yet, when it was time for the brass ring, the same attention to detail and commitment to the brand that helped sell all those records were called into question by the boys. Confirmation that being on the grind does not always guarantee the shine.

"Initially, *Illmatic* had the Ruffhouse logo on the record, and I said [to the album's executive producer MC Serch], 'What the hell is this? He's on Columbia. There's no way I can be a credible head of rap promotion if my own logo isn't on it.' And I got the logo changed. And ironically it was another Nas project that had more cooks in the pot, like [Loud Records founder] Steve Rifkind and Steve Stoute, telling me I don't know what I'm doing. My credit card got Nas state-to-state and got his publicity photo taken when the label wouldn't pay for it. After *Illmatic*, Nas became a rock star. Steve [Stoute] comes in, and *he's* the expert. I then went from being the person in the room who laid all this groundwork to being the one who was a bit difficult and not credible enough, when I've been going to Queensbridge [the projects Nas grew up in] at 3 AM and getting outfitted for [bulletproof] vests to run around Oakland in with Nas. At that point, I should have gotten the VP stripes, big money, and all of that," Tyesh reasons, given the natural order these promotions take when men are on the receiving end. "But my next move was being sabotaged."

After nine years with Columbia, Tyesh was taught the biggest lesson of her fast-tracking career. "I had been there too long. When you're being told to go, go. Even if you have to keep moving while you're afraid, move on." With matriculation inside Columbia no longer part of her career plan, Tyesh put her presidential skills to the test and established her own promotions and marketing company. The crash course she put herself through to become The Chief showed her some disturbing things about the decline in respect that women executives garnered from male executives. She saw this affect her business from two angles: when she pitched to get label clients and when she hired employees. It was as if the stock of women in power—especially Black women—had plummeted. Tyesh attributes it to the misogynist turn hip-hop took in the mid-1990s. So often we hear debates about how lyrics affect consumers and children. She actually experienced it shifting the mind-set of the Black male executives who were *marketing* the records.

"Going into 2000, there was a shift," Tyesh explains. "During that time from 1996 to 2000, the music was different—but to be more disrespectful and go beyond misogynist became even more *mainstream*. The depth to which the music has sunk has impacted the minds you encounter as far as men go, with both consumers and executives. When you see Black males become so incredibly detached . . . desensitized—where nothing affects them—now this disrespect is bleeding over into how they interact with women executives. And now there is a new guard that says they have no respect for women. This is a new generation of male executives. These men are not hiring women to even be their right hand, yet they're not capable themselves. And if any of them were to bring a woman like me in, they'd be afraid that I'd do better than them at their own job. There is no differentiation between the women who come in as accessories and the ones who are about something. This is warfare. It's open season, and the message is for women to stay in their place."

As CEO of her own business, retaining employees is important. There is no time for turnover when records are being promoted to radio stations on a weekly basis; revolving-door staff impedes cementing relationships. Tyesh creates an environment for developing employees that includes weekly one-on-one meetings, feedback on regular reports made to her, and an open-door communication policy. She also stays "in tune with what is being said about me among my staff and tend to any sores that show up. Some things you can't defuse," she notes. "As a business owner, you always have employees who think they can do a better job. But once the person decides they can't function inside the company, it may be time to have them exit." This *You can't tell me nothin'* ethos made a few of her male employees impossible to mentor and, sadder yet, impossible to trust. Tyesh caught one worker in a lie about a family emergency he concocted in the interest of parlaying a new job. "He said he had to leave," Tyesh recounts. "I told him, 'When you go, take your bag and don't come back.'" For Tyesh, leadership means never having to say you're sorry for saying good-bye.

"I don't think firing someone is extreme. And sometimes letting go of someone is required. Some people do not deserve the privilege of being part of your organization. Who's gonna be in your first two rows at your Broadway show? Are you gonna just let anyone sit there? It's my program. You don't like it? You don't have to be there. And there will be people who just don't like your program."

Thirty-five-year marketing, promotion and artist management veteran Sharon Heyward, former president of Perspective Records, contends that Black music lost its executive juice inside the labels when it treated hip-hop, it newest member of the family, like a stepchild. She believes that "staying connected to your people and the culture they represent" separates the good presidents from the great ones. What Sharon witnessed instead was a separation of another sort.

"We gave Black music away. Black radio kicked hip-hop to the curb from the beginning. Then it became a cross-cultural thing. We gave it to crossover departments to promote on crossover radio stations. We jacked ourselves up when we separated Old School and New School. It left New School execs with nobody to train them. They got a paycheck and thought they were all that, but they didn't understand the corporate environment. So for that hour and fifteen minutes that they got to live, we *all* got messed up. The senior execs were lumped together as folks who 'didn't get it.' And the youngsters got put out because they couldn't perform. It's a mess; artists aren't developed, our artists are not on the road like they once were. We got Hoobie and Shoobie managing their cousin and they don't know shit! Instead of pairing up with a veteran, they stumble through it thinking they know it all." And it created a real Catch-22 for the young generation of executives, who stockpiled anger and hurt over being abandoned by the generations before them. They were running departments for the first time with no acumen, and very few elders willing to reach back and teach them.

Sharon was one of the few. One of her presidential secrets was to create multigenerational teams long before the media got hold of the conversation about how Baby Boomers and Gen Xers coexist at work. Unfortunately, it was not in the cards for the label that Jam and Lewis built.

"We had a good team, we had great producers. Good people and great records make for success. By the same token it was also the thing that was limiting and what got me fired," Sharon explains. "I wanted the next level: I wanted hip-hop, rap, and film. And it wasn't what Jimmy and Terry were about. They didn't like hip-hop and they never got into it. And for me it was all about the future. It was obvious hip-hop was here to stay. Times were changing; the 'good music' approach was not enough. We needed a mix of music in the house. We needed Mint Condition and Sounds of Blackness but I also needed some street flavor. They replaced me, changed the direction of the label, and the next level never happened."

....

F IS FOR FIRED
....

Once Sharon found herself outside the system, she learned the value of having "a good lawyer who will believe in you during the in-between times." She also got a cold, hard lesson in who her real friends were both in and outside the business. She highly recommends "finding that power mentor before you're sitting on the outside. At my level, the air gets really thin. The young people I had mentored who became VPs never asked about or looked out for me," she confirms, true to her theory about the impact of the generational split. "Ray Harris has doubled as a friend and mentor. I chose men outside of music, Barry Mayo, Charles Warfield; Dyana Williams was cool with me. During my transition I reached out to a lot of women, and the only one to respond was Cathy Hughes. That was an absolute surprise, and very painful after all the time I put in [to relationships]."

Painful is the very same word Lisa Cortes uses to describe the impact of being fired as the CEO of Loose Cannon Records, a division of Poly-Gram Records. She'd already experienced success as vice president of A&R within the PolyGram system for Mercury Records. During her four years in A&R, she gave poet and writer Reg E. Gaines (*Bring in 'da Noise, Bring in 'da Funk*) the first major-label deal the spoken word genre had seen. Cortes also signed and had commercial success with Black Sheep and Buju Banton prior to heading up her own imprint. As CEO of Loose Cannon, she had the vision to acquire the comedy albums of Redd Foxx and Richard Pryor. However, after two years in her new position, it became clear to her that the playing field was far from level for her as the sole African American woman label president among PolyGram's US and international divisions. Declining to comment in detail, Lisa puts things in terms so simple, you can do the math. "Here's what I *can* say: I filed a suit based on sexual and racial discrimination. And there's no PolyGram Records, but there is still Lisa Cortes. Or as Maya Angelou would say, 'and still I rise.'" Now head of production for Lee Daniels Entertainment, which she joined during production of the Oscar-winning film *Monster's Ball,* she's just fine not saying much more about the whole experience, as much as it would enlighten presidents walking in her footsteps.

"Revisiting is painful—and that's not gonna help me with what I gotta do. I feel I dealt with my integrity and my truth. There were people who had worked hard to get me where I was and I had to honor their spirits, because that's what I'm here for. Both my parents were dead when it happened, but they told me to *never* let myself be taken advantage of. And I may be a polite Yale graduate and speak nicely, but I ain't no punk! Staying anchored in hatred and negativity would not have allowed me to move; to be attracted to the light and to growth. These situations drive you to deep analysis, and you realize you never want to be in that place again. [I asked myself], *Are you going to stay with that story or take what you've learned and write a better ending?*"

Lisa's testimony demonstrates that even at the top levels of executive power, the same women who manage multimillion-dollar budgets and make global superstars experience levels of uncertainty. We all do. When it's time to choose what's next, *you* must steer your career, not life's circumstances. This will require consistent action on your part and will not be easy. It will however, be the difference between a humiliating fall and a triumphant return. Lisa made sure she had the latter and claimed her victory. "As humans, we're limitless in our capacity. What I love is that during that jour-ney there was a lot soul searching, dramatic changes I took upon myself to make in my life. I thought producing film was going to be where I made my mark, but I didn't know how I was gonna get to the next place," she recalls. "It didn't happen right away. I worked at it for a long time. When I made the transition from music to film, I went to film school. I took a production course because I knew I wanted to produce movies. I volunteered at film festivals and did music supervision on shorts to help people out. I started producing and editing EPKs [electronic press kits], which furthered my creativity and leveraged my music connections. You can't decide you want to do something and then just add water," Lisa jokes. "You have to educate yourself from ground zero."

In Lisa's view, having solid footing in the *process* of doing the business at hand and moving it forward is the cornerstone to success as a CEO. For her, it starts with the question of ownership, something that is often hol-low when it comes to label deals. "Are you really the CEO?" Lisa asks out loud during our interview. "If you don't own it, you're really not in complete control. It affects your process understanding. And if who you are and what you're doing are being misinterpreted, or not presented with a 360 view, then you're not fully realized in the job. Really own your shit. When you are hired by someone else, you don't. When you own it, your sense of self remains solid. You're not at the whims of others."

It is in this independent spirit that Lisa joined forces with Lee Daniels at a crucial time of transition for him from being a talent manager to direc-tor and producer. Lee's eye for talent, particularly in unexpected roles, put the Oscar in Halle's path. Lisa remembers her talks with Lee about casting Berry. "We discussed his desire to cast Halle for *Monster's Ball* because he was encountering resistance; and we talked about it a lot. He taught me to look at her in *Jungle Fever* as a crackhead, which was so convincing and pow-erful. It's about the material and the direction. If the diamond is there, it's there. You gotta put that diamond in the ring; put it in the right setting."

Having wrapped production on the film adaptation of Sapphire's best-selling novel *Push* in 2008 starring Mo'Nique, Paula Patton, Mariah Carey, Lenny Kravitz, and newcomer Gabourey Sibide, Lisa is clear that she's found her own right setting in the world of independent film. All that Oscar did for Lee Daniels was crystallize his mission. "After *Monster's Ball*, the stu-dios were a-calling. They wanted him to do material he found derogatory to

Black people. That experience was part of why the shift at Lee Daniels Entertainment was to raise the money ourselves and make the movies we want to make. The plus was the Oscar win propelled Lee to make the company's focus production. But it did not propel Hollywood to support the vision of a filmmaker who wanted to tell diverse, moving stories."

Lisa presents a powerful example to further illustrate that Lee Daniels is not crazy for rejecting Hollywood's Black box. "Tyler Perry has had three number one [box-office debuts] out of four films, and finally on the third one, the studio decides to support the films internationally," Lisa points out. Tyler Perry has box-office receipts, a huge fan base, and consistency on his side. Does the double standard come down to race at that point? Had white characters been at the center of his films, would he have enjoyed immediate support? "It's an arbitrary process, but *you* can't be," says Lisa. "You have to have your hustle on and stay focused on what you want to have happen, not what *they say* can happen." Like Lee Daniels or not. Hate Tyler Perry or love him. If nothing else, Lisa's comments merit taking notes.

....

CHALLENGE ACCEPTED

....

In chapter 2, Radio One and TV One founder Cathy Hughes explained how she persevered through thirty-two *nos* for her first loan to her first *yes*. That story is an incredible example of staring a challenge in the face without blinking. And yet, what I found more amazing still about Cathy is that her high school experience actually prepared her to be able to withstand thirty-two rejections long before she tried to own her first station. This challenge is one the business magazines never ask about because they tend to focus on the woman Cathy is today. Her journey as a teenage single mother is seminally relevant to who she she has become in the business world and, as such, can no longer go untold.

Cathy was the first African American to graduate from Duchesne Academy of the Sacred Heart in Omaha, Nebraska. She paints a picture of this bastion of faith and propriety where she studied Latin and French: "We wore stockings and gloves between classes and curtsied to the nuns. I was sponsored by a priest who was Eisenhower's roommate at West Point, but decided he could not kill. He felt the school needed to be diverse and crammed me down their throat." Cathy was a senior with a secret of the highest order, one that constituted a sin at the academy. She was pregnant in 1964. Now,

Cathy already stuck out as a student of color. When she started to literally stick out, the rumors threatened to swirl into a tornado. Fortunately, her school friends quelled them when confronted by the staff. "Their parents were major contributors to the school. 'She doesn't look pregnant to me,' they said," recounts Cathy. Their word and their net worth carried enough weight to close the conversation. "I was five months' pregnant when I graduated." As I listened to her tell this story, I tried to put myself in that scenario, being pregnant at a time when not even being sexually active before marriage was discussed publicly. Add to that the weight of representing an entire race on that campus. The more I imagined it, the more I understood what a fighter Cathy was. That fight in her has taken her to the head of the boardroom table, right along with her ability to discreetly play the game to her advantage. "I'm not trying to rush it. I don't think I'm a mogul. I am still a work in progress." Here are some pearls of wisdom for you CEOs in the making from the 'work in progress' with her own radio conglomerate and television network.

"Research first and foremost." And your level of formal education is not a determiner of your success, Cathy says. "If you can read, write, and count, you can be successful. Once these rappers who dealt drugs have the opportunities to count money legally, they flourish. Business-wise, it's no different [in media] than any other business. My number one priority is to enhance shareholder revenue. Keep expenses at a level where revenue generates a profit. It's the management, coordination, and development of staff that makes or breaks you. I wanted to be the boss so I could provide opportunities for others. If you take care of your front line, your bottom line will follow. When you're struggling—as all new businesses do—instead of obsessing about the money put that energy and commitment into your people. They will make the business profitable. Never get discouraged. Never did this country girl from Nebraska imagine that I'd ever be given a million dollars," she marvels after three-plus decades in business. "I did an interview with Jesse Jackson. He said, 'The only marriages that fail are the ones where the husband and wife give up on them.' It was like God was talking to me about business [through him]!"

Tomica Woods entered the music industry in 1989. The bright, ambitious receptionist for Tabu Records founder and CEO Clarence Avant "never wanted to be in the business" but wound up learning every label function by doing them all. "He had his hands in so many things. He was a consultant to so many people. He even had a publishing company, Avant Guard Music," Tomica recalls. "Four people worked there when I started. I would assist the promotion rep and call radio. I would be on the computer designing congratulatory ads. For a minute he was managing Johnny Gill, so I worked with Motown when he went on tour for his solo debut album." With all of this going on, Tomica had the presence of mind to do more than execute tasks. That opened the door to her becoming Clarence's right hand and mentee. "I would read everything that came through [the office], legal documents, contracts, correspondence, filing requests for publishing. He had three or four assistants who kept leaving. I volunteered for the gig. He agreed, on a 'trial basis.' And I was on that trial basis until I didn't work for him anymore," she laughs. "I got raises, of course, but whatever he dealt with, I was dealing with. I picked up his ability to be candid, not caring what folks thought about what I had to say. He gave me insight into the business, free information, and knowledge that would help me later on. He was a good mentor. I didn't realize how much I learned until I wasn't with him any-more. It was a lot easier when I worked for him," she reflects. "Sometimes I wish I still did. It was fun."

On March 26, 1995, the fun came to a traumatic end for Tomica. Her four-year relationship and recent marriage to Eric "Eazy-E" Wright ended when his life was claimed by AIDS. All at once, Tomica Woods-Wright becomes the pregnant widow of Eazy-E, CEO of Ruthless Records, the label that pioneered West Coast gangster rap, the guardian of a seminal force in hip-hop, and the executor of her late husband's estate. She barely had time to worry about her own health and potential exposure to the virus that took her husband's life, let alone the rumors and acrimony that ensued. What mattered most were the two promises she made to him in his last days. "I promised I wouldn't abort the baby. I told him I would not sell the company, and that I wasn't mad at him. I just wanted him to hold on," she explains on the verge of tears. "I never had time to grieve. All of a sudden I became Eric." She became a CEO out of love, duty, necessity. Regardless of what people had to say about their relationship, the most important people in it—she and Eric—made the choices together that would set her path in the business.

"The hardest thing is people being judgmental. The other mothers of his children ask why it's me and not them. No one can take away those memories or moments they [his other women] had with him. They can't be compared. But I had a personal obligation and commitment to my last words to Eric. I had to be responsible for my own children *and* the extended family." What is conveniently omitted from the story of Ruthless's survival is that as soon as Eazy-E passed away, Tomica was being urged to sell it, in some cases by the same parties who resented her inheriting it. She cites this as the time when she stood her ground most successfully amid a cacophony of doubt and questionable intent. "Everyone told me to sell Ruthless because they didn't think I would be able to run it," she says. "Friends, family, the baby mamas, they all said sell it. Everybody said I wouldn't be able to handle it. Sony was even offering money for it. I said no. I didn't really know the value then; I was [going by] my gut—and my promise. And I was still pregnant. There were still issues; we didn't know the worth of the company. But I wasn't here for the money. There were lawsuits and attachments—and all I could do was count on myself. Everyone was saying take the money and run. I didn't get here by myself; but in that moment if I hadn't followed my intuition I would not be here now. It stood the test of time and the company has grown in value—and it's still growing." While the label took a beating in the court of public opinion for slowing down on signing artists, Tomica literally took inventory of the label's publishing assets (approximately 350 songs spanning twenty years), organized them, and leveraged them to annual seven-figure profitability.

Tomica credits learning all the aspects of the business early in her career for giving her the confidence to step into her new power amid great resistance from her husband's label partners and all six mothers of his first seven children. (Tomica is the mother of his youngest two, but has pledged to help support all nine until they are at least eighteen.) "In our business we have some people who are the blind leading the blind. Don't go off of what you think you know. You want to put the research and the work in and get the facts, using resources that are readily available, then do the steps it takes to get it done. Don't just go through the motions."

Tomica echoes Sharon's sentiment about a crisis in executive leadership, but she also thinks some corporate consolidation is healthy as a means of eliminating incompetence.

"We have a generation retiring and dying off, so the new generation is coming into those shoes—but they are not handling the business and there's no one teaching them. The ones who do know the business are off into other areas. There's a generation *and* information gap. Fifty percent of me thinks consolidation is good. It bleeds out the extra luggage that didn't need to be in place; the skimming and unnecessary titles run down [the major label's] resources."

But what about the people who are casualties of layoffs and cuts made on paper—capable executives who knew what they were doing, even if the parent company didn't, chopping their heads seemingly at random? For Tomica, it comes back to "knowledge of the business, no matter what side of it you're on." It is important to gain knowledge in areas that were once unrelated but now impact your specialty directly, be they new media, intellectual property, or finance. If the days of a secure record industry job ever existed, they are now officially over. As the revenue and deal-making models change and grow, so must the players.

"The world is evolving and the indies will continue to be able to operate. The [music] business is just shifting and reconfiguring itself to fit today's world. It's slumping now, but it isn't going to disappear."

And based upon what Tomica has in store to preserve her late husband's legacy, Ruthless isn't going anywhere, either. The year 2008 marked the label's twentieth anniversary. Tomica's role as CEO is now as much about closure and honor for Eazy as it is about sheer perseverance against the worst odds imaginable while being underestimated at every turn.

"I had a life before I met Eric. [Neither the industry nor the media] knew my struggle, my education, my background—they had a preconceived notion of what I was about. It was either I'm not street enough, or I got here by lying on my back. They insulted my intelligence by judging a book by its cover. And then, for some I wasn't what they expected. I had gone to college for a short while, but my work experience was my education. Yet I was in court dealing with probate; people challenging his last words and demanding paternity suits. People tried to say I drugged Eric and took advantage of him on his deathbed; they even contested the will. Both Jerry Heller and Mike Klein were claiming they owned 50 percent of the label, which would mean I didn't exist. I was in court March 27, 1995, the day after he passed. It's been a long haul." She sighs.

"I am taking the time to solidify the legacy and accomplishments. There's more light shined upon his passing and how he passed, along with gangster rap. I want to look at the positives of him being an entrepreneur and opening a door through which so much was able to come. I want to set the facts straight and give proper credit and due justice to who he was, with proceeds going back to the HIV/AIDS cause. I want to get NWA inducted into the Rock and Roll Hall of Fame," she says with a smile. "I have interest in doing films. I would eventually like to go that route to bring closure to him. His legacy will continue to go on."

....

NEW RULES OF ENGAGEMENT
....

Tisherman Gilbert Motley Drozdoski (TGMD) president Vanessa Gilbert co-owns the talent agency that represented the late King of Movie Trailers, Don "In a World" LaFontaine, among other hugely successful voice actors including George Del Hoyo, Peter Cullen, Nick Tate, and Jean Smart. She has seen three decades worth of changes in the world of voice-over. She jumped into it as the assistant to legendary Hollywood agent Don Pitts at Abrams-Rubaloff. For Vanessa, the key to her success in dealing with per-sonalities was having a personality that clients appreciated. Sounds simple, but when interacting with heavyweights of that era like Casey Kasem, Gary Owens, and Wink Martindale, not to mention her own rainmaker clients, it's a subtle art that takes perfecting.

"I loved it from the first minute. We had a game show division—and they'd use us to play the games with them to test the flow of the shows. Don[Pitts] relied on me, so I carried a lot of responsibility. The clients really appreciated me. The lesson here is personality," she affirms. "Actors can be very sensitive and they want simple and clear details; if you go the extra mile, you get the details. Sensibility, sensitivity, and trust are very impor-tant." Vanessa would ask thorough questions of producers and vendors, then relay the answers to clients.

Her penchant for being honest, hardworking, and thorough made her a mainstay at the Tisherman Agency, where she represented LaFontaine and others. Vanessa was making it rain for eighteen years, generating hundreds of thousands of dollars in commissions for Tisherman. Toward the end of her tenure, things started to unravel, and Vanessa couldn't put her finger on why. As it turns out, Tisherman had been trying to sell the agency. "His wife would always say, 'Someday this will all be yours,'" she recalls. "But it was hurtful that he never even asked [if I was interested]." Well, Vanessa got over the hurt and got to strategizing on how she would buy out her boss. Here's how and why she became president.

"Kevin Motley and Ilko Drozdoski, my two partners and me, got all the money we could together and did this deal. I refinanced my house and we did a two-year payoff. We found out it was difficult to try to do so much in such a short time, but we did it," she remarks. "Kevin is from New York." Vanessa laughs. "He put together some of the biggest deals in the on-camera VO business. He got the bright idea for us to open an on-camera department. We hired two women—Sally Kadison and Jennifer Bernardi—who were both ready for their own opportunity. They book their asses off and they got great actors to come with them. And they now get a cut for the bigger picture. You have to profit-share," she emphasizes. "I could have gone anywhere because I had the biggest client in the world [Del Hoyo], and he was loyal to me. But I had been there done that and I wanted to be able to bring my dog to work if I wanted. Thank God the big clients stayed!"

They stayed because she would ride or die for them, and she refuses to waste an actor's time. She shares a story about learning just how disloyal networks can be when she as an agent is being client-loyal to a fault. "George Del Hoyo and Don LaFontaine were the voices of Fox. George was so loyal to Fox for so long, we would tell the other networks no because he was making five figures a week. Then, without giving us notice, Fox started to hire other voices. So we held out for them for a while. Then we did an upfront for ABC that was only supposed to be internal, but it ended up on-air. When Fox saw it they got pissed, but we only had a gentlemen's agreement [no written contract]. We weren't in violation, but when the networks want you they want you. And when they don't want you, they don't take your calls. I'm into compromise. But it's the absolute abuse I won't tolerate. Just be clear. Don't try to act like you're doing me a favor as you abuse me." Both actors continued to voice for Fox after the incident, a testament to their talent—and Vanessa's. "Voice-over is a small town; keep the bad vibes out of it," she says. "It's about the work."

She will also work with a producer to make something new, historic, or exciting happen. I can speak to this personally. As the creator of the 2007 BET Awards campaign and director of the VO for the promos, I wanted to hire Don LaFontaine. It was a first in that no white male actor had ever voiced the awards campaign. My attitude was, if we're gonna go there, it needs to be the biggest voice in the business. Not only was Don voicing nearly every big movie trailer of the summer, he was now a household face thanks to the Geico commercial where he boomed, "Payback . . . this time, it's for real!" Vanessa loved the concept of "The Main Event" and made it possible for Don to voice the promos. The awards was instantly on par with Hollywood blockbusters in perception, and in addition to being the number one telecast on cable the night it premiered, it garnered the largest African American households rating in the award show's history.[1]

And while I saw it as an opportunity for the campaign to reach a new level creatively, Vanessa saw it as a chance for Don to voice an awards show that he had never done before. Vanessa was just following her grandmother's advice, which she lives and works by: "Take what's showin'! If you see an opportunity you better fucking take it, Lord knows when the next one will pop its head in," Vanessa says. For me, there was no "next one" with Don. With his sudden passing in September 2008, a legend was lost. I am so glad I seized the opportunity to work with him.

"We're not all horrible and slimy. That cracks me up, but there [are many who] are, so [the misconception] makes sense. I try to be an honest person in this game," Vanessa offers. "What gets me off? The gratification of knowing I did the best job I can and the people I represent did the same thing."

Former Violator Management president and newly self-appointed CEO of her own venture, Monami Entertainment, Mona Scott-Young is on her way to a career as long standing as Vanessa's. As a pioneer in urban talent representation, she was in the trenches and on the forefront of aligning hip-hop icons with mainstream brands. She did it with Busta Rhymes for Mountain Dew and with Missy "Misdemeanor" Elliott for Gap. At a time when many corporations were skittish or sloppy about their execution, Mona was the quality control and the iron will that got deals done without sacrificing her artists' credibility. Which means don't look for her to play nice—or make nice all the time. "In life you don't get what you deserve. You get what you negotiate. Don't sit around thinking that just because you're doing right, others are doing the same. That's Lesson One. I've had to fight that battle for all my artists all the time," Mona says emphatically. "I'm always leveraging and maximizing the [client's] success potential against maintaining their integrity. I'm all for 'get it while you can,' but don't sell yourself in the process. I like to think that I'm strategic because I will tweak and mold something until it works so it has mutual benefit."

Mona's got a word for corporations looking to cash in on hip-hop's billion-dollar cachet. Artists need revenue more than ever as CD sales decline, but not at the cost of their relevance in their core communities and disciplines. "You can't cannibalize what I have to the point where you suck us dry, and spit out the bones," says Mona matter-of-factly. "I have to maintain my positioning as much for you the brand as for me. I'm your only path to the consumer you seek—and when I'm no good to my consumer, I'm no good to you, the corporation. When I look up and there's no one at the dance, you [as the co-brander] are not coming, either."

The understanding that all money is not worth taking leads Mona to debunk another myth. "The biggest misconception is that this is fast money—that you can come in, get it while you can, and get out," she states. "That exists and it does happen, but it doesn't lend itself to any kind of staying power for the people that subscribe to that mentality."

Mona will be the first one to tell you that deal making can be protracted, convoluted, and even nasty between the parties involved. Mona's presidential secret is to be "single-mindedly focused" with a touch of cutthroat. "It's not from intentionally going after someone; that's just what happens. Because I am single-mindedly focused on accomplishing the goal, there are casualties in that process at times. You can be ruthless with a level of integrity, even if it's [integrity] to self, the project, and staying true to the objective." So what does it take to close deals? Mona breaks it down from her point of view. "The ability to cut through clutter and stay focused on the goal. Part of the game that's played is to divert and confuse the issue. That's why things remain in play but don't yield any fruit financially. People get caught up in the process instead of the result."

········

REAL MONEY TALK

········

Mega-star stylist (Jamie Foxx, Halle Berry, and Quincy Jones) and Dawn to Dusk Image Agency founder and CEO Dawn Haynes has been about results since she was a little girl. Though she now advocates for some of the industry's most talented hair, makeup, and wardrobe stylists to get paid and keep working as their agent, she admits to being "in love with money" herself, and had a hustle for every season as a youngster. "My aunts and uncles would come for Thanksgiving dinners at my house. I would gather my cousins up and we would have a car wash. I would put each one of my cousins on a different car and I would negotiate with my aunts and uncles how much it was going to cost for us to clean their cars. Then I would break each one of my cousins off and take my percentage. In the wintertime I would sell Christmas trees with the local Christmas tree dealer. For Halloween I would sell pumpkins. I grew up in Playa Del Rey and in the summertime, I would go down to the marina and work on the yachts. Well, people who owned yachts normally have a lot of money, and they would pay you a lot of money to sand down the teakwood. So I got a crew and I created a yacht-cleaning business."

While Dawn loved the money she made, she enjoyed the freedom it afforded her that much more. "I was able to buy my mom things, go away for the weekend to ski, and I saw that the more I worked, the harder I worked, the more money I made, [the more] I was able to do the things I enjoy doing without asking anybody to help me."

Dawn's relationship to money has always been a healthy one where she controlled it instead of letting money run her. This is vital for success as an entrepreneur, particularly one who is responsible for the income of others as their representative. She admits to being disturbed by the material ethic of this generation of young women, who seem to operate in reverse: They get caught up with the result of having money instead of focusing on the process. This makes for bad business in any business, but in entertainment especially, given that it's so easy to start believing the hype you generate as someone who works in the world of imaging.

Dawn explains. "They want to live up to what the videos are showing them. It's disappointing to me because I feel like across the board right now young girls don't have high self-esteem. They're not looking into actually developing their own dreams; they want to live vicariously through someone else. Or they want to take, and they're willing to give their body up for a purse or a pair of shoes. It sickens me because if they just dedicated that amount of time to themselves, if they just focused on their own dreams, they could take care of their entire family." The disappointment Dawn expresses here may very well be a source of career conflict for women who work on videos as either producers or stylists for the models who transmit these imbalanced messages about beauty and body image. At Dawn's level, you can turn down the gig, or you simply aren't dressing the extras.

I had those same conflicting feelings myself working on the ads for the Bravehearts' hit single "Oochie Wally" while at Sony. Here were these rappers using a girls' playground game as the basis for a song about explicit sex, and here I was charged with helping it to get airplay. What I remember thinking with relief was *Thank God these projects are few and far between.* It hurt that my womanist views had no place on the page. I simply created a headline that didn't make matters worse. For sisters on the grind to pay the rent consistently doing this level of work, the question becomes: How much of a contribution to misogyny can you live with?

If your answer is *I've reached one disgusting job too many,* Dawn has some practical steps you can take to get your dreams in motion. Her first order of business after establishing her DBA (doing business as) Dawn to Dusk was going after other people's money. "Knowing that there were grants out there and that the government had things set aside for minorities, I studied all of that. And I filled out the applications and I did all the things that they asked me to do. Little by little, I got grants." She also kept her own books to save money in the beginning. Once she had expanded past the point where she could do it all herself and still manage to work as a stylist in her own right, she committed to being organized with her accounts, receipts, and invoices, and intimately aware of all her line items. "So now I'm at a place where I have an accountant and a business manager. Still, organization is important," she notes. "At the end of the year, you can pay someone five hundred dollars to do your books, or you can pay someone five thousand dollars to do your books depending on how organized you are and what you bring to the table. By doing things myself, I learned the more organized I am, the more I can save. I can walk into my accountant's office and spend an hour with him as opposed to four hours explaining things." And if we've learned nothing else from Ron Isley's jail sentence for tax evasion, we know that no amount of evasion is worth your career. By all means have sharp tax accountants to keep as much of your money as possible in your pocket, but there's a difference between working the system and red-flagging it to come after you for what they feel they're entitled to.

Dawn sheds light on the big-picture impact of doing the tax thing the right way. "I file taxes every year and I tell the truth. It's more important that you say you made a lot of money. I hear a lot of people say, 'Don't report everything or show a loss.' But why would I show a loss? If I have a loss, then no bank will ever support my company when I want to go get a loan or a line of credit. I want to show that I'm a good businesswoman and that every year I make more money; that my company grows. So when I decide to walk into a financial institution, I show years of taxes, [the returns] show growth, and my company shows growth."

....

SUMMARY OF SECRETS REVEALED

WHAT YOU THOUGHT YOU KNEW:

All that CEOs want from their assistants is someone who takes orders and messages.

WHAT YOU NEED TO KNOW:

"There is a support group solely comprised of my former assistants who meet once a week for therapy," Mona jokes. CEOs may wear assistants out, but the ones that last are the ones who are a mental and executive match for their bosses. "Assistants are invaluable because that's your infrastructure, your backbone, your support system. All the strategy in the world without implementation means nothing," Mona continues. "It makes more sense to me that assistants should be able to do much more than take calls and give messages. Having come from a small-company mentality, there needs to be a certain amount of overlap in terms of their skills. It always makes more sense to have people who can extend beyond their primary function."

WHAT YOU THOUGHT YOU KNEW:

I should follow everything a potential mentor says.

WHAT YOU NEED TO KNOW:

Dawn got some advice from talent manager Ramone Hervey that she was able to channel for the better, but not without considerable heartache. This is also a lesson for mentors: Be realistic, but also be careful about poking holes in the dreams of your mentees. Even if you mean well, you may never know how devastating an effect it can have.

Dawn gets specific: "You always want someone to say yes. But sometimes you get no for an answer; you have to wonder why and you just have to let it be. [Like] some of the advice that I got from Ramone Hervey, who at one point was married to Vanessa Williams and was an attorney himself as well as a manager. I was just coming out of college, Cal State University Long

Beach, I was applying to go to Pepperdine, and I was very excited about the law profession. Because I respected him and knew what he did, I came to him and said, 'Hey, listen, this is what my plans are, this is what my dreams are.' For whatever reason, he basically told me that [law] would not be anything where I would find success, and there weren't very many African American women who were successful in the entertainment industry as an attorney. I'm happy where I am; my life has been amazing so I thank him in a way. I'm peaceful with it now, but at the time it really shook me. I was very depressed and didn't understand why he would say that to me."

WHAT YOU THOUGHT YOU KNEW:

I have to know exactly where I'm headed and how to get there to make it to the top.

WHAT YOU NEED TO KNOW:

Lisa Cortes didn't know how to become a producer, so she went and found that out, then acted on what she learned. It's okay to be uncertain about the future as long as you're willing to get clear as you move forward. She did so by immersing herself in the world of production, never doubting that she could make it. Her approach came out of her early years at RUSH Management/Def Jam Records working with Russell Simmons and Rick Rubin back when they were both very hands-on. "I learned about devotion from them; their singular commitment and focus," she acknowledges. "The word *no* does not exist. It is someone else's reality. There were too many forces that didn't want hip-hop to happen! If they ever stopped to doubt themselves, [Def Jam] and its far-reaching legacy could not have happened."

CHAPTER 10

Have Passport, Will Prosper: Going Global

....

Ebonnie Rowe ✳ Fatima Ouanssaidi ✳ Karine Plantadit ✳ Les Nubians ✳ Sasha Dees ✳ Thami Ngubeni ✳ Vivian Scott-Chew

....

We are so limitless. In this lifetime it would be wonderful if we could only focus on how limitless we are. Whatever you want to be, it's beyond beyond.

—KARINE PLANTADIT, DANCER-ACTOR

The world gets smaller with every click, page view, and download. Artists and films are being released on one worldwide date to avert piracy. Television shows like *America's Next Top Model, Survivor,* even *Pimp My Ride* have taken their concepts to international locales and found audiences intrigued by cultures as they clashed or found common ground. As English becomes the language of the business world, American offerings are more appealing than ever. Now that hip-hop has recalibrated the way the world hears music, the music and its culture of urban lifestyle have crashed through barriers of race, class, and gender sensibilities.

America's creative exports have drawn foreign nationals with a passion for expression to its shores. They don't want to be citizens, but they mean business and utilize the entertainment meccas and infrastructure of the United States to their full advantage. So it is fitting that Americans are picking up on that cue and turning their skills into profit abroad. This chapter will check in with Americans who work all over the planet, as well as

women from Canada, the Caribbean, Europe, and Africa who are workin'
it in America and bringing their knowledge home to empower and enrich
their communities.

Women of the world, read the testimony and paths of your international trailblazers. And to my American sisters, this is your global wake-up
call. Just as the digital era has dropped the world into your lap(top), the
future of our business lies across our borders and oceans. America is not
the only place to make money. The world's emerging entertainment markets
can benefit from your contributions while you benefit financially, culturally, and even spiritually. It's all in the approach. The time for us to learn
from one another and get paid together has arrived.

....

THE REBELS
....

Born to French and Central African parents, Alvin Ailey dance legend
turned Broadway actress Karine Plantadit (*kah-RHEEN PLAN-ta-dee*) was
turned out by Debbie Allen way over in Cameroon, and they'd never even
met. "I saw a bootleg tape of *Fame*. That's when I realized dance had school
and was a real profession. So I moved from Africa to France because I wanted
serious training. Once I was in school in France, I found out about Alvin
Ailey [American Dance Theater]." Karine was studying dance in Cannes.
Not coincidentally, Ailey was touring Europe and performing in Paris. If
Fame was Karine's introduction to Black dance, Ailey was her first crush,
one she pursued relentlessly. "My mother saw the show and the next day she
sent me tickets for the flight and the show. It was clear from the day I saw
[Ailey]. At fifteen, I realized I was going to New York to be in the company.
I was already finishing school early so my trick at the time was to pass the
national exam so I could go to New York for a year. At seventeen, I went to
New York on my own. My dedication to my art was so big, it didn't matter
where I was. If Ailey had been in Thailand, I would have gone there."

Karine took a huge risk leaving the foundation in dance she'd laid in
France by coming to the States as a teenager. And while she had the natural gifts of an African dancer packaged in the body and face of an African American, Ailey represented a culture shock all its own. Though she
enrolled in the Ailey school, Karine's blessing came in the form of Judith
Jamison, founder of the Jamison Project, the company she joined. "I found
out about the audition and got hired right away," she recalls with a smile.

"Each choreographer comes with their own planet. You can inhabit it or not. I was born on the Jamison planet," she explains. "Judith didn't know me from Adam, and she served as a mentor for me through dance. She guided me, pushed me to do it better . . . [gave] me compliments or [didn't] give them, all through movement. I will never be able to stop saying thank you to her for that."

She also had Jamison to thank for smoothing her entry into the country. Anyone who is not a naturalized American citizen living or working in America will tell you that immigration laws are a bitch, and they've only become more stringent and obtuse in post-9/11, Patriot Act America. They become as much a part of your training as your art. Karine was fortunate to have a renewable student visa as an Ailey attendee, but she knew she would need professional help to remain in the country. "Things have changed a lot since I entered to come to Ailey. I hired a lawyer, and my next move was to get a green card. I wasn't going to get married to do it, so I created a file to establish that only I could do what I did for the company. My file was initially denied and I had to appeal. The rules of immigration are impossible to figure out and are almost subjective. They require navigation." They also require skilled immigration attorneys who can wriggle through the system and are aware of its ever-changing requirements. Let foreign nationals who've had success with their lawyers refer you, then be prepared to pay and wait through every step of a very complex process.

Karine followed Jamison to the Ailey Company when Jamison was appointed artistic director. When Karine's creative planet moved, her career path began to shift as well in ways she had not anticipated. She talks about finding her zone with Ailey, which took three years of her seven-year tenure.

"For my first two years, Ailey didn't know what to do with me. I may have looked African American, but as soon as I speak or dance, you know I'm not. I didn't have the cultural reference for Ailey's historical suites and works, so my aura was different. We know the body doesn't lie. It took me a little longer to get the pieces; it had to do with my maturity as well. In the beginning, I was young. I needed to sit and learn though I was dying to dance. I got to watch stars of the company who were fifteen-, twenty-year veterans and had worked one-on-one with Ailey [himself]; a lot of what they gave me just by dancing was a master class."

As she watched and learned, Karine found her rhythm inside this new dance culture of which she was now a part. "When the more modern pieces came into the repertoire, I was more attractive to the choreographer. There was something about me at that moment that was able to be molded into my third year," she reflects. "The second year, I was cracking my shell. My biggest break was with Donald Byrd's piece *Dance at the Gym*. He saw he could use me in a way I could understand. We were all of a sudden speaking the same language."

And the conversation went well until she was called into being as an artist on other levels by her own desire to expand. She had spent her entire career working to fly with Ailey, and in her eighth acclaimed, exuberant, and grueling year on tour around the world, her departure time had come. "The creative team sees your color and they want to use it a certain way. If they see orange and need orange, I become the Orange Girl. I wanted to use all my colors, not just orange. It was an emotional choice. My curiosity was kicking. As a dancer, learning how much of an actor I was also shifted things for me."

Karine obeyed the shift and headed for the Great White Way. Her mastery of African and modern movement landed her a role in *The Lion King*. As further testament to what a journey a career can be, Karine—an accomplished dancer from a world-renowned company—was faced with yet another culture shock: the demands of Broadway auditions, rehearsals, and performance. Fine dancers with Broadway dreams be advised: Check your ego at the stage door. Karine elaborates: "Many dancers might have an ego about the level of training they undergo for dance—and not be fully prepared for the totality of Broadway stage performance. For a dancer in a company that desires to move into theater, there is a way of approaching the art form that has to change completely. We are used to using our body as an instrument. It has been created for your own self-expression since you were young, especially for women, usually from five years old. What was the best of me was not what was asked to be front and center. In the theater world, the dancing is lessened; it comes after the acting and the singing.

"A [Broadway] dance audition can last three hours while they see if you can vibe in their planet," she continues as she outlines the process. "Then you go into a rehearsal period where the singing [and] acting are all coming together—but the dancing is last. We did one-eighth of what we were doing in auditions in rehearsal. We are now moving puppets, learning Zulu, and singing. That was another time to sit and learn. In any transition there is a moment for sitting. It is a gift to realize this, so you don't fight against yourself."

Not surprisingly, Karine's experience with the vision of Julie Taymor and the acceptance of her own newfound abilities as a Broadway star aligned for a cinematic debut. She won the role of a Parisian chanteuse who shares a bed with embattled artist Frida Kahlo, portrayed by Salma Hayek. She relied heavily on Taymor's direction for her first film role, where she not only had to be naked but also had to perform a love scene with Salma Hayek. No pressure.

Karine giggles at the memory. "My husband was possessed that I was going to Mexico to make love with Salma Hayek! I was hearing *action* for the first time and going to bed with a woman on camera for the first time as well. I was unveiling physically and emotionally. Because I trusted Julie completely, I was able to go into that space. I trust who she is as a woman and her voice as an artist," she states, elaborating on how Taymor guided her through another wave of culture shock. "Julie knew I didn't understand the extent of what I was doing. She showed me where the camera was placed, the technical parts of the set, and what the audience was seeing on the monitor. Once I saw that, the character was not the issue so much as what I would do spatially. I had to reduce the space but keep the intent and focus of emotion of it intact. And it was my honor to play inside that vision."

Karine has come across three continents to realize her own vision as a master of dance and stage while blossoming as an actor in film (*Chicago, Across the Universe*) and, most recently, in television as a commercial actor. Her travels into unfamiliar territory demand that she trust herself, the only constant in an ever-changing career. Karine's greatest challenge has been that of negotiating her chameleon-like power as an artist without sacrificing herself. She poses the one question she has yet to answer fully. "What is the line where you become nothing and nobody, become what you think they wanted—and on the other side, are liquid enough to accept it, dance with it, create with it? I am still learning about how to do it. Learning to remain whole while being able to offer. [Learning] how I can be transformed without losing who I am."

Though there is no blood relation, Karine's Cameroonian sisters Celia and Helene Faussart have also spent their careers extending the boundaries of rebellion with their creativity. Known professionally as Les Nubians, Celia and Helene have become the most successful female R&B/soul act of

African descent in France, a nation where recording artists of color can easily be ghettoized under the banner of world music. Celia attributes this to the exclusive, nepotistic nature of France's music industry, one that mirrors the colonial consciousness of the European's dominance over the African. Her description of France's modus operandi can give a new appreciation for the American system, which, by comparison, is much more accessible for artists.

"In France, the business is very oligarchic. The people who are in it are all related," she says. "So doing business is about whether you are an outsider or an insider. As the average French person has very little knowledge of the industry, it's easy for the labels and managers to screw the artists. It's a pity. There are eight [prominent] entertainment lawyers in the whole country. So if you want to take them to court, they discourage it. They get paid from the labels more than they do from [representing] artists, so as an artist you're very much on your own," she asserts. This dynamic is compounded for artists of color who cannot rely on their music icons for guidance. Sounds exactly like what Black music executives experience stateside: a gap of information widened by the hoarding of knowledge.

"[French] Black artists don't communicate and exchange information about their experiences in the business, so each generation has to start afresh. You have to force them to tell you even a hint of how the business works," Celia laments. "They've been through a lot of things, so they blame themselves. They view it as a personal failure instead of seeing it for the game that it is, where the more you play, the more tricks you learn and the easier it is to win."

At fifteen, Celia was studying to be an ethnomusicologist. Helene, her elder by four years, was in pursuit of an intellectual property law degree with the goal of organizing music publishing for African musicians. At first, the Faussart sisters had not planned on becoming Les Nubians; they simply enjoyed singing. However, putting together a band at their young ages proved difficult, so they chose to perform a cappella at small venues in Bordeaux. Neither of them banked on being spotted by a female emcee named Casey, who created enough buzz among industry players to generate interest in the duo. One indie-label executive named Elpidio Sitty became the girls' manager and got them a spot on a Virgin France jazz compilation album called *Jazz à Saint-Germain*.

"Thierry Planelle was A&R for Virgin France. He came to see us recording that song, and he asked us to do an album on the spot," Celia recalls. "My mother would never sign for me; the family wanted us to stay out of the business. We asked Thierry to wait seven months so I could sign the deal myself at eighteen." This was the start of Les Nubians' own French Revolution with their stunning debut, *Princesses Nubiennes.*

Helene elaborates: "We were quite brilliant in how we could, for our first record, be in control of so many things for our album: artistically, the cover of the album, the track listing, what we put out as our message. A lot of artists didn't have that much control. We had huge support from our A&R, and that control is the most important thing," she emphasizes. The album was released in June 1998 to little fanfare. The ladies were visually, lyrically, undeniably self-proclaimed "Afropean" soul singers, and it was a shock to the French. "We weren't politically correct; we were talking about being pro-Black, and we were perceived as being aggressive. And because of what we represented, doors were closing off to us."

As the doors to the French industry closed, Les Nubians were welcomed by an overwhelming organic response to their album in the United States. Omtown/Higher Octave licensed the album for American release in September of the same year, calling upon ShoreFire Media to blitz the album at college radio and service the video to BET and MTV. The subsequent radio and video play led Virgin America to pick up the album's distribution. Celia describes the slow but steady build they experienced in America. "By January 1999, we had sold eighty thousand units in the US and we were appearing to support the album. A year later we were at over three hundred thousand sold, with one single video. We ended up getting nominated for two Lady of Soul Awards and it was so unexpected and beautiful that we won [Best New Artist, Group or Duo]. We couldn't believe it because we were singing in French!"

Helene had an epiphany about the duo's future with Virgin France in the wake of the success the young rebels experienced abroad. They had signed the typical French new-artist deal, which was less than favorable. After becoming America's most successful French-language album in more than a decade, it was time for Les Nubians to renegotiate. "That deal said [Virgin] got 50 percent of all sales outside France, and we were mainly selling outside. I realized we'd have to organize our next deal differently. So I asked our manager to get us a new contract where we would get our own publishing, and have our royalty shares change," says Helene. Easier said than done.

"We tried to negotiate our publishing shares so we could be co-publishers of our next albums, and the label began to get really angry. They took so much time to sign, I refused to go into the studio without the signed contract." Well, it's more accurate to say that the ladies refused to go into the studio for Virgin without a new contract.

Their stalemate with Virgin did not quell their desire to record. In the spirit of Chuck D and Public Enemy, these rebels without a pause created their own label, Nubiatik, and produced *Echos,* a spoken word compilation that sparked the live poetry movement in France. "We knew our fans would appreciate it. Spoken word at that time was not something France had; there was no spoken word scene. We knew that we could do an album with poets without spending a lot of money. And in the process, we did a documentary to show France what [spoken word is]. MCM [the French equivalent of PBS] aired the show for the entire year of 2000. Then spoken word blew up in France. I received thousands of e-mails from kids who were doing it in their bedroom and [because of us] now knew they could do it." Les Nubians' documentary led to their being commissioned to curate the first three seasons of *Slam Opera,* a live event that brought poets into the spotlight for the first time, among them award-winner Grand Corps Malade.

As architects of the "slam" movement in France with an album they produced, Les Nubians approached Virgin France as owners with a licensing deal. Now, being outspoken self-defining young singers is cute and even tolerable. But coming to the table as creators and licensors of content was another proposition. What Helene thought would be a positive shift in their label relationship turned into a powerful lesson. "We came to them [with *Echos*], and offered them a licensing deal since we produced it. They loved it. And I was a bit naive, thinking they would be my natural partner since we did the first album together." The label responded by demanding co-production rights for an album it did not commission. Les Nubians rejected their counter immediately, but the label persisted. "Virgin sent co-production contracts, and I refused them," states Helene, still incredulous at what happened next. "And worse, they sent samplers of the project without our authorization to test it and see how the journalists would react. They tried to release an album later and called the same poets we had on our album—and it didn't work because it was crap and no one could eat it. So all this shows me that Virgin France was not good for us, and not our partner," Helene reflects.

"We were in talks for four years. That's when you start to say, *It's racism because they just want to kill my business*," adds Celia, echoing her sister's sentiment. The pair continued to perform to earn their living, and the clamor for a new studio album began.

"Eventually the [label's] PR reps started saying the reason it took so long to make a new album was because I had kids, which was so disgusting to me," Celia insists. "That was unacceptable to me when I was making so many sacrifices. We were still touring in Africa, [promoting in] Brazil, going into new territories for Virgin France. And we are now in 2002 and ready to do a new album, and we are unable to move forward because the new contract is not complete," Celia continues. "I was touring with a month-old baby breast-feeding in one hand!" This sent Helene and Celia into a less diplomatic mode for their next round of negotiations with Virgin France. Their career sales and hard stance paid off for *One Step Forward,* their sophomore studio album. "I had hired a new manager to get a new contract," says Helene. Their first contract's advance was for seventy-five thousand francs; this one offered Les Nubians a million euros and a co-publishing split, precisely the victory they had envisioned. "He was [a] shark, so it worked. They sent us a contract we could sign for the second album, and we got back in the studio." The album garnered two Grammy nominations in 2003 and sold more than two hundred thousand copies in the United States from the release of one single.

When the ladies met to discuss going to the awards with the label, they were handed the proverbial straw that broke the camel's back. Celia recounts the meeting that led to their departure from the label. "They tell us that our categories are not on-camera, so they won't pay for us to go. So now we stand up and walk out. And this is the last obvious proof you don't want us to do well. We went anyway. And it took eighteen months to get out of the deal," she says with a mix of disbelief and disgust. "We released *Echos* through a US company a few years later." The trials of this top-selling, Grammy-nominated duo give you a window into how difficult being a recording artist is. You can imagine what it looks like when you have neither sales, name value, nor acclaim to use as leverage.

Celia believes that being women in control of their collective identity as both French and Cameroonian and being determiners of their own destiny as businesspeople affected their major-label experience. "If we were male, it would have happened differently," she insists. "They would have talked to us man-to-man, even without a manager. We say we are French and we fight for the part of our identity they don't want us to represent. And since we are not world music artists, we're not their type. They want to tell you what you can and should say about your own culture! What is African about our music? Us. And that's enough."

....

THE TRANSPORTERS

....

As a daughter of Barbados and Canada, Ebonnie Rowe splits her time between the Caribbean island and the T-Dot, Toronto. She came into the record business from a unique place: as a youth advocate who used music to reach the students in her mentoring program Each One Teach One. "At the time, we had a 60 percent dropout rate for high-school-aged Black youth. I also noticed that when I'd have events for the program . . . there was a hostility of the young men toward the girls and toward me. It was imported rage; they'd watch the videos and just decide for no good reason they'd be ignorant and angry, too. I saw that it wasn't just what these girls were telling me; it was a much broader issue. I knew music had the ear of the youth, and the power and reach of music attracted young people. I patterned the program in a very specific way so it was unlike the others," Ebonnie says. "I didn't want to make the kids feel like here was this woman in a suit saying, *You're doing wrong, let me show you the way.* I dressed in jeans and Chuck Taylors and went on Much Music (our MTV) to reach the youth. I just wrote or called them and got on their programs to talk about mine."

Since American music influenced them so heavily, and Toronto in the early 1990s was a burgeoning urban music industry market with limited resources, Ebonnie went where the action was, the US of A. Her mission was to get the knowledge, bring it back, and apply it in the interests of the youth in her program.

"Hardly any of the things I've wound up doing were learned in school. I attended seminars to learn: *Gavin, VIBE* Music Seminar, Jack the Rapper, New Music Seminar, Canadian Music Week, North by Northeast. I went to How Can I Be Down? in Jamaica and met Younglord, but no education was going on there." She laughs, describing a fertile time in the new urban music business propelled by hip-hop's foray into the mainstream. "The best thing that came out of them for me was the networking because everything was happening south of my border. So being in the mix and the energy of those players was great. Lauryn Hill was sitting next to me in panels. Suge Knight was a panelist. Puffy was sitting by the pool. This was before everyone needed protection. I was standing next to Aaliyah at a *VIBE* Music Seminar after-party and she was thirteen! Now it's all so plastic. Everyone's overpolished, with attitude and egos. No one felt like they were above anyone else. Now everyone's roped off in some VIP area.

"Chuck D was talking about this weird thing called the Internet that we needed to pay attention to thirteen years ago; the street team was a new thing; Puffy and Will Strickland were instrumental in that change of promoting artists. I was the only Canadian woman of color at most of these events," she recalls. "It was a new world."

Ebonnie started out responding to a crisis among black youth in Canada. After fourteen years of importing the knowledge and wisdom of her American counterparts, she is credited with developing Toronto's urban music industry as the founder of PhemPhat Productions (no relation to Phat Farm or Baby Phat). Her company spawned two seminal franchises for the advancement of Canadian women in entertainment: Honey Jam, an annual women's talent showcase, and the Women in Urban Music Seminar. Providing a performance outlet for women was critical, but it became clear to Ebonnie that she also had to educate women artists because men in the industry had other things in mind. She was not only on the receiving end of blatant sexism from her male counterparts herself, but also saw how men would come to her showcases to pounce on women.

"Unscrupulous men would tempt them with deals and midnight trips to record songs. I saw this darkness among the men; then I'd experience a weird vibe as [one of the only women] at clubs. The people I asked for guidance and info from were all men, and I would get approached in a sexual way. And when I would refuse, they would call me bitch or tell other people I was a lesbian. I didn't want other women to go through that. They were bright-eyed and eager and I felt like the Mother Bear, so I wanted to educate them about the business. I created a seminar to remove the sexual harassment casting-couch mentality from the process."

In addition to spotlighting female emcees and DJs, Honey Jam's standing-room-only lineups served as the launchpad for singers like Jully Black and Nelly Furtado, who were both discovered on the Honey Jam stage. "The girls would be too embarrassed to demonstrate or mention their ability to rhyme or DJ. The moment when these women owned the stage was so positive. PhemPhat has directly contributed to the breakers, DJs, and emcees who are women that come out of Canada. We showed girls that it can be done. The artists tell me they do it because they saw it done at Honey Jam and knew they could, too. The guys would come to Honey Jam standing front and center and just staring, like they were at a zoo. They thought the [girls] were pretending to scratch like there was a tape running and they were mix-syncing."

Nothing brings out overt sexism like women standing up for themselves in full control of their expression and their environment. Ebonnie's events and connections to the industry were immediately targeted for sabotage. PhemPhat experienced "an almost violent backlash from certain men in the industry that I would have never expected," she notes. "I actually had male rappers come to my show, get in my face, and call me the C. DeLores Tucker of Canada. These men contacted labels and told them not to support what we do." She was confronted with how unwelcome women really were to the industry in her city, and had a choice to make about whether she would go hard or go home. "For many years, I was a people pleaser brought up to make sure everyone liked me. And here I was going into the arena that no one invited me to. I created my place the way I wanted it to be, and they took offense. It made me ask myself, *What am I made of? Am I gonna sit down and cry?* And I did, but at home, because I don't like aggression. It wounded me, and was very sad, but it also emboldened me. I wasn't going to let it stop what I was going to do. I was shaken, but not stirred."

So when it came to dealing with men, Ebonnie did what so many of us find we must do to win at the game of the entertainment business, no matter what country we're playing in. She chose to go hard, literally. "I developed a rep as a hard-ass. I'd be a bitch. I created a hard exterior on purpose. I needed to be taken seriously because I was a woman, and I didn't want to be seen as a groupie. You're nonthreatening if you're the woman these men would want to sleep with. I wasn't going to bat my eyes, use feminine wiles, wear super-tight clothes, or play that game." Ebonnie had her armor on, and she learned a few clandestine survival tactics for dealing with the boys. "When they requested to meet at ten, I'd very specifically say to them, 'Oh, for breakfast? That'd be great.' I didn't want them to know where I lived; I made sure they knew there was a finite end to the meeting. I would skew meetings toward the daytime so we never met at night. And e-mail made things easier, too; I could reply to calls via e-mail and keep them out of my business or from calling my house. I may have lost opportunities, but I needed to do that for myself. I definitely had a real chip; something I had to prove. They think that we at Honey Jam are anti-men because we're pro-women, walking around with nutcrackers looking for balls to break every day of the week—but we only do that on Tuesdays and Thursdays," she jokes.

All the nut cracking has paid off powerfully, both for Ebonnie and for the women of Toronto. In 2005, Toronto's YWCA conferred upon her its Woman of Distinction Award. PhemPhat has expanded to become the PhemPhat Entertainment Group. Ebonnie plans to bring Honey Jam into Canadian living rooms as a performance-driven reality series, and to offer educational development opportunities to Honey Jam performers. Her mission to smooth the path for women was fortified by the sudden loss of three of her best friends, all Black women in their twenties in the business: Renée, a model-painter; Maxine, a hairdresser; and Paula, an event planner and boutique owner. "My closest friend [Paula] committed suicide by throwing herself before a subway train. They had so much promise. I wanted to continue doing things they would have wanted to be part of. I wanted my life to count for something. I didn't want to leave the planet without leaving a legacy behind." Ebonnie Rowe can most definitely check the legacy thing off her list.

A content and business development executive for the production company Bounceback Media, Fatima Ouanssaidi is a Moroccan woman who calls London home while doing business primarily in America and South Africa. She completed her studies at the University of Bristol and earned a law degree by the age of nineteen. After all that accelerated study, she found that law was neither her passion nor her calling. "I did an internship at a big-city law firm in London and after six weeks there over the summer I realized my personality was not suited to be a fuddy-duddy," she reflects. "My intention was always to become a lawyer but I realized that I didn't want the hours or the lifestyle of that career."

The hours of a guest list girl in London's hottest, most exclusive clubs were more Fatima's speed. She went from deeming people worthy of the VIP section to being assistant manager for Creation, Brighton's premier nightspot, where she eventually put on events of her own. "I became [the manager's] right-hand woman, counting money and advising him on who to book. We did the MTV Lick parties with Trevor Nelson, Cosa Nostra, and garage nights, which was popular at the time. I started putting on successful nights of hip-hop, soul, and R&B; or we'd do fashion shows with performances, and nights with well-known DJs," Fatima enthuses.

Planning themed nights and booking talent like spoken word artist Metis sparked her inner marketer, leading her to plan a historic event for the BAFTAs, which are the British equivalent to the Academy Awards. She was hired as the marketing representative for Cinnamon Films, the production company helmed by BAFTA-winning director Alrick Riley. "I put on the premiere of his short film, generating a lot of press for it. Cinnamon Films [then] put on the first-ever event celebrating Blacks in film at the BAFTAs in 2007." Top-notch awards shows have a tendency to propel careers, and Fatima's took off soon after the event.

"Bounceback CEO Colin Gayle asked me to be his director of business development, building the programming bridge between the United States and post-apartheid South Africa, which is ripe for new ventures in entertainment. I help Colin create programs that wrap American content with African hosts and sensibilities. It's a fresh market, and people are open to ideas and new programs. I get to travel to the States to shoot [shows] for South Africa," says Fatima. "I'm associate producer for a program we're shooting featuring [first-ever Black Emmy-nominated actress] Brenda Ngxoli. It's a huge deal for South Africa and the SABC network. The challenge is to get Americans to understand this whole new world of opportunity. We know Africa is the next China, and the potential there is huge. It's exciting to be part of this new business. For them, it's not as big a deal."

With entertainment revenues down sharply in the first decade of the new millennium, Americans better recognize! Fatima's path to becoming a global businesswoman started with her passport. If a career outside the United States appeals to you, it's time you boarded a transcontinental vehicle of some kind and saw the world. Read: seeing the world as a *resident,* not a tourist. This has been the best education for Fatima, who believes the key to doing business abroad is to "respect their world, not coming in with an attitude that West is best." Fatima was very creative about traveling the world and doing so while interning or spending very little money. And while it is not imperative that you speak other languages, it certainly increases your value. Fatima was able to leverage speaking three languages and her educational background into a three-month internship in New York with an ambassador to Morocco. But the States was just one of many stamps in her passport. "I speak French, English, and Arabic. Having to learn the language of the people changes your view," Fatima insists. "I knew whatever I did had to be an international job, mixing with international people. I took a year off after university and traveled the world. I waitressed and worked in clubs all summer and saved all my money, lived on my cousin's couch, then went to Brazil for six months, Mexico for a month, saw Europe, North Africa. It tested what kind of person I was, my strength, my ability to do things on my own. It was about personal life experience."

....

THE BRIDGE BUILDERS
....

Screenwriter-producer, spiritual author, actor, and radio personality Thami Ngubeni has mixed American formal education in film and television with hands-on work experience in her native South Africa to create a dynamic career that both heals and entertains, all before turning thirty-five. "The experience–academia relationship is symbiotic. There is no substitute for experience, but an academic qualification can give you the confidence you need to be bolder and more daring. You tend to trust yourself more," she notes. Thami studied film and television at the University of California at Los Angeles and wasted no time putting what she learned to use back home. "Even after I had studied film and TV, I was still photocopying scripts and making tea for everyone. But it's important to pay your dues," she affirms. "It's in the seemingly menial tasks that we hone our skills and lay a solid foundation in whatever field we wish to excel in." She eventually secured acting roles, playing in the popular soap opera *Generations* and the medical drama *Jozi H*. She worked as a writer-producer for Fremantle Media for seven years before establishing her own production company, Thamzin Media. In 2005, she was part of the bridge that brought the American hit series *The Apprentice* to South African viewers on SABC (South Africa Broadcast Company) as its producer. "Producing *The Apprentice: SA* was a rare opportunity of watching the dynamics of the business world unfold right in front of my eyes," Thami reflects. "In this microcosm was the competitiveness, strategizing, forming of alliances, betrayal, planning, management, leadership and lack thereof that is at the center of all business interactions."

You'd think that after that show wrapped, she'd be eager for a break. Instead Thami released a book on spirituality and self-love called *My Sacred Spaces* the following year, to wide acclaim. She extended the conversation of her book to *The Sacred Space,* a weekly radio program on relationships and creating life balance for Metro FM.

She is a beacon of inspiration for the women of South Africa, whom she describes as "ambitious and driven by a desire for a holistic success that encompasses their professional and personal lives." Sound familiar? The key difference for our South African sisters is that their pursuit of happiness is taking place in what Thami calls "our teenage democracy. We're still in the early days," she says. "We have yet to find that perfect balance that fulfills our needs and nurtures our individual talents and ambitions while fostering a common vision for family." The lesson of self-sufficiency is one confronting South Africa's professional women en masse like never before. "We generally cannot rely on the stability and security of a marriage. Many young, dynamic women are single or divorced. Along with our economic transformation, we are undergoing a cultural metamorphosis. Relationships just aren't what they used to be." While this realization can be sobering, it represents a powerful opportunity for the women of South Africa, who are taking full advantage. "South Africa is one of the most progressive countries when it comes to empowering the previously disadvantaged—and women are on the top of that list," says Thami. "They are running their own businesses and heading large corporations."

Thami is right there with them, securing financing and producing content as the owner of Thamzin Media, right down to her book, released by Thamzin Publishing through Pengiun. But wait. There's more. From May 2007 to July 2008 she was editor of *O, The Oprah Magazine South Africa*. In her newest role, Thami built more bridges, these among the many races and cultures of a nation healing wounds centuries old, reconciling the injustice of apartheid in every area of life. Media is no exception.

"When *O, The Oprah Magazine* first hit the shelves in SA, it entered to serve a market that was historically divided along racial lines. There were 'Black' magazines and 'White' magazines. For the first time, here was a magazine beyond race and cultural boundaries. It spoke to the essence of who we are as women, what we yearn for and struggle with. Here was a magazine that said, 'At the core of who we are, there is more that binds us than separates us. We are more than our skin color,'" Thami notes. As a steward of one of the world's most successful print properties, she had her hands full, and she put it all on the pages of *O.*

"We made sure that we had a good racial and cultural mix, because inasmuch as pain is pain and triumph is triumph, in a country as culturally diverse as South Africa there will be experiences that are not shared—like being involved in a polygamous marriage, choosing religion over love, or deciding to allow your daughter to undergo virginity testing. I can distinctly remember the overwhelming reaction we got from mothers when we ran a story about the relationship between Black dolls and raising Black girls with a healthy self esteem. We dealt with issues of self-identity across the board, and those really go beyond race, because white women also have self-identity issues. Our models and fashion and beauty sections also reflected our diverse demographics."

Having worked and studied across continents, Thami shares several tips for doing business globally for those at the entry level and for professionals who seek broader horizons. Whether you're new to the world of work, or just new to working around the world, the ideal way to make the transition to doing global business is at your own pace, and at minimal cost to you. Even if you're new to the game, to make it on an international level you have to have been playing the game, not just been warming the bench from the sidelines.

Thami elaborates from the angles of an aspiring writer, producer, or actor. "You can work virtually anywhere in the world if you develop the necessary relationships and secure the relevant legal paperwork. If you're looking at relocation, a track record and display of exceptional talent will have to be demonstrated to both prospective employers/partners and immigration departments because the entertainment industry is so competitive," Thami admonishes.

"Traveling is much easier when you're younger and you're able to gain experience in various industry departments without having to worry too much about how much you're getting paid. For example, members of the commonwealth can apply for a two-year work visa to the UK if they are under the age of thirty. That visa will allow you to work in whatever field you choose. Relocation always costs money, but [you] can be creative by finding someone from your chosen country to do a home swap for a specific period of time.

"If you're a writer, director, cameraperson, find an interesting angle or story about your destination of choice and pitch your idea to a magazine or TV show. If they like your idea, *they'll pay you* to travel there and get them the story. It's always best to get someone else to pay for you.

"As an actor, getting representation is probably the hardest part of going into another country. It helps if you've got special talents or characteristics that will distinguish you from the sea of already existing talent on the agents' books. Don't expect to be an overnight sensation. Just because you've already developed a name in your home country does not guarantee that the new market will receive you as well. Be willing to do the work. Make use of preexisting relationships and contacts.

"Whether you are a producer or artist, do your homework. Have a plan of action; set appointments before you even leave your home country. You may not stick to it to the T, but it will set a framework for you and may even be your backup plan.

"Have a lot of savings and live as frugally as you can until you have a reliable source of income. Accommodations can be your largest expense, so try to stay with friends or friends of friends if you can, until you are sorted out." This note about frugality cannot be overemphasized for Americans seeking opportunity abroad during times when the US dollar is weak compared with the Euro and the British pound. And even if you travel to a country where the exchange rates are favorable, unforeseen expenses will pop up. You may find yourself spending more than anticipated simply by adjusting to the new way of life.

Thami also knows what it's like to be approached simply because of her association with world-class brands, from *The Apprentice* to Oprah. But relationships by definition are about more than name-dropping, and the best businesspeople forge lasting alliances by presenting mutually beneficial opportunities, not by leeching like parasites. "Relationships should be authentic and be based on mutual respect. When the foundations of those relationships are solid and are from person to person instead of a *what can I get from you* mentality, you can go through extended periods of not making contact. But then, when you finally do, you will pick up where you left off. In a world and industry where people want to be associated with you because of a particular profile or position you hold, it's refreshing to meet someone who is unaffected, honest, and nonmanipulative in their relating to you. On such foundations you can build real relationships that result in win–win situations."

All right reader, I can hear your mind clicking. You're on the plane settling into that first-class seat, destination Cape Town, courtesy of *O* . . . I know she's one degree from Oprah, and I'm no hater, but *please* take her generous advice to heart before you approach Thami—or any of the women you read about in these pages for that matter. Remember: Mutual opportunity and professionalism rule the day. None of us wants anyone regretting that she shared this precious information, right? Riiight.

Obstacles abound for women in business, no matter where in the world you choose to conduct it. Thami gets down to the nitty-gritty on how you surmount them, whatever those obstacles may be. "There's a saying: 'The only cure for racism, ageism, sexism, or any other -ism is excellence.' It is the power of focus and persistence that will disarm any resistance," Thami proclaims. "Believe in your vision, have your own back, love what you do, and run your own race. We give people permission to treat us the way they do. I have found being clear and not avoiding having uncomfortable conversations to be empowering. You have to take care of you."

Vivian Scott-Chew vowed to do just that. In 1997, she ensured that her professional life would mirror her personal experience. She established her groundbreaking promotion and marketing firm, Time Zone International. She had come to learn the power of international business as an A&R executive, first for PolyGram—where she signed Third World and Sa-Fire—and then at Epic Records, where she catapulted Shabba Ranks to worldwide success and back-to-back Grammy wins for Best Reggae Album. In both positions, she learned how to work the label system, even if it meant subverting it.

Vivian opens up about the Shabba Ranks deal, the one she says taught her the most about the industry and herself. This project had the right mix of executive confidence in her vision from her department head, teamwork between label and manager, and victories with the small details that maintain an artist's authenticity.

"Hank Caldwell was my boss. Hank said, 'I don't hear what you hear but I respect your passion, so I'm gonna make sure everyone takes your lead.' I was allowed to partner with his manager to steer [Shabba's] career in its entirety. I was excited to win the battle for the *As Raw as Ever* cover with his nose flared and his eyes cast down. I wanted the imperfect necklace not to be retouched. I loved quarterbacking the project; I was extremely involved.

"That project taught me that I was really a marketing person," Vivian continues. "The Shabba project also showed me international was where I would do my thing. And the company didn't get that he was an international artist *before* we signed him." Vivian had the courage to challenge Epic's understanding of Black artists as global sellers using guerrilla tactics. Vivian elaborates: "At the time, Babyface and Luther [Vandross] were not even being marketed internationally. With Shabba, we took the back-door effect and let him perform in cities around the world [without a product available for sale]. We made palm cards that said 'In Stores Now.' And just like clockwork, the kids went asking for the record. Then retailers called their nation's distributors, and they [in turn] would call the home office." She smiles. "The [international department] asked me to get an international version of the record ready. And I already had it on my desk. He sold so many records abroad; that's how I was able to buy my first house."

Vivian also had help from mentors, both male and female. Her career was divinely ordered, with powerful, generous people guiding her along a twenty-plus-year tenure that began as the assistant to entertainment law icon Louise West, whom you met in chapter 6. Of Louise, Vivian says, "She was the architect of my entire music industry career. I learned so much from what she taught me, but I more importantly I learned from how she conducted herself. She was a lady. She was not intimidated by men; she was a friend to the artists and had a sensitive heart to the artistry of music. I try to keep a balance of all of those things in my work." Vivian also worked alongside renowned producer Kashif, with whom she got a firm grasp of touring, production, and the inner workings of running a music studio as he wrote and produced for Meli'sa Morgan, Whitney Houston, and others.

In an industry where mentorship is increasingly absent, especially from men, Vivian attests to how important it was for her as she gained knowledge and solid footing in a male-dominated arena. "Sisters talk about how men don't help them; and I've had many helpful women in the business, but the men were incredible for me. Merlin Bob, Bill Underwood, Don Taylor—these brothers were all in sight. If I needed them I could reach out, but they stayed far enough to let me be me. From 'you should have fixed it in the mix—but let me show you how to fix in mastering' right down to stepping to somebody to say, 'Leave her the fuck alone.' [Music producer] Timmy Regisford was the one who told me I couldn't lose with Shabba. He showed me how to make the deal work and gave me the confidence that someone had my back." Today she makes sure to surround herself with people who can mentor her as she mentors those who walk in the trail she blazed. "We as women tend to hang onto our Fave Five. If you're the smartest one in your

Fave Five, then you need a new Fave Five. Don't be afraid to stretch out and find some twenty-five-year-olds and seventy-year-olds," she offers.

Vivian takes this philosophy a step farther in her global business. As an American who speaks one language and relies on foreign nationals when she executes plans or takes on clients, it is vital for her to retain a circle of intelligent colleagues she can trust regardless of the market, cultural mores, or the project on the table. "I always have a local rep in meetings with me. They guide me and protect me and sift out a lot of bullshit. It's amazing that even in this political climate, America is still seen as all things big and best. As a result, I attract a lot of projects that may be a waste of time. Or conversely, there may be someone my rep has history with but presents a great opportunity. All your relationships should be one phone call away. If you can't, you should know someone who can. It's more about knowing the culture and etiquette that is needed to conduct business." And how does that etiquette look exactly? Well, that's just it: It varies depending on the border you cross, and you have to know the rules of engagement for the location.

"The Japanese offer a great example. They are so much about order and things being right. If I'm meeting a new client, I bear gifts. I wait for them to extend their hand before I do. It's about respect. Going in there having done your research. Sitting back and being quiet. Watching and having respect for how [others] do things. We cannot come in like the Big Bad Country that does everything better. I hire residents who are my on-the-ground personnel. This is how I weed out who's serious. I also depend on them to keep from offending people. If you're gonna talk concept with people in their language, have a command of it. Otherwise it comes off as 'awww, isn't that cute.'"

While all Vivian wanted was the kind of work that would allow her to travel the world and listen to music, being the only company of her kind was far from a vacation. It came with all sorts of challenges, from how to show her label clients they needed her services to how and how much to charge for them. "I come in as the specialist for the international departments. I try to do the groundwork for them; to create the awareness to a level that their affiliates can pick up the baton and go from there. But because no one has done this before, clients think they can do it without me," she says of her entrepreneurial Catch-22, which has caused her to choose clients carefully and charge competitively but creatively. "I had to learn the hard way," she reflects. "I turn down more work than I take. They either don't have a realistic take on what it will require to make it happen, or if I don't think it's gonna happen, I won't take their money. I charge based on my man-hours, knowledge, and contacts—and it varies. Once you get me on the phone, the clock starts running. Then I charge a fee for my services, and we'll offer à la carte services as things come up. Sometimes I'll do the tour and commission what I bring in. But the number one rule is: Never spend a check until it clears!"

Since Vivian was one of the first successful A&R women of color, I asked her what she thinks of what Black music is offering up to the world, since she is now in a position of marketing it on a global scale. Her response is bittersweet. Alongside her victories in breaking 2008 Grammy nominee Ledisi in Europe five years earlier, and helping guitarist Kem tour and deeply touch the lives of people like Edith, a fiftyish German woman who is a huge Kem fan but at first glance has very little in common with him, there is the rabid proliferation of denigrating words used by and about Black folks to contend with. "For the last ten years, I've been bringing music to the world. I love being in Tokyo and hearing the crowd go crazy when somebody says, 'Is Brooklyn in the house?!' Black people need to give the world a variety of good music again," she insists. "The images of us overseas are making me sad. I hear 'bitch' in territories where the word 'bitch' would never have been spoken—and ten-year-old Black boys are saying it. We have the Africans rapping and using the N-word. What have we done?'" The short answer is that Black music has ceased to be fully developed. And in Vivian's view, the decrease in women working A&R in hip-hop and R&B is no accident. "It's tough to sign artists who disrespect us at the same time," she asserts.

Sasha Dees is a bridge builder who is also big on respect. The twenty-year veteran producer and manager of artists and events splits her time among Amsterdam, where she co-founded the spoken word event CrimeJazz: Words, Poetry & Beyond, along with Blacksoil, Europe's first hip-hop film festival; New York, where she scouts spoken word and music talent for performances abroad; and Suriname, where she promotes creative and cultural exchange between its people and those of Holland, its colonizer. Sasha transferred her skills as a corporate strategist and organizational executive into the world of the performing arts at the request of her artsy friends, who needed counsel. "Organizing came naturally to me. The guy I lived with was a composer-musician and he asked me to organize his business, ask my opinion about a contract.

Casual and informal advice is how it started. Then it evolved from music they recorded, to theater people who knew writers and video people," she says with a laugh. "After a while I would have friends of friends coming to me. But then some would offer to pay me, so I wondered how I would set that up; I had no company. I formed SashaDees Production and Management, and the work came organically, totally from word of mouth."

Her big break into the mainstream was also the experience that told her she preferred the underground. "My most commercial success was Jörgen Raymann; he's the Chris Rock of Holland. He was a restaurant owner in Suriname and I was doing cultural exchange projects. I would exchange free meals for performances in his venue. He made a show with a friend and invited me to see it." Sasha went into action to bring his one-man show to Holland, knowing the community of people from Suriname would love it. "I applied all the skills I picked up, PR, marketing, and putting my own money down and calling everyone I knew. Luckily the one journalist that came was from a big daily paper. He didn't get the humor but was surrounded by all these laughing Black people, and he gave us the front-page color review that propelled Jörgen. There was such a need for him: a successful Black person who could say things without being threatening. He was a crossover hit. With the right talent, all the things I learned worked. He toured Holland for a couple years and I got my small [Manhattan apartment] from part of my earnings. But once the big bucks came rolling in, the work got boring, and that's why I left Jörgen. I am a builder. I start things off, and that money is fine for me. When I stopped working with Jörgen, I founded a nonprofit organization called John 106 together with Philip Powel. We created Crime-Jazz and Blacksoil to give emerging artists a platform to showcase their talent."

Sasha is an inspiration for all you entrepreneurs out there who strive not to be gazillionaires, but to live comfortably doing creative work that will let you sleep at night (on the rare occasions you get sleep, of course). Sasha's secret to being a successful global businesswoman is accepting compensation in all its forms, from money to services. She truly has a global point of view about doing business that puts collaboration before exploitation and people before process.

"I have an artist's view in the business world," says Sasha. "With everything I do, I need to like the people, feel the project. I don't take a call and work for people I don't know. And it's also about fairness. I don't do a lot of commercial work. I ask what the budget is like and charge accordingly. If they don't make all the money they wanted, I will go down in price, too. Even my Web site was a gift from someone. I get a lot of payment like that. Part of my payment is also my freedom," she notes. "I do live in two countries, so I must be doing well."

This is not to imply that Sasha doesn't understand how money works or its importance in the transaction, however. It's simply not her primary motivator. And living in our American capitalist society, we can lose sight of the idea that this is actually okay. The European commitment to funding the arts on a governmental level also helps take the urgent need for profit out of the equation—something that American government has sacrificed. The dearth of federal funding makes art for art's sake a tougher proposition. Sasha sees fund-raising as part of her role as producer and scouts for sources like she scouts for talent. "[As a producer] you make dreams come true. I also help people find money, because you need that to make the dreams come true as well. I find out about subsidies and foundation grants. Before the Internet, I'd look at who was thanked in the program, and then call them for more information. You get a lot of *no* at first, but you must be persistent and prove that you're good at what you do. You have to learn the language of asking for money and explaining what you need it for. If I can't get the money, I get the value with in-kind sponsoring."

Her gift for getting the value has turned Blacksoil into Europe's premiere hip-hop film festival since its 2003 debut. She may be a white European, but she has the passion for art and the security in her own identity not to repeat the colonial cycle as the festival's curator. Cultural understanding goes both ways, and Sasha knows the difference between supporting a culture and co-opting it. Her work with spoken word artists in New York helped her see a void in Amsterdam and fill it. "You don't have to be a jazz musician to like jazz," Sasha says, offering up an analogy. "I'm not this woman shouting about the ghetto. I get irritated when folks get dropped off in a Volvo talking about a ghetto they never saw. Sixty-seven percent of Amsterdam is non-original Dutch, so it's very diverse, and it's been that way from the start. I wasn't a B-girl, but I did a lot of spoken word and hip-hop theater was a given for me, I grew up in that crowd. [Blacksoil] started with screenings. Then we made it a weekend, and it kept going annually. Meanwhile there's a network of festivals all over Europe that we work with, advise, and program in. I still don't rap or wear baggy pants, but that was never the culture's foundation to begin with. I don't feel the need to pretend to be a B-girl, writer, or emcee, or that I grew up in the South Bronx. I feel I can be me with my background, wearing the clothes I do, and still be part of a culture." Being yourself is all it takes to expand the global conversation. Remember: People from other places want to do business with the real you. Besides, they can spot a fake just as well as you can.

....

SUMMARY OF SECRETS REVEALED

WHAT YOU THOUGHT YOU KNEW:

I can play this game like the boys and still be a lady.

WHAT YOU NEED TO KNOW:

Vivian warns that you've got some reevaluating to do. "Never take it personally and never assume. Women get caught up in those two the most. If we all read [Don Miguel Ruiz's book] *The Four Agreements* we'd be a lot better off," she says.

WHAT YOU THOUGHT YOU KNEW:

My fee should be what I think I should get paid.

WHAT YOU NEED TO KNOW:

"We undercharge as women," Vivian states matter-of-factly—especially when "there's no frame of reference for what should be charged." As a new enterprise or service provider, be creative about how you get paid and don't be afraid to put your true worth on the table. You never know; they might not even blink at your number. Why sell yourself short? The worst that can happen is you start negotiating—or you lose a client who would probably be a high-maintenance headache anyway.

WHAT YOU THOUGHT YOU KNEW:

I should stick to what I'm good at, or at least what I'm comfortable doing.

WHAT YOU NEED TO KNOW:

Reinvention by definition requires that you throw out the old ways of doing and being and apply new ones. Shake off the idea that doing something you could take or leave is what it means to be a working woman. You can and should strive for the career you love. If the one you have now is not the one you love, Vivian recommends "knowing what you're good at, then making the decision that you're never gonna do anything you don't want to do ever again." The other side of this pearl of wisdom is to recognize when you're good at something and when you're passionate about something. Just because you can do it doesn't mean it's the best thing for you to do, especially if you wake up uninspired by it daily.

Thami has this to say about taking the leap of reinvention: "The biggest challenge is change and the uncertainty that comes with it. Ironically, this is also the biggest thrill. Change is pregnant with possibilities and potential. The greatest reward is the fulfillment that comes following your heart and giving yourself a shot. Whether the outcome is what you had hoped for or not, the true victory is in having had the courage to move beyond your comfort zone."

WHAT YOU THOUGHT YOU KNEW:

If a business relationship is going south, instead of ending it I should just deal with it, even if I go down with it.

WHAT YOU NEED TO KNOW:

Sasha says the opposite. "There are times when you think you start out wanting the same thing but halfway through, you see you don't. It's good to count your loss and graciously leave or solve it well at the end. I'm so intuitive that I'd feel irritated when it wasn't working; now I know what that is. You learn that from years of experience. I'm also better now at telling people why I can't work with some people."

Thami agrees, and recommends drawing the line before you pay a personal price. "Don't compromise who you are and your self-worth. Don't be afraid to walk away if you have to," she says. "When one door closes, it probably wasn't the right one for your highest benefit. So move on and keep your head up high."

CHAPTER 11

The Revolution Will Be Feminized: Women of New Media and Mobile

....

Alyce Emory ✳ Camille Hackney ✳ Eleanor Blattel ✳

Emily Griffin ✳ Kathy Baker ✳ Lakiya Oliver ✳

Nana Brew-Hammond ✳ Rhonda Cowan

....

If you play the scarcity game, we all lose. Safe is easy, but you're not gonna grow.

—EMILY "MS. E" GRIFFIN

The entertainment industry battles content piracy on an unprecedented global scale. The music business specifically is working feverishly to restructure its model so that it can capitalize on the power and reach of the digital space. Content copyright holders are trying to collect royalties to which they feel they are entitled on a new income-earning platform. Trying to grasp the opportunities and revenue in new media is like trying to scoop up a bag of spilled marbles in roller skates on a well-oiled floor. The whole experience can make your head spin, and inevitably some of the marbles are going to elude your grasp.

It is the sheer vastness of this swiftly mutating space and an urgent desire to stabilize within it that makes it so easy for entertainment to vilify digital. The platforms themselves, however, are not the enemy. Like the people who operate them, companies tend to fear what they do not understand. And our companies have operated in the tangible worlds of film, vinyl, tape, brick-and-mortar stores, and theaters for hundreds of years. Having songs, shows, and films reduced to ones and zeros in a computer file is a shock to our culture, our pockets, and our souls. Unfortunately, from the Napster crackdown in 2002 to suing individual downloading consumers, the industry's knee-jerk responses to the rise of digital business have at turns been punitive, desperate, and downright ugly. Suddenly, content creators found the value of their assets being set by technology companies. Labels' best hope for a single became the 99-cent price point on iTunes, $9.99 for an album. Some might say, "Serves 'em right. No matter how many tracks the CD contained, labels were only paying artists royalties on ten songs per album anyway." But no label could have anticipated the rabid decompartmentalization of albums that iTunes made available to music buyers. The BUY button let users click to take what they wanted to hear, and leave the rest of the album behind. Not only did this cannibalize album sales online, but it also undermined delivery of the artist's vision as each artist intended. In the online space, the exercise of listening to the whole album and finding favorites after the buyer had committed through purchasing it in its entirety waned, leaving the listener's album-loving muscles to atrophy as a singles-driven consciousness took hold.

I am the first to admit that there is a lot I don't know about the digital arena. What I do know is that as an employee of a major music and film conglomerate when downloading shanked the traditional revenue model, I found it scary. It felt like one day Napster was being sued by Dr. Dre and Metallica for infringement, and the next I was writing anti-piracy campaigns to run in *Billboard* and on television.

Labels were crudely introduced to a generation of computer users who became file sharers. These people were not the loyal music lovers they had come to rely on, who roamed record store aisles with fresh ears and open wallets. This was a new crop of music lovers who had no idea what music cost to make. They just knew that at roughly $18.99 a CD, music now cost way too much for them. In their minds, the record company had been stickin' it to them for years. The CD's bloated price was the last straw, especially when there were only a few tracks worth listening to once they pushed PLAY.

This new crop of users' collective file-sharing experience gave them instant gratification and connectedness in a once impersonal medium. Its subversive immediacy was also a vindicating middle finger to the record companies, which — to downloaders — seemed like abusive pimps leaving their talented recording artist and filmmaking hoes out on the track to fend for themselves and accept pennies on the dollar for their art. Prior to the emergence of online piracy, labels and studios never felt the need to educate their public on what it costs to make music or movies; they just collected the public's money and kept putting out products of increasingly questionable quality. Labels became the Bad Guys. They also found themselves painted into the ninety-nine-cent corner out of fear and ignorance about selling music online. The perception that music ought to be free—because hell, it sure *felt* like it was after hitting a button and getting a file—was born for a generation. Once the per-song price was set and contractually locked by iTunes at roughly a dollar a jam, labels found the value of their assets being determined by an outside power, a predicament that is coming back to haunt labels as online retail grows. The film industry was not immune to the downloading frenzy. Among otherwise law-abiding citizens, there was a collective return to the notion that a movie should not cost more than the five dollars it used to in theaters. If that means rolling the dice with a bootleg off some Manhattan street or an LA swap meet, so be it. The more savvy online users were ripping entire films without ever leaving the house.

What made this so scary for labels and studios alike was that digital theft was instantly a global problem. Their marbles were scattered and rolling away from their reach at unimaginable, uncontrollable speed. The initial scramble to recover any of them was inordinately frustrating and fiscally painful—our own version of a war on digital terror. Today our business continues to reel from the impact as it makes adjustments to protect assets and reclaim revenue.

And yet, with innumerable profits lost, new models are emerging, presenting fresh opportunity for legal online acquisition of media content. Amazing avenues for exploiting this content and extending the brands of entertainers have been invented between labels or studios and technology companies; we've gone from online chats with artists to streaming video of live performances and now, the recording of exclusive albums for mobile service providers (Timbaland's mobile album for Verizon, an industry first for artists, mobile, and record companies). In recognition of the fact that they needed to protect themselves and regain control of their assets, record companies and film studios have also stepped their game way up in the digital media space.

New media is one of the few growth areas in entertainment, which is good news for women seeking a career where the present meets the future. I spoke to executives who make up a dynamic group of veterans, innovators, and relative newcomers to the digital world from other sectors in business and entertainment. These eight women are a sample of the executive talent in this exciting and highly profitable area and represent just part of its broad spectrum. I invited them to introduce us to their world behind the computer interface and contribute to this critical dialogue.

In this chapter you'll meet film festival and new media consultant Alyce Emory, who helped to pioneer the "Webisode" during her tenure at HBO; Camille Hackney, senior vice president of brand partnerships and commercial licensing for Atlantic Records; former Sanctuary Records director of new media Eleanor Blattel, who is currently VP of digital sales and marketing for Alternative Distribution Alliance (ADA); Zune Programming manager Emily Griffin, who got her start in radio and made her mark as an electronica DJ before going digital; real-world mechanical engineer turned Columbia Records senior director of digital marketing Kathy Baker; Lakiya Oliver, who leapt from director of video promotions with Universal Motown into a post as North American marketing manager for Fox Mobile Entertainment, home of Jamster; freelance writer, film acquisitions executive, and current writer-producer for Bluefly.com Nana Brew-Hammond (whom you may recall from chapter 8); and longtime music industry veteran Rhonda Cowan, who transferred her marketing and talent relations skills into the online space as vice president of music development and network convergence for BET.com.

Each woman featured took a different road to her career in new media. Some came from record labels or radio; others from the general market corporate world. We have a wide range educationally, but interestingly enough, no one studied computer science, which cancels the whole *must be a nerd-genius to work in new media* theory. Their paths into the digital world combined with their insights and experiences will open your mind to new possibilities and confirm for you that even in a brand-new world, some of the same good, bad, and ugly principles of the old world remain. What they shared certainly helped me wrap my head around what their part of the industry is up to and going through—and how it all affects their careers. These women took me into the proverbial rabbit hole of new media 2.0, from online retail and social networking sites to Webisodes and lifestyle destinations. They also had a wide range of opinion about where new media is taking the business of entertainment, offering further proof that nobody has one right answer. At least not yet.

MUSIC'S DIGITAL MELTDOWN

How did record companies end up at the mercy of digital pirates, technology companies, and even their own consumer base? Based on the responses of women working in the field, it sounds like a perfect storm of missed opportunities, thrusting upon labels a need to redefine and expand their revenue models. Digital marketing director Kathy Baker works under the Sony BMG umbrella in her digital marketing post at Columbia Records. You might think that because Sony makes computers, it could have anticipated and acted upon the need to monetize its content in the digital space. In speaking with Kathy, however, I learned that just because a company makes computers doesn't mean it's in the business of e-commerce. And even if Sony was working on it, no conglomerate can move with the speed of a curious college student on the cutting edge of technological advances. "Labels are not technology companies," Kathy reiterates. "They could not have anticipated online piracy, and they were never gonna beat some young kids figuring file sharing out there on their own. Labels still think we can actually stop songs from leaking. Once it's out, that's it."

Eleanor Blattel created Sanctuary Records' new media department, where she negotiated deals for the exploitation of its extensive rock and pop catalog, oversaw marketing for online releases, and launched the label's own online store. She maintains that even if labels had jumped online before piracy exploded, their problem was twofold: a singular revenue stream and an imbalance of new media executive talent to grow additional revenue streams. "The labels' 'miss point' was that they put all their eggs into the artist's basket and all they reap is income from a record they may or may not sell," Eleanor explains, noting that even as a fairly diversified independent record company, Sanctuary did not fully realize its potential online or in the areas of touring and merchandising. "Sanctuary had a world-class merchandising company and a publishing company, and they [still] didn't take full advantage. When we had artists like Morrissey or Robert Plant who could benefit from all the resources, we could do so much cool stuff. Everyone benefited and the artist was always happy. The mistake made by labels wasn't not getting online fast enough; their model doesn't sustain itself. Intellectual property is not enough; you need income from concrete things as well. It should be like expert mini units that fall under one umbrella that all work together. Why isn't the label participating in all the revenue streams? [Because] the labels the way they are now have no right to ask for all that. I was dealing with old-school record men. These [executives] are either music guys or business guys; you've got to meet somewhere in the middle."

Zune Programming manager Emily Griffin echoes Eleanor's sentiment and adds to it, noting that majors were too heavily vested in real-world retail, which contributed to a slow ramp-up in the virtual space. "The indie labels and smaller companies always got that the Web was a marketing [tool] for them. They always collected from tours and merchandise. The labels were so dependent on brick-and-mortar retail, they were not as quick to harness and realize the opportunity to their advantage," asserts Emily. Was there an all-or-nothing perception about retail the online space? It is doubtful that major labels knew enough about how to operate in the digital world to make it that cut-and-dried. But with a bird in the hand that they could see, feel, set prices for, and earn money on, these labels' choice to hold on to selling music in stores was familiar and comfortable if nothing else.

Trouble there is, consumers were familiarizing themselves with new ways to buy music that did not involve a real-world store of any kind. To use Dr. Spencer Johnson's phrasing, the labels' cheese was moving faster than they were initially willing to chase it. Enter Apple, Inc., whose iTunes store opened its virtual doors on April 28, 2003, with flat-rate pricing. Most songs cost $.99 in the United States, .79 pound in the United Kingdom, and somewhere around .99 euro elsewhere in Europe. Songs encrypted with anti-copying software called Digital Rights Management (DRM) initially cost $1.29 in the US. iTunes did what labels were unable to do collectively: provide one user-friendly service by which music could be downloaded legally for profit. As of January 2008, the service has sold more than four billion songs.[1] According to Adam Penenberg of *Slate* magazine, iTunes' take is four cents of the ninety-nine-cent price.[2] A $160 million service fee for the platform is not a bad take by any stretch of the imagination. Especially after selling well over a hundred million iPod devices on which to play the songs, as music sales took a hit during the same five-year span. Interestingly enough, while song pricing has essentially remained flat for the last six years, the pricing on the iPod hardware has been variable from the start, ranging from $399 for the Classic to $99 for the Shuffle. I wonder how Steve Jobs would feel about iPods costing ninety-nine dollars, regardless of model. No one has posed this question. And in Apple's defense, the prices have come down considerably since the device's inception. Universal Music Group is the first label to act on industry displeasure with iTunes pricing by opting out of renewing its iTunes contract. Consider this from a 2007 article on SiliconValley.com:

> In what may signal a shift from simmering discontent to open hos-tilities, Universal Music, the world's biggest music company, has reportedly decided not to renew its annual contract with Apple's iTunes and instead wants to continue the arrangement on an at-will basis, giving it an easy exit should disagreements over pricing or other terms become a problem. Universal's move reflects the gen-eral unhappiness among the major record labels that Apple, by dint of its ubiquitous iPod, is calling the tune on digital music sales. In particular, they're not crazy about Apple's restrictive Digital Rights Management scheme and iTunes' flat-rate pricing; as Warner Music chief Edgar Bronfman Jr. recently told investors, "We believe that not every song, not every artist, not every album, is created equal."[3]

Label heads continue to question the one-price-for-all-songs arrange-ment in the interest of earning more per track, since album sales have plummeted in both the virtual and real worlds. This coincides with a new wrinkle: the emergence of Amazon in 2007 as iTunes' first formidable online retail competitor. Amazon immediately offered songs for less at 94 cents and undercut iTunes album prices by as much as $2, offering albums at $7.99. So the already low price of music keeps getting lower, and while free is the rock-bottom price, the paying cost floor has yet to be agreed upon.

Now that MP3 players offer a video feature, the downloading of televi-sion shows and films has delivered the pricing conversation to the door of the studios. According to Wired.com, NBC Universal president Jeff Zucker weighed in on the subject during a recent interview. "We thought it was video who killed the radio star, but NBC Universal president Jeff Zucker claims that Apple killed both. While being interviewed by *The New Yorker*'s Ken Auletta at a benefit for Syracuse University, the executive claimed that Apple has made millions on its iPod 'off the backs of our content' and that the software maker 'destroyed the music business in terms of pricing.'"[4]

What has boggled my mind, and I'm sure the minds of many in the entertainment business, is how consumers have no problem paying three dollars for a ringtone while balking at paying the same amount for the actual download of the full track when a ringtone is a thirty-second snippet that may not even be the part of the song you bought it for in the first place! According to Eleanor, it starts with the unfortunate precedent set by illegal file sharing. Since music started out online as free of charge, paying any amount for it is counterintuitive, even though anything else constitutes theft and robs the artists people claim to love and want to support. Sadly, the consumer is paying for the convenience with a ringtone, not for the music. Eleanor elaborates: "Music started out as free [online]. It's hard to get anyone to pay more for it unless there's a reason. Napster ran amok and people were putting up music on FTP servers, so a whole generation is ripping and thinks it should be free. With the [retail] co-op, artwork, and packaging, peoples' perception is that a physical CD has things that go into making it. Not so for the MP3 file," Eleanor clarifies. "They will pay more for convenience, and since they can't convert the song into a ringtone they will pay to have it done for them."

From the point of view of a label executive, whose company's directive is now to make as much money as possible in the digital space, the ringtone conundrum is a boon. Kathy speaks to this firsthand, noting that ringtones have such revenue-generating power that they can mean the difference between an artist getting more attention from the record company and that same artist being shelved or deprioritized. "Ringtones are our friend," Kathy says, noting that artist and label divide a minimum of half the ringtone fee with the mobile provider. "A ringtone can save an artist's project because it is revenue that comes in and can sometimes pay for an entire budget. It's grown so much, they've become their own area of business for us. It's something we can sell that kids can't steal." Meanwhile, Sony BMG has begun to combat ripping with what is called spoofing of music files to protect their intellectual property. "We go out to all the illegal services and flood them with fake files," explains Kathy. "So if you go to Limewire for 'Pony' by Ginuwine, for example, and get our spoof that sounds terrible, you'll get frustrated and buy it legally so you can hear it." The chase for real income in the virtual space continues with the monetization of widgets, wallpaper, "whatever it is to collect money," Kathy emphasizes. "We can't just sell CDs anymore. We run ads on our sites now, something we didn't do in the past."

Lakiya actually jumped ship from her position as director of video promotion for Universal Motown Records and hitched her star to Fox Mobile

Entertainment. She had seen the revenue- and buzz-generating power of ringtone sales with artists from her roster like Akon and Chamillionaire, both of whom are many-times-platinum ringtone sellers. And while at first glance, a mobile company hiring a music executive may seem like a stretch—especially given that Lakiya had no technological experience on her résumé—she was an attractive candidate to Fox Mobile, which claims Jamster as one of its acquired companies. Jamster is always advertising on music video channels. Lakiya was the label's liaison to those same channels. Her knowledge of the outlets and their viewership made her instantly valuable. And the marketing focus of the Fox Mobile position appealed to Lakiya as well. "Video promotion was not something I wanted to do for the rest of my life, let alone the next five years," she says. During her job hunt, Fox was the only mobile company to whom she submitted her résumé. Though it was a lateral move, it was in its own way a promotion, because it took her out of a field facing a downturn and into another experiencing growth. And while she waited for the right job offer, she worked on pop music projects including Drake Bell, the Rapture, and JoJo to diversify her experience and keep from being relegated to the fateful "urban box." "My title is the same as it would be at Universal in terms of rank, but I am doing more," Lakiya effuses. "I oversee TV, print, and radio marketing. I also create synergy between the Jamster and Fox brands and make sure Fox content is cross-marketed on the Jamster side. I even deal with customer retention and label partnerships." Lakiya is also seeing the mobile company morph into an A&R source as well as a revenue stream for musicians, right from her inbox. "I get at least a hundred e-mails a day from people looking for us to turn their songs into ringtones," she marvels. "I see artists who may not have deals, but want more control of their projects; they have definitely changed, wanting to retain control and have more input. They can make so much money from ringtones, they don't need a label."

....

NEW MEDIA FRENZY: PROMISE AND CHALLENGES OF
A NEW PLAYING FIELD

....

The field of new media has an interesting dichotomy happening within. On the one hand, it's a tiny community of executives, scientists and engineers, creatives and marketers. On the other, it's a growth area that attracts all kinds of passionate people of disparate backgrounds. It's probably the most level section of entertainment's playing field simply because it's too new to have been trampled through. New media is not the rest haven for nerds that common perception makes it out to be. In fact, you don't have to specialize in writing code or building sites to have a fruitful career. The online business is only as strong as its compatibility and accessibility in the real world by real people. In the digital space, common sense and agility are prerequisites just as critical as book smarts and practicality.

"I learned to be nimble and not be on one track," explains Nana Brew-Hammond, who after careers in journalism and film is now an established new media executive with AOL and Bluefly.com on her résumé. "I wanted to focus on magazines, but when a magazine's funding would not go through it was a mess, so I went into film. I left film because the money wasn't good and there was no mobility. I was converting a lot of content from the [cinematic] space to the online space, so that was a natural transition for me."

I asked her how much about programming she needed in her role as style and beauty programming manager at AOL. The answer is surprising: There is "a little bit of code and HTML, but I know it well enough to get some coding done. I oversaw the blog, site features, and polls. We piggybacked on AOL Music's shoots and shot our own makeovers. It was the perfect marriage of my branding, interactive, and editorial experience," says Nana, confirming that a computer science degree is by no means a prerequisite for a successful new media career. Not saying it won't help, but it won't hurt if you don't bring one to the interview table, either. In fact, both Eleanor and Kathy mentioned actually teaching themselves HTML before or upon securing their new media posts. If you're not the self-teaching type, put yourself in an HTML class. What's important for you to hold on to as you take on the field of new media is this: The mosaic of experiences you bring from wherever and however you worked before is what you will draw upon the most. Because new media is an entirely new destination, every journey that leads there will contribute to your productivity and growth in the field. Yes, you need to understand how technology works, know what happens behind the interface, and have a working understanding of the languages that computers speak. Just know that you can acquire this on the job or in school without getting a degree centered on computer science. Not one woman in this chapter has such a degree; the degrees held include mechanical engineering, sociology, public relations, and business.

Emily is the only one who "does what I went to school for," majoring in communications with an electronic media emphasis. She got the degree at the University of San Francisco, and loved that it combined "liberal arts with production; it's important to have both. I did sound editing, radio production with razor blades and tape-to-tape, scriptwriting, newswriting, audience research, and studied the sociology of media. Too bad the program is defunct." The knowledge base is always shifting anyway, so the best thing to do is to keep up with all the advances by reading trade sites and blogs or by attending conferences. The ones recommended by women in this chapter can be found in the Recommended Reading and Resources guides at the end of this book.

Camille Hackney came into new media when it was being called "business development." After more than fourteen years in new media, she can safely say that the field molts its skin and is rejuvenated approximately every three years. "Everyone reinvents themselves," she marvels. "I've seen four generations of reinvented executives. Gone are the days where everyone had jobs for twenty years with one company. Someone across the table from you one day may be your boss the next."

Camille graduated from Princeton and worked on Wall Street for a couple of years. That was all she needed to find another line of work. "I needed a job that I would intrinsically love," she explains. "I took time to go to business school and learn about finance, other businesses, and myself; and it brought me to the music business. I could do my job without a Harvard MBA, but it gives me a different perspective . . . I ask how I can help solve a problem. As a problem solver, people continue to come back to you. That's how I've built my business and my relationships."

Rhonda Cowan's path was the opposite of Camille's. She began her career on the record industry side, working for Russell Simmons at Def Jam, back when the now Zen co-founder was hands-on and in the office daily. Listening to her, I saw the parallels between the early Def Jam and a dot-com in its seminal stages conquering the world with a new set of weaponry. Def Jam's arsenal just happened to be hip-hop. "I learned how to hustle and get it done with little or no resources," Rhonda reflects. "New media is a natural progression for music to go in, and for me to grow into from a traditional label situation. Because I still work on the music side of the Internet, it allows me to transfer my skills seamlessly." The hands-on work experience is just as valuable in this brave new media world, where everyone has to roll up their sleeves and solve problems. Rhonda believes that formal schooling alone won't cut it. "You need a combination of both," she asserts. "I have worked with everyone from high school dropouts to Ivy Leaguers and everyone in between. At the end of the day, if you don't have integrity and honor, your degree or lack thereof won't make folks take your call."

Camille went without getting her calls to Sylvia Rhone returned for months, advanced Harvard degree and all. Ironically, Camille started out inviting Rhone to speak on her campus, which never happened. "I stalked her and [her assistant] May Attaway three or four times a day every day," Camille recalls. "I was always nice, never mean or threatening. I would call early in the morning. At 8:45 AM one day after a snowstorm, Sylvia actually picked up the phone! She knew I had been calling and invited me to come in [for a meeting]. Asking her to speak at Harvard turned into her giving me a job," says Camille. "I owe my start in the business to Sylvia." Once Camille got in the room, she unleashed all her preparation, from reading industry books to studying *Billboard* for the past year. "I gave her a landscape of what I would do if she hired me," Camille continues. "The Internet was just starting up; it was about developing the Web as a distribution strategy. I was a heat-seeking missile for new ways to do business. With Sylvia's guidance and faith, I built the department from the ground up. I came in as director of business development. I ended up managing a staff of five and a host of freelancers. In three years, I was [promoted to] VP."

Kathy's gift for math and engineering ran in the family. She looked up to her father, who was an aviation engineer, and competed with her brother in the field of mechanical engineering. She was doing great in school until the fourth grade, when she recalls falling behind to the point of her parents meeting with her teacher and making her catch up on math through the night at home. "I'd be staying up until 1 AM, but it helped me get into the advanced math program and stay in it until I graduated," Kathy notes. "By the time I got to Rutgers, I was literally sleeping through calculus. But there was nothing easy about mechanical engineering, believe that! My mechanical engineering major let me know I could do anything I could put my mind to."

What Kathy had not bargained for was being one of a staff of two in her new media job at Columbia Records after six more semesters of school at Columbia University, where she studied Inter- and intranet management and design. She found out quickly that her undergraduate degree was not specialized enough for this new area of science and engineering. She also got a taste of how fast the dot-com bubble could burst. She started job hunting before completing her certification. "I went to a dot-com called AKA. com (Also Known As, not the sorority). When they were getting bought out, I knew it was time to leave. AKA was shut down in a month. Some of us moved to labels. My role was in production and managing the sites. I came to Columbia in 2001," continues Kathy. "That back-end experience did help. I managed all the urban sites for the label. I literally split the roster with another girl who managed all the rock [sites]."

Kathy was so busy managing this near-impossible workload, she had no idea how much she was contributing to the success of individual projects and specific artists overall. "I was managing digital campaigns for all the urban sites. This includes online public relations, e-mail marketing, managing partnerships with iTunes and Yahoo!, et cetera." Kathy now has a staff of four, but it took her second pregnancy to show her how badly she needed a staff in the first place, not to mention an increase in salary. "When I went on maternity leave and someone else stepped in my shoes for a second, that's how I started to see how valuable I was to the company," Kathy remarks. "[My replacement] was in disbelief at how I was managing it all. It took me four years in the trenches to see how important a piece of the puzzle I was. That's when I realized I was a senior executive."

For Eleanor, her male counterparts had to make some adjustments to a senior woman executive who was half their age. "I felt like a standout because of my age, not my gender," remarks Eleanor, who recalls getting comments like "'she's a blond girl in her twenties; what's she doing in this position?' Once I opened my mouth [to speak], they knew I wasn't the ditsy blonde." Eleanor notes that while there were other women in her department wherever she worked, her approach to interacting with men is what distinguished her among her male peers. In a field that can switch from geeky to ultracool on a moment-to-moment basis, the key is making yourself relatable. "I never had a problem hanging with the boys. I was never flirting or hooking up with them, and I never dressed provocatively. They forgot I was a girl; I was a person they worked with. I was treated with respect."

Emily supports Eleanor's strategy. "You have to tolerate the dudes," Emily echoes. "You need to be able to talk about sports even if you don't care about it. They have their monthly moments just like we do, they're just not as in control of it. Guys can attack and criticize in a way where they try to one-up you on the tech stuff. They want to show their competence in different ways, respond to the pressure of the environment," Emily continues. She goes a step farther by noting that how the women in these very masculine environments work together and support one another is also crucial. "I see a lot of women get threatened by other women who come in with an impressive skill set that would rival their own, and [consequently] not doing everything in their ability to collaborate, align, and pull each other up to come up collectively," Emily emphasizes. "We are really the blood, bones, and glue of these companies."

Web producer Alyce Emory took a path less traveled into new media. After working as the assistant to the dean of student life at Georgia State, she relocated to New York. While temp jobs filled her basic needs, she lived with family until she found an apartment in the Bronx she could afford. "Thank God for the support of my family! It was a hard eighteen months of living with my dad," says Alyce. "I had signed up with ten temp agencies to do secretarial work, and there is an inordinate amount of racism and ageism going on in that world. I would read up on the [media] industry at the business library twice a week." As she temped by day, she would freelance as a writer for film Web site Cyberspace Soul City to nurture her love of the medium and get her byline in front of tastemakers.

The salad days were well worth it for Alyce, who during an interview with a Time Warner executive revealed that she wanted to work in the African American marketing department of HBO. Her communication of this desire is a testament to the power of speaking what you want into existence. After more than a year of the corporate temping grind, Alyce eventually landed a temp job in the lodging and commercial sales area of HBO. Here she was taken under the wing of other women executives, who helped her sharpen her skills as a producer of content, much different from the event production experience she'd gained putting on concerts and screenings for students at Georgia State. "I was transferred to African American marketing, where I worked under Sherron Currette. Under Sherron, I worked on *4 Little Girls* and *First Time Felon*. On paper I was an administrative assistant, but I was really a marketing coordinator," explains Alyce. "I was the in-house marketing liaison for all the departments, which allowed me to learn who all the stakeholders were that make things happen."

As she coordinated marketing efforts, Alyce took the lay of this exciting land of opportunity called HBO. Perhaps not coincidentally, the woman she'd freelanced for on Cyberspace Soul City, Diane Jakacki, had gone on to become an executive producer for HBO.com. The Small-World Law worked in Alyce's favor. "It pays to grind it out with excellence in mind, because you never know what that opportunity will lead to," Alyce reflects. As writer-producer for HBO.com, she brought the on-your-feet thinking of her Georgia State world together with the marketing savvy she gained in her previous post at HBO. It was 1997. Networks were still navigating the waters of the Web as a tool to get more eyeballs to the TV screen. "At that time, HBO was still about driving subscribers, still trying to figure out where the Web fit. They thought Web sites were cute," she muses. The stakes were high for *Oz*, the first drama series the network had ever produced. Alyce took a revolutionary idea to the show's creator and writer, Tom Fontana. "I was part of the team that developed the first known Webisodes for *Oz*. I suggested we launch a new character exclusively for the Web. Tom and my boss Diane loved it. Today, every HBO show has a fan site with separate story line, virtual worlds," says Alyce. "That all started from the *Oz* Webisode." She was promoted to producer, interactive ventures, after her first year on the job.

Although Alyce enjoyed the creative accomplishments her tenure at HBO provided, she got an education in coping from the strain and insensitivity of its corporate environment, from bosses and co-workers alike. She shared how she recovered from a confrontation between her and one of her bosses. After securing approval on a Web site redesign with the initials of the show's executive producer, that executive producer later claimed he'd never approved them. Thankfully, Alyce had a paper trail, but it did not account for the man-hours wasted in design that was now mysteriously not approved. "This meant that our HBO.com production team had to go and create new templates, and then start the design process with the client all over again. The template required so much more changing, the designs created wouldn't have worked. That pissed me off. All of us in that room heard him—and I had a copy of the template that he initialed. After my meeting with him, I just went downstairs with my cell phone and called my aunt so she could hear the story and help me cool off. I had to go outside and take a breather. I'm so glad I did that. They expect us to go crazy [as people of color], but I just held my own and documented everything that happened." The lesson for her was that "you have to function in a system that sometimes can allow for people to undermine you without consequence," Alyce admonishes. "I left the office early that day and returned the next day with more resolve to do the best job I could but to continue staying even more current on professional options. I knew I had to be prepared to make changes to continue my career and not necessarily be focused on the limits of the job."

As for the coping lesson Emily got from co-workers, Alyce did not benefit from the female camaraderie that Emily has. Alyce attributes this to the notion that corporate sisterhood is not always authentic or in your best interests. She offers to debunk a myth for both white women and women of color with respect to this dynamic. "The myth that [some] white women work under is that we're in this together as women, but we are not always together. There are many white women I admire and respect, but when you run across someone who says something that doesn't sound right, look at it. And be careful about who you are partnering with. We need to be diligent about who we allow into our circle and our space." The world of digital media may be new, but the old trappings born of patriarchy and racism continue to wreak havoc here as well. Alyce's suspicion is an unfortunate consequence of patriarchy and the toll it takes on relationships between women. The hoarding of knowledge, stifling progress in our business, is to blame as well. Alyce puts it very bluntly when she echoes Emily's theory on scarcity: "In media industries, they don't share with you the tools that are specific to the industry. It's all about coveting and protecting individual success." It behooves us as women to study and understand these dynamics so we are prepared to interact respectfully and powerfully with women of any and all backgrounds. White women can no longer hold up the feminist banner and expect their nonwhite sisters to stand under it with them. As women of color, we can no longer write off all white women as being racist and insensitive. And as we learn, we must educate the men in our respective groups. We all have some housekeeping to do.

....

WHERE TO FROM HERE?
....

I asked the ladies where they saw the future of entertainment heading as the virtual world turns. From the super-niched explosion of social networking sites to the recording of music fully sponsored by nonmusic companies, even songs sold on a sliding scale and album rental, the predictions offered by the women of this chapter are definitely thought provoking; only time will reveal how accurate they are. Regardless of what we don't know about the digital world, we do know that competition in virtual retail is now driving the cost of music down instead of up. We also know that Apple's dominance via the iPod is no more assured than that of the Sony Walkman before it. And as Nana succinctly puts it, "Single-handedly the biggest shift in our business is artists and entities as brands. The new media field has not exactly been leveled, but it has extended into the stands for the everyday person to take advantage of."

Which means a smarter cookie at the computer terminal. Emily was hired as a programming manager at Zune to satisfy Consumer 2.0: the savvier, hungrier, and more discerning user. She says, "People are getting smarter about media. They know how much advertorial they are seeing. They don't want more hype. They feel it when someone is paying to tell them something. Music is sounding amazing, and fans feel closer to artists than ever. I want to relate to people; give the audience a sheer discovery opportunity. At Zune we want people to get that there are actually people who love music doing this." This is an important distinction because working in technology does not guarantee executive colleagues who are passionate or knowledgeable about music, as Kathy attests. "A lot of decision makers I deal with aren't listening to urban music. I have to compare my artist to some pop star so they understand. They couldn't pick Soulja Boy out off the street, but if they hear he has sixteen million hits on YouTube they want it. When I have an artist who is developing, I have to pitch until I'm blue in the face. I get blank stares in these meetings." Kathy sighs as she cites Three 6 Mafia, a prime example. "These executives didn't know who Three 6 was until the Oscars, but the group was already rich and multiplatinum. The work it takes to get a Three 6 recognized by the mainstream is the kind of work I do; it's about getting artists promotion real estate on sites."

Jobs and careers aside, as music lovers, we will need to be as vigilant as ever about actually buying it, because according to Camille the sales will get worse before they get better. Napster was the proverbial tip of the illegal downloading iceberg. "We have to figure out fully how to protect music as sites like Limewire wreak havoc on our business. Labels are continuing to contract; we'll be doing that until 2010. We'll see digital sales making up for the decline in physical sales."

But at what price? Prepare for the day when artists will wish they'd gotten that ninety-nine cents for their vintage smash hit. According to Emily, songs will be sold on a sliding scale just as Radiohead's album was, but based on age and staying power. "I think there should be variable pricing in music," offers Emily. "New music should be at a premium, but if I want some vintage Madonna, there should be other options, maybe paying less for deep cuts and old songs." Perhaps the price becomes sponsored and the consumer is relieved of having to pay for the music at all. Sponsorship from cellular carriers that have traditionally not created music, but use it to super-serve their customers and create exclusivity for them, has already begun. "There may be a time when labels offer music free and run advertising around it, or offer a subscription service for those users who will pay for other things [aside from music]," Kathy says.

Kathy remembers meeting with MySpace when it had forty thousand urban users. It's now well past 217 million total users. "As a one-person team, I couldn't really work with them [then]; it would take too much time. Before I knew it they blew out the gates! You have to recognize when they are pitching you early," Kathy reflects. "Within a year of that meeting, we were actively marketing through and creating campaigns with MySpace. It's a whole new world we have to manage, because now artists and managers can see their competitors' friend numbers." From Facebook, Twitter, and Bebo to LinkedIn and specifically artist-as-brand sites like 50 Cent's ThisIs50.com, hundreds of other social networking sites have taken hold worldwide and are not necessarily entertainment-centered. This wave of virtual worlds has yet to crest, so watch it as a real growth area in the years to come. But we should also be on the lookout for some sort of tracking technology that can identify real, distinct users from the software-generated kind that friend adders generate. "Social networking will be around for a while," confirms Kathy, "but it will segment off, get more specialized. Now we have whole companies emerging from social networking, like iLike and SplashCast."

Emily, a self-proclaimed "big fan of social networking," is looking for more from it as a platform; chances are she's not the only one. What's missing for her is cross-network functionality. "I don't need to collect friends like baseball cards, I want a way to better keep in touch with them, that helps me track whether I've spoken to them in three months or not," says Emily. "What all current networking sites lack is the ability to sync up. I also want the possibility of entertainment; to have the virtual space enhance the human connection." Like these women and most of the world, I can't wait to see what's next. It might be coming from you.

....

SUMMARY OF SECRETS REVEALED

WHAT YOU THOUGHT YOU KNEW:

New media is such a small niche area, getting in is next to impossible.

WHAT YOU NEED TO KNOW:

Getting in at the top is next to impossible, but getting in — from wherever you enter — will most likely hinge upon your relationships and ability to deliver results. Eleanor elaborates: "There's no competition for a vice president of new media because there are only a few of us qualified to do it. We're doing things so specialized, it's hard for new people to catch up to us. To get started, work in an outside company's online department, like places that sell music online or a mobile company. They may have more patience with people who need training, and labels want you to deliver results fast. Get your feet wet so you can get qualified and go further up the chain inside a label."

WHAT YOU THOUGHT YOU KNEW:

Move back home?! Oh hell no! Not only am I too old for that, but it's just embarrassing, even if it's the key to jump-starting my career.

WHAT YOU NEED TO KNOW:

There is no shame in the boomerang game if you're actually up to something! In Alyce's case, she was relocating from Georgia to New York, saving for a place of her own, and looking for full-time work in film. Emily also relocated back to her parents' place in LA from San Francisco in order to launch her own business. She shares an empowering point of view about what is normally seen as a humiliating step backward. "Moving back home at thirty wasn't my picture of success, but I risked it on running my own business. How many times in life do we get to learn, fail, and be happy we did it? It gave me a chance to hang with them before I started my own family. I wouldn't say I failed, I had the company for three years — but we had a simple idea that I overcomplicated, and we had too many partners. And when you don't have a lot of funding, you've got to be simple and focused. But I wouldn't have known that unless I did it myself."

WHAT YOU THOUGHT YOU KNEW:

Being a mother in the new media world is probably harder that most other jobs because it's so fast-paced.

WHAT YOU NEED TO KNOW:

Well, yes and no . . . As a mother of two young children, Kathy contends that new media is a great career for working women, even with the downside of not meeting up after work with colleagues. "One beautiful thing about being in digital and being a mom: I can do my job from home if necessary. I can conduct all my business from the computer." There's a cloud for that silver lining, of course: "I think men can do more personal life stuff without being judged. A guy has to leave early for the anniversary dinner? No problem. Meanwhile, I'm nervous about taking my child to the doctor. I have to be aware that [colleagues] don't think of me being a burden on the team as a mom with duties."

WHAT YOU THOUGHT YOU KNEW:

In a new media job, I'll be working normal hours from a desk, nice and stable.

WHAT YOU NEED TO KNOW:

If nothing else, the political shell game is heightened by the mercurial change of the industry and the rush to innovate and profit in a field where, as Eleanor points out, "no one knows what the right answer is. Many women pigeonhole themselves out of decision-making roles because they are afraid to speak up or take on the responsibility. Stand up, raise your hand, and say, 'Why don't I work on this?' Be super-resourceful and unafraid. You have a lot of freedom to design a role for yourself." Kathy recommends that you "be prepared for long hours and managing the male executives so they understand your worth, value, and experience. You have to get their trust because there are always senior executives turning over and coming in. You should also come open to new ideas, creative ways of executing, and adjusting to their expectations and personalities."

WHAT YOU THOUGHT YOU KNEW:

In new media, there is no room for error.

WHAT YOU NEED TO KNOW:

On the creative side, trial and error is how you strike gold in new media, so embrace failure by learning from it. Emily talks about how learning the uses of real-world technical equipment as a DJ and engineer prepared her for understanding how the digital world works. "I had to get past a lot of fears about equipment: having a heavy hand, breaking it, not knowing how to work it, practicing . . . over time that made me less afraid of technical stuff. My brain was able to understand the flow of information from Signal A to Signal B or, in the Web world, from the home page to other pages. Women totally have technical minds, but there is this social, gender-based boundary of 'only guys do that.' It didn't even cross my mind that I could DJ until I saw a girl named DJ DRC [pronounced *darcy*] doing it."

On the business side: This is still a myth, but the margin for error narrows considerably. Lesson number one for Eleanor in one of her early new media gigs was "never sign anything! It seems so obvious, but you need someone to tell you that," she notes. "A colleague of mine signed a streaming agreement before streaming even existed, then went to a new company a week later. We got out of the deal because he wasn't authorized to sign it, and no harm was done. Educational mistake. I align myself with the [company's] lawyers and make sure they are behind what I'm doing."

CHAPTER 12

Exit Stage Next

....

Alexis Levi ✳ Dolly Turner ✳ Echo Allen ✳ Jasmine Vega ✳
Mykah Montgomery ✳ Tageré Southwell

....

*As a woman and as an entertainment executive, you have to
be thinking about reinventing yourself, just like talent does.*

—Dolly Turner, marketing veteran

Now you know that the only wrong path into and through this business
is on your knees, unless of course you are praying to your Higher Power.
The good news is that same integrity, faith, and resolve it takes to survive in
the business are all you need to make your exit, along with a plan. I understand, however, that inspiration works best with examples. For some, the
exit was a necessary break before surfacing anew like the phoenix. For others, the break was a clean, complete one into a new field altogether. As with
the entry, the exit will not be without fresh pain or new practices. Let the
incredible stories of these six women encourage and assure you that it's 100
percent okay to be done with the industry where you've spent a significant
part of your life. Not only is it okay, but you will be, too.

GOT OUT, GOT STRONGER, GOT BACK IN

We begin with Dolly Turner, whose exit served to give her clarity about her truth, which is that she loves entertainment. She just needed the perspective you can only gain from going to work like folks I call civilians—those who consume entertainment instead of driving it. "This was part of God's plan even though I kicked and screamed," says Dolly, who had logged in fourteen years as a senior marketing executive for many labels before being spun out as LaFace was absorbed by Arista. "The biggest blessing was, it allowed me to rebalance my life. I had a chance to spend more time on me, spend invaluable time with my family, reconnect with a lot of old friends, develop new ones, and develop my next career plan. I now have a theory that you don't advance to the next phase in life until you get the lesson."

The lessons Dolly got were that "it's tougher for women over forty than men." And overall, Black executives have a different challenge than white executives at forty. "We have to dye our hair and lie about our age, but I can't tell you how many long gray ponytails I've seen in [record company] hallways," Dolly says. "Men are allowed to age; their aging is considered relevant. Whereas for women, you're considered outdated or out of touch a lot sooner, unless you put forth a lot of effort of keep yourself connected to the younger demographic and the younger executives in the organization," she adds, offering a caveat that brings little comfort. "It's okay for men who become senior and disengage to get comfy in the executive suite. Women cannot afford to do that, insulate themselves, and feel like their accomplishments give them the right to live in the Ivory Tower."

Dolly couldn't rest on the laurels of marketing artists like TLC and Toni Braxton to multiplatinum megastardom. She took a partnership marketing job at global hotel coporation Choice Hotels. During that time, she also sought professional help. This was not therapy; she hired a career coach. "I'm not twenty years old anymore, and I needed some extra tools to make a successful transition. I was at a point in my career where I was beyond coaching myself. I also needed an objective opinion from a third party outside of my family and friends, who can sometimes project their interests onto you. My coach helped me break from the addictive part of being in music. I took for granted that I was doing something I loved, and she showed me it was a true privilege."

Though it was far from the flashing lights of entertainment, Dolly's position with Choice Hotels offered her the kind of opportunity you should always take advantage of: to learn while you earn. "I enhanced my marketing skills; worked on Web projects, which was a great new experience; and learned a lot about franchising," Dolly explains. While she knew that record company life wasn't it for her anymore, hospitality wasn't, either. "I was struggling with the fact that I was going to a job that I didn't particularly like," she recalls. Instead of taking that frustration out on the job, she volunteered for the American Black Film Festival (ABFF) to plug back into the entertainment world on a pressure-free level. "Working on the festival gave me an opportunity to engage myself in something that made my heart feel good. It satisfied my need to work in entertainment and I got to network," Dolly says, describing her two-summer stint as a volunteer. It also wound up being her access pass to the film world as an executive. "The sponsorship executive left the festival, and [festival founders] Reggie Scott and Jeff Friday offered the position to me."

ARTIST MANAGER TO TEAM OWNER AND GENERAL MANAGER

After spending years promoting artists in the Oakland/San Francisco Bay Area as both a manager and host of her own local TV show, Alexis Levi has positioned herself as a history maker in the sports world. She's the world's first African American woman owner of a professional male basketball team, the Las Vegas Stars. This is all the more astounding when you realize that she's a mother of two sons on her third career. She spent the first fourteen years of her working life outside the entertainment world altogether as a registered nurse. When a debilitating car accident sidelined this career, she educated herself in business and earned her sports agent's license. "I've always had this thing of multitasking. I had a stable job, but I always had something creative I was doing on the side. I co-produced the Bay Area Showcase at the Holiday Inn in Emeryville. I also managed Suga-T and Turf Talk, but eventually it got so draining I stopped doing it."

Alexis transferred her skills as a music industry hustler directly into the sports arena. The onetime high school basketball player became an agent and completed the process of acquiring a team in less than four years. Even she admits that this was ambitious, but she has regrets about taking the fast track to team ownership, where she was met with less-than-open arms. "I was perceived well in the music business. I had even done events in the business world. But in the sports world, it was the flip side. Other owners were pissed that I was a woman with a men's team, and they were really pissed that I was getting all the publicity I received. Me owning a team made the whole league more visible. Thankfully, the commissioner of the International Basketball League [Mikal Duilio] was very supportive of me," says Alexis. The hate was so strong, she was willing to be a silent partner. "At the time, I was gonna have two other men work with me, and have [one serve as the] figurehead. I wasn't sure if they were ready for a woman owner. Ultimately, God wanted me up front—the commissioner said he would give me the team solely," she says, smiling. "It was a good feeling to know I could not be denied. I did the same thing they did to get their teams, so I commanded my respect."

Alexis chose to go the IBL route because it "takes a couple million as opposed to tens of millions," she explains. She also gets to be a killer whale among sharks. And the lifestyle ain't bad, either. She splits her time between the Bay and the Strip. "I live in Vegas January through June. Players and coaches arrive in the spring, and we play from April through the play-offs in June." Alexis remembers how building this team from the ground up "almost killed me. The commissioner told me to purchase in 2006, wait a year, and debut in 2008. Me being strong-willed, I thought I could just whip it together, but it was a lot to do in a short time. I got an offer to bring a women's team to Vegas, but I learned from that," she says. "I have a staff of twelve and a lot to oversee. And now I'm diversifying because as Carol H. Williams told me, I am the product. I am doing it like Diddy and Trump mixed together." She also reveals that she has already written her memoir. "I finished my autobiography and I have a screenwriter for my life story," she says with a twinkle in her eye. When I try to process how this woman gets all this done, having raised a twenty-two-year-old and a fifteen-year-old while beating back her players' groupies on road trips, I am reminded that once we become the masters of our own schedules and destinies, so much more is possible!

....

ACTRESS AND MODEL TO REAL ESTATE MOGUL
....

Enter Echo Allen, an architect who discovered the power of that possibility after a wild, rocky decade or so spent between modeling, acting, performing stand-up comedy and her own one-woman show, and ultimately exotic dancing before she hit her bottom in the business and chose to turn her entire life around. Ironically, the trade with which she started her work life is what brought her full circle from being thousands of dollars in debt to having a net worth in the millions as a real estate investor. "I was a poor girl from the Bronx. Coming out of the ghetto, I wanted to create great housing for people. It was architectural school that gave me the resilience to do what I do now, but God gave me another way to provide housing: real estate investment," she remarks.

Echo's career as an architect ground to a halt at the start of the Gulf War. She thought her degree from Syracuse was going to keep her employed no matter what, especially as a member of what her mother called the Power Four: accountants, attorneys, architects, and doctors. "I was working as an architect, perfectly happy, and I lost my job. It was all I knew. I didn't even realize I could lose my job. Reagan had me thinking the world was coming to an end. I cried to my mother because she told me if I got a good education, I'd be fine! I was told that the Power Four would always be safe. That was a lie."

With no plan B waiting in the wings, she took inventory of other talents she had. "I had this attitude that people who made money from their looks were dumb because they ought to be using their brain to make a living. I was always trying to be like the boys in achitecture; I never thought of myself as being pretty. I had designer friends who used me as a model. So [one of them] took some photos of me and entered me into a calendar contest in the summer of '89. I never shaved my legs, wore makeup, any of it. I had a complete awakening about being a girl," she effuses. "The top three women selected got to work with Grace Del Marco, the modeling agency of color of the moment, for six months. I won third prize. My whole life shifted from that moment on. All of a sudden I was surrounded by gay men telling me they were gonna 'beat my face' and I went from being a tomboy to being glamorous. I went from fifty grand a year as an architect to unemployment to modeling money, which was twenty-five thousand for the year back then, but I had the time of my life." She entered another modeling contest with a flyaway to Paris for a week of auditions as first prize. She won, stayed for three weeks, and returned an official model with steady print work, frequent appearances in *Essence,* even a few magazine covers. As is so often the case, her leap to the next lily pad started with an innocent question. "Then one after the other photographers at my shoots would ask me if I was acting or would get into it. After the third one, I spoke to my agent, who just started sending me out [for roles], even though I didn't know how to act. I was going out for model roles where you don't talk. Then I started taking classes at HB Studios for about a year. I also studied at the Actors Studio,"

Echo says, retracing her path to the defining heartbreak of her acting career, *Boomerang*.

"Grace Del Marco sent me out on the casting call for *Boomerang*. I walked up in there lookin' like Mahogany did on the runway—the Asian-inspired one." She laughs at the memory. I knew how to be over the top, and I knew I couldn't beat [the other girls] with height, so I went there!" Echo was hired for a bit part in the dating montage. As far as she was concerned, she was on her way. The star treatment blew her mind. "I was on set for a week working with Eddie. I had a trailer with my name on it. I told the whole world I was in the movie—and I ended up on the cutting room floor. I didn't get the word until seven months later, along with the paycheck. At the time I wasn't smart enough to ask for the footage. And I was devastated that I was cut out of the movie. That was my big break! I learned that just like in architecture, I could be cut out of a job. It took me years to get over that, especially after I watched everyone's careers take off from that film. I was depressed for months, hiding out from my friends and people who had me repeat the *Boomerang* story," she says with a mock cringe at the memory. Her trial by fire with *Boomerang* did bear a seedling, however. "I got an agent just from doing the film. They sent me on an audition and I got a job on *Hangin' with Mr. Cooper* playing Raven Symoné's mom." Her recurring role led to more work on *Livin' Single, General Hospital, Law & Order Special Victims Unit,* and *Swift Justice*. "It was God's way of saying, 'Let me help heal this girl.' And just like that, I was an actor. People go to school killing themselves to do it yet never book anything—and I was right there," Echo marvels.

Sounds like everything is going peachy for Miss Echo, right? Yes and no. Hers was a classic case of *All work and no play makes for a woman with no personal life*. She made a move to settle down and took a job at a strip club to supplement her acting income during the slow months. It was just performing, or so she reasoned. She could not have anticipated how far down she would spiral chasing quick money. Echo takes us back to some of her darkest days.

"At one point I wasn't making any money, so I became an exotic dancer. The only thing that saved me from going over the edge was having a degree and a family that taught me I didn't have to this. I chose to do it. Acting slowed down and I couldn't get design work, and I was so bad at waitressing, I got fired the first week. A friend of mine waited tables at a strip club. I went for waitressing, but they only had a dancer position open, so I danced. The money is insane. I was easily making a thousand dollars a day back in the 1990s. The illusion is that you're partying all the time and your ego's being stroked, but what it did to me psychologically was make me distrustful of men."

Echo gives a sobering account of what can really go on for women working in strip clubs. The videos and reality shows have young girls thinking this is a sexy, harmless career. For most it's a dead-end job, a dream and self-esteem killer. Echo testifies to this, sharing the telltale signs of her higher self fading to black.

"I hid [stripping] from everyone but my sister. I even kept it from my live-in boyfriend by dancing while he was bartending. I would shower the smoke off me in time for him to come home from cleaning the bar. I started to feel like the only light in a sea of darkness. It began with allowing men to touch me while dancing, something I swore I wouldn't do. My boundaries of not drinking or sleeping with the men were starting to come down. Those are golden handcuffs. I wouldn't recommend that to my worst enemy. I stopped auditioning from being tired and sore from dancing. That was a low period in my life. It took me years to undo the emotional damage that did. And I only did it for two. I was so messed up from it that I didn't act for a year. I started on the path to self-help with Deepak Chopra, Iyanla Vanzant, and Landmark Education. That's when I wrote my one-woman show, *Tales of a Bugged Out Black Chick*." Her show beat unimaginable odds opening on September 12, 2001, a day after laughter was stolen from New York City and, indeed, the world. In the face of tragedy, Echo found a way to give back and heal through her show. "Twenty people showed up on opening night. I was devastated, too, but I had to get onstage and be funny. I wanted to cancel it because I didn't think I could make jokes after 9/11. But the following weekend it was sold out because the city *needed* it. Artists get a lot of flak, but we are the ones who keep the rest of the world in check when their relationships or lives aren't working."

Certain areas of Echo's life weren't working, either, and 9/11 brought that into sharp relief. Time was moving on without her. The change to real estate was motivated by a need for stability. The writing was on the wall. "I had been living in studio apartments all my life. I was addicted to the highs and lows. All my college friends had families. I [was] thirty-eight at this point, I was single, had traveled the world, but I was unstable emotionally and financially. I had nothing to show for the times when I had made large amounts of money. I would always lose the money out of feeling unworthy. I had no love life and no intimacy in my life. It all added up to me not being happy. And because I had been in the public eye, it made it harder to share the truth of who I really was. I felt like I needed to be an *adult*."

After taking stock of what her life had become, Echo started to own being grown. She used her 401(k) savings from an earlier corporate job as seed money for real estate and began the hunt for her first property, a Los Angeles fourplex. The sacrifice was demanding on every level: time, effort, and money. "I got a ten-dollar-an-hour job telemarketing for a mortgage agency. I worked fifty hours a week and just saved my money. I ate bag lunches and made that hourly wage look like a fat paycheck. I strategized to get an income property because I didn't want to end up like my actor friends who bought single-family homes only to lose their acting jobs and subsequently lose the house. From six to nine each morning, I searched for houses then worked from 10 AM to 10 PM, even on weekends. Three months later I found my first building. It fed the architect in me, and I learned the streets of Los Angeles as a result," explains Echo. But buying the first thing she found would have been too perfect; y'all know better than that! At least her lawyers from her acting days came in handy. "I lost seven grand in attorneys' fees fighting to get out of a bad buy that had illegal tenants and mold. I ultimately had to use my SAG [Screen Actors Guild, an actors' union] attorneys to fire my Realtor, who had been steering me to the building for his commission. I was bruised from that but eventually I met the developer from whom I ultimately bought the fourplex." In less than five years, Echo has made many times what her career in entertainment generated for her. "I started out with a net worth of minus thirty-four thousand dollars at the age of thirty-seven. I thought to myself, *How is that possible after working as an architect, working on the strip club floor, and working on the television screen?* Now I have eight buildings. My primary residence is in a trust. The other seven are in three other states, Alabama, Florida, and Tennessee, so I created LLCs in each state to hold those homes." Echo is also over the superwoman syndrome that has so many of us trying to do everything on our own. The only millionaires who get to the seven-figure club by themselves are lottery winners. "I have a team of investor friends that own more than me. They keep me inspired and show me my problems aren't so big. I have an accountant and two attorneys, one for California and one in Alabama. I have six property managers, a slew of handymen, contractors—all outsourced. And I have a personal assistant on my payroll to help me—my goal is to have her manage it all full-time along with my accountant. The properties are worth three million dollars. My net worth is $1.9 million. Sometimes there are days where I don't have the cash on me to put gas in my car, but because I am asset-rich, I can laugh about that now."

RECORDING ARTIST TO MASTER IN LEADERSHIP

As one-third of the talented but naive vocal trio Emage, Mykah Montgomery didn't have cash on her most of the time, but for her it was no laughing matter. As the granddaughter of piano icon Buddy Montgomery and grandniece of West Coast jazz architects Wes and Monk Montgomery, she was a natural talent surrounded by music but uneducated about the music business. Her story is a cautionary tale that happens far too often, that of newly signed baby recording acts who get taken for a ride, and not because they were robbed necessarily, but because they had no clue about the business or how to stand up for themselves before it chewed them up and spat them out. Mykah and her group members Taura Jackson, now a successful songwriter, and Kimbre'ly Evans, a background vocalist and commercial actor, came into the game just the way the industry likes its artists, young and gullible, ignorant to its inner workings. Mykah explains, "I was nineteen years old and it was a total whirlwind. One of the girls met [emcee and producer] Dres at the lake [Merritt]. He was trying to get at her and he said he was looking for a female group—and when she sang for him and told him she had a group, he was blown away and wanted to meet us. We all met at Lake Temescal in Oakland and sang for him—and he said, 'Let's do a deal.' We cut a three-song demo to take back to [then Mercury A&R executive] Lisa Cortes the very next week. She loved it and we started negotiating contracts, which were signed several months later."

Unfortunately, Mykah's contract had one thing missing. It seems small at first glance, but would have made life as a developing artist a lot smoother. Mykah says, "We received ten thousand dollars each. That felt like a lot of money to us. It was more money that we'd ever had. But because we were not at home in California, we should have been paid per diem"—a daily stipend for food, transportation, and essential expenses. Does this mean Lisa offered the girls a bad recording deal? Not necessarily. Contracts are what the two parties negotiate, and the label is not going to advise artists on what to include. "That was our attorney's bad for not telling us, the artists—and his clients—what we needed to have in our deal," says Mykah. "Then Dres moved us to New York to record. We started out at his apartment for a month then we got our own place in Manhattan. But we were in New York for eight months. We had no idea what per diem was, so consequently, our [advance] money ran out, and it was like pulling teeth to get more. In fact, we never really got it. We could have stacked our advance money and lived off per diem. If you're not smart enough to ask, you don't get what you need."

In the meantime however, Emage were Dres's golden girls, which carried considerable cachet in the mid-1990s, when Black Sheep was riding high off the success of its gold debut album, *A Wolf in Sheep's Clothing.* Mykah and her girls were out of Oakland and livin' the life of recording artists in the Big Apple. At the time, little else mattered. "We were on a strict schedule every day: gym, vocal lessons, recording every day. At night, we'd go to clubs with Dres, who was a star at the time. It was a lot of fun, but it happened so fast," Mykah recounts. It wasn't long after their album *Soul Deep* was released that things started to slow to a stalemate. They seemed to be on a perpetual promotional run but with absolutely no say in how the music they uprooted their lives to make was actually promoted. Once the group realized how low on the food chain they were, the music business started to lose its luster.

"We wanted a second single; we didn't like their first single choice. Even though he had the label, Dres didn't have creative control on marketing us. He was signed to a label under a label, and the buck was always getting passed so we never got any kind of closure on what we needed. We never got paid for the gigs we did and never got the benefit of making money as artists. No one would take responsibility for the group's progress—so we asked to be released from the label. We didn't have other real plans. We could have shopped for another home and then left the label, but we were hotheaded personalities so we just got upset and left the label. We didn't have a plan as a group and I was unhappy in that situation, so I left the group and never looked back or regretted it." After shooting one music video and recording "Happy Kwanzaa," the first Kwanzaa song released to urban radio, Emage barely sold five thousand copies of their album. Mykah was back in the real world, so she hit the pavement for a job. "The Emage experience wasn't the best one for me as a person. Musically it was great but I was ready to go back to corporate America so I could have a check, some stability, and have some money. I worked at an entertainment venue called Geoffrey's Inner Circle, then I went into the technology industry so I could eat," she jokes, noting that as supportive as Geoffrey was, in the Bay Area technology was paying much better than the music industry.

And yet, something just wasn't clicking for Mykah on the grind with her nine-to-five. She chose to advance herself educationally, earning her master's degree in leadership from the New School of San Francisco. Achieving this educational goal gave Mykah a new perspective on both music and work. "I will never give up music, but I needed to dig out of the industry at the level I was in it, which was not that high. Once I finished my BA and got my master's, I knew the corporate world was not where my heart is," she explains, noting that she is plotting her pathway back to being an artist on her own terms. No longer content to depend upon others for music, she got serious about honing her craft as a consistent songwriter, gifted arranger, and, recently, music producer. "Up until about four years ago I was working with producers, and they were cool, but I didn't have money so I was at the mercy of their schedules. Months would go by before a song could get done. I have a song from seven years ago that's still not done," she says, laughing. "So I finally bought my own equipment and started teaching myself how to play; listening to the things in my head and trying to produce them. Now I can direct players to play what I envision. I don't need producers unless I want another sound, and that feels awesome. I had trials with being confident as a writer and certainly as a producer because no one ever even thought I could produce—and I just kept doing it even though I wasn't being nurtured that way. And without the group or any negativity, I was able to focus on me. Producing and writing are second nature for me now. I'm not having the *Oh my God—I can't believe I did that* thing happening anymore." Mykah is more than a master in leadership. She is now the master of her destiny as an artist. And her timing could not be better, with all the access to consumers artists can command via new media.

"I have my own companies now: Mylaan Entertainment, M.E. Records, Black Ram Publishing, and Black Ram Productions. I am now in the space where I *want* to be in the music [business again]. So if I'm working, it's only so I can put it into my music and make the music work for me: to perform, to pay the band, to finally get my CD done. My work experience in account management and sales plus my master's all help me build my business," asserts Mykah, the independent solo artist. "It's all preparing me to run my label—and, with my own single on iTunes, it is coming full circle."

....

PUBLICIST TO ESTHETICIAN
....

For media relations veteran Jasmine Vega, after upward of twenty years in Black music publicity, working it from the clubs to the suites as the head of major-label media departments, it was simply time to get gone and stay gone from the business. Jasmine shared her industry story in detail for chapter 5. At some point, she realized she was just bouncing from label to label like a Ping-Pong ball as internal support for music and artists waned. That wasn't what she'd signed up for. The thrill, as B. B. King so eloquently put it, was gone. The independent spirit that attracted her to Delicious Vinyl and Priority Records was being squelched by the mainstream's acceptance of hip-hop. Once rap got some real attention, it started acting a fool, right along with the labels that were blinded by the astronomical profits they raked in as a result.

"It all kind of started shifting for me with Priority. I started feeling less of a purpose. I started seeing it was about the [label] making money, not about all of us on the grind. I started seeing this was definitely a man's world. Going over to Virgin, I felt like I had a purpose again; we were a team striving to create this urban division that was going to be great for this major company. And it was. But then, the industry was changing a lot, visually with the videos, lyrically in songs, and with how business was run. It was about 'This is what I have' instead of 'This is what I'm saying.' Artist development departments didn't exist at all; there was no teaching the artist about the business side, about how to act or how to be. It was no longer about the music. I started losing the passion for the industry, and contemplated, 'what do I really want at this point in my life?' I was definitely working sixteen hours a day almost seven days a week for somebody else's pocketbook, and that wasn't what it was all about for me. So I kind of did some soul searching while I was working, took a couple months off, came back, fulfilled my contract, oddly enough signed another contract, fulfilled that for about a year. Then I was just ready to leave. At that point I was in my midthirties and said, 'Well, you know what, it's time for me to just start doing me for a change.'"

Jasmine's soul search led her to a career—one where she "could be in an environment where people felt good about what they did and had a passion for it"—as a medical esthetician alongside a doctor in Beverly Hills. "I felt the industry was a very unhealthy environment, spiritually, mentally, physically. I got in touch with what I'm about and became whole again. Now I'm working on creating my own skin care line for women and men of color, because now the men are about [skin care], too. I work with products that are nontoxic and nonharmful. It's all about health from the inside out," Jasmine concludes with a smile.

....
MUSIC VIDEO PROMOTER TO CHEF AND FOOD STYLIST
....

Chef Tageré (say *tazure-ray*) Southwell took a page from Master P's book when it came to getting in the music industry; She was truly 'bout it 'bout it. While most young people can barely hold down one internship these days without making more work for their mentors because they are so dense, unfocused, or fixated on blowing up, Tageré worked three internships simultaneously. She wanted a career in the music business so bad she did two things many of us refuse to do: move back in with Mom and go without cash. "I started interning at Big Beat/Atlantic a couple days a week right out of college. I also interned at *Rolling Stone* one day a week in the sales department. And I worked at Arista two days a week. Then I broke off from the other two and did a full-time internship at Arista for a few months. All I got was transportation and lunch. At that time Arista was the biggest label. They felt no need to pay us. I was living at home and giving Mom some money, but really had no other job. I would do hair on the side but that was pretty much it," she recalls.

Tageré's persistence and hustle won her a job assisting in the rap promotions department with Jeff House, J. C. Ricks, and Jean-Pierre Diaz briefly before being promoted to video promotion manager. She loved a fair share of the work, but the cold reality of the business hit pretty fast. "I enjoyed meeting people that I probably would not have met any other way. I learned how to network. It took away my fear of talking to anyone at any time, from the mailroom guy to the chairman. What was missing for me was loyalty. There were a lot of people I thought were my friends . . . we stayed in the office from nine to nine most days. I thought I had built these family-type relationships. A colleague told my boss I didn't like a project. That turned me off to making my co-workers my friends. I realized I had to keep them separate. That's when my relationship with my boss was affected, and it ended up going downhill from there. That was my last industry job."

It sounds unreal, but it was literally Tageré's stomach that led her out of the record business, long before she found her calling in the culinary world. "It was getting to the point where I was waking up with a stomachache. I was physically ill going to work," explains Tageré, who realized that she worked for an abusive boss. "He was completely oblivious to how he treated me. He was berating people on calls, and he threw the fact that Arista was doing so well in my face. I was depressed." All it took to go along with that constant stomachache was a few more terrible baby acts and a bad boss getting worse to give Tageré a real bad taste of the business overall before she snapped. "I gave him a two-day notice. He said I might as well not stay. He called HR and had them watch me as I left to make sure I wasn't stealing anything. I just said good-bye."

I asked Tageré what sparked her transition from pushing records to pushing pies. Turns out, she was doing both at the same time, but she hadn't chosen the latter as a career option until she left the label. "I was depressed for a good six months. That was what I really wanted to do. I had a degree from Syracuse in retail and fashion business. And I really wanted to do something creative. And working in college radio really showed me I wanted to get into the music business. And yet, I didn't see myself anywhere else after Arista. I was good at computers so I went to school to take some HTML courses. I looked into jobs that combined music and the Web. I went to Net-Media, where I helped them build sites for BMG artists; oversaw Strauss Zelnick's site and a couple other corporate sites. And I really enjoyed that, but I knew it wasn't really my thing." Then she realized she could turn her love of cooking into a way to earn a living.

"While I was at Arista the security guards would ask me to bake for them. And that made me feel good . . . I was feeling so bad at work, the cooking was cathartic for me. I felt like I wasn't working, like I was playing with food. I was using my great-grandmother's bowls, and still do to this day. I left NetMedia and went to New York Restaurant Schools, now the Culinary Art Institute. Once I got into culinary school, I excelled. I got straight A's and I never missed an hour of school. I couldn't be away from it! I took a two-month externship at Chanterelle [a fine restaurant in New York]. That was great experience. I worked under a female sous chef who took a liking to me and let me do everything, which is rare. I knew this was it."

Tageré let her passion and skill carry her forward, pursuing every cooking opportunity she could find to get her name out there and gain experience. When the chance to cook at the Cannes Film Festival presented itself, she jumped at it and was selected for a two-week intensive, learning from the world's best chefs on the French Rivera. She'd come a long way from having to pretend she liked a terrible single just to get its video some airplay. "I was crying the day before I left saying, 'God, if this is it . . . this will be the event that will change my life.' We were cooking on the beach in the American

Film Pavilion where non-French-speakers hang out and eat and surf online. We went to St. Tropez, shopped at all the French markets, I was livin' it up! I got to cook with Roger Verget, a world-renowned chef, for the American Foundation for AIDS Research dinner. He fed five hundred people in less than ten minutes. It was like the culinary Olympics. Just being in the midst of his greatness was incredible. I met all these people who actually lived in New York. I even ended up working with them when we returned."

Tageré's powerful networking skills combined with her culinary acumen put her on the fast track in her new career, where she tried food styling and serving as personal chef. "From Cannes, I did some recipe testing with a friend who worked at a magazine, and I worked at the institute as a freelancer. While doing that, I met Sarah Moulton and Peter Berley. I assisted him with his wealthy clients in the Hamptons. That's when I saw how much money you could make cooking for individuals. Right out of school and assisting, I was making five hundred dollars a week at the most. I was getting five hundred dollars a day working with Peter. In the Hamptons it goes up to seven hundred a day. These people have money to burn and I've never had trouble getting my money from anyone," notes Tageré, the intern who used to be made to feel like the label was doing her a favor by letting her intern there for free. She used to settle for music and concert tickets as compensation, but none of that pays a single bill. Now she gets paid what she's worth and still gets great free stuff, from gourmet knives to admission into food conferences. "The fear gets people," she says, empathizing with the courage it takes to make the leap. "I prayed a *lot*. I know would have been miserable working somewhere else otherwise. I'm glad I did it."

REALIZATIONS IN TRANSITION

Echo recommends "being open to the synchronicity in your life. Let the universe support you even though there are disasters going on," she says. "I was devastated about losing the money on the first property I tried to buy, but three weeks later I was right next to the man who sold me the next one at Kinko's, even though I was telling myself to quit."

Jasmine's realization was more about the underlying premise of publicity itself, and the fact that it was not really in alignment with her operating principles. "With age comes a lot of realization and self-acceptance. You never want to be driven by ego, and I felt publicity was all about feeding somebody's ego. Ethically, I had an issue with that, but I didn't think that I had anything else to fall back on. I didn't have this huge education. I didn't have parents with money. My drive to make something happen for myself is what's gotten me through everything. I think for anybody that really wants to do anything—whatever it might be, if it's to make the best ice cream ever—then go for it. Find out the ingredients. Find out everything you can about making ice cream, and make that best ice cream!"

"I remember each day to be true to myself," affirms Alexis, offering another secret to success in whatever game you choose to play. "The business and its hype can suck you in. I didn't sleep my way to the top, and I don't do drugs. Be about the business but don't get caught up in the business, and you'll come out on top." Mykah echoes Alexis's sentiment, reflecting on the wake-up call that she got from being a major-label baby act with the 20/20 vision only hindsight and wisdom can provide. "I came out of college to record my first album, and that became college for me. By and large, the corporate [label] people don't respect you as an artist. Half the time, they are frustrated artists themselves! They'll laugh, smile in your face, and buy you drinks, but they're making the money. You're not."

Dolly's advice is straight no chaser. Just read the exit signs. "You're stressed, hair falling out . . . that's God giving you the signals that its time to go. If you ignore all that, it's your fault," she warns. "The check, the career, the position, the access—none of it should become more important than your personal life."

....

SUMMARY OF SECRETS REVEALED

WHAT YOU THOUGHT YOU KNEW:

I can't resign now. I have to stay here to stay relevant, even if in my heart I am ready to move on.

WHAT YOU NEED TO KNOW:

Be careful in assessing how long is too long to stay. Admittedly, it's hard to quit your job so you can find a better one, but sometimes we need to release a negative situation to open our lives to positive ones. A hand that is full cannot receive. Dolly weighs in on this point: "I used to believe positive could prevail. When you are in a negative environment with negative people, it has the ability to overcome the positive. There were times when I stayed way too long, and that's been an important lesson for me. What I do now is go into a situation assessing it honestly, knowing the negatives from the start, determining what I will and won't accept."

WHAT YOU THOUGHT YOU KNEW:

The only way to find a better or different job is to hit the pavement.

WHAT YOU NEED TO KNOW:

Interviewing for another lane in the rat race is not your only shot at career fulfillment. Release the notion that you will not survive the transition; you absolutely will if, to quote 2Pac, one of my favorite lyricists, you "plan, plot, strategize, and bomb first." Volunteer in the next arena you think you might want to play, as Dolly did with the film festival. After two fun summers, she had a new gig in a new field. Try on going back to school like Mykah, Tageré, or Jasmine. Mykah went for her master's, but Tageré and Jasmine went for professional certifications. Both Tageré and Mykah went to school on weekends while they worked, so flexibility works in your favor. You don't have to break the bank or spend years learning new skills. Tageré recommends that "you think about how you're going to pay for school if you'll need it to make a change. I was sucking up my 401(k) to pay for school, and that was not cool."

WHAT YOU THOUGHT YOU KNEW:

It will all feel so much better if I just choke, smack, or sabotage my colleague, boss, or client, even if the feeling lasts for a moment.

WHAT YOU NEED TO KNOW:

Do your best to stay cool and take care of yourself when you're having thoughts of "taking care" of the next man or woman in a not-so-nice way. None of whatever you are going through is worth catching a case. Take a note from *The Four Agreements* here and don't take it personally. "People make decisions based on how it will benefit them from a business perspective, be they talent or executive," Dolly maintains. "That's the bottom line, and it can be very disappointing and lead to heartache if you don't understand that. Therefore, you have to be strategic about everything you do. I maintain the high ground with professionalism and positive interaction. I draw on my faith and belief in God."

Recommended Reading

Spiritual & Self-Help Books

Castaneda, Carlos. *Tales of Power*. New York: Pocket Books, 1976.

Chideya, Farai. *The Color of Our Future: Our Multiracial Future*. New York: Harper Perennial, 1999.

Coelho, Paulo. *The Alchemist*. San Francisco: HarperSanFrancisco, 1993.

Gibran, Khalil. *The Prophet*. New York: Knopf, 1942.

Giddings, Paula. *When and Where I Enter: The Impact of Black Women on Race and Sex in America*. New York: William Morrow, 1984.

Greene, Robert. *The 48 Laws of Power*. A Joost Elfers Book. New York: Viking Penguin, 1998.

hooks, bell. *Sisters of the Yam: Black Women and Self-Recovery*. Boston: South End Press, 1993.

Machiavelli, Niccolo, and William J. Connell. *Machiavelli's The Prince*. New York: Bedford-St. Martin's, 2005.

Maxwell, John C. *The 21 Irrefutable Laws of Leadership: Follow Them and People Will Follow You*. Maxwell Motivation, Inc. Nashville: Thomas Nelson, 2007.

Morgan, Joan. *When Chickenheads Come Home to Roost: My Life as a Hip-Hop Feminist*. New York: Simon & Schuster, 1999.

Ruiz, Don Miguel. *The Four Agreements: A Practical Guide to Personal Freedom*. San Rafael, CA: Amber-Allen Publishing, 1997.

Schucman, Helen, and William Thetford. *A Course in Miracles*. Mill Valley, CA: Foundation for Inner Peace, 1975.

Somé, Malidoma Patrice. *Of Water and the Spirit: Ritual, Magic and Initiation in the Life of an African Shaman*. New York: Putnam, 1994.

Somé, Sobonfu. *The Spirit of Intimacy: Ancient Teachings in the Ways of Relationships*. New York: William Morrow, 1999.

Tzu, Sun. *The Art of War*. Hertfordshire, UK: Wordsworth Editions, 1998.

Walsch, Neale Donald. *Conversations with God: An Uncommon Dialogue* (Book 1). New York: Putnam, 1996.

Industry Books

Banjoko, Adisa. *Lyrical Swords: Hip Hop and Politics in the Mix*. San Jose, CA: YinSumi Press, 2004.

———. *Lyrical Swords, Volume II: Westside Rebellion*. San Jose, CA: YinSumi Press, 2006.

Chang, Jeff. *Can't Stop, Won't Stop: A History of the Hip-Hop Generation*. New York: St. Martin's Press, 2005.

Churchill, Sharal. *Music Supervision 101: The Indie Guidebook to Music Supervision for Films*, rev. ed. Los Angeles: Filmic Press, 2002.

Cooper, Martha, and Nika Kramer. *We B* Girlz*. New York: powerHouse Books, 2005.

Dannen, Frederic. *Hit Men: Power Brokers and Fast Money Inside the Music Business*. New York: Times Books, 1990.

Fong-Torres, Ben. *The Motown Album: The Sound of Young America*. New York: St. Martin's Press, 1990.

Kashif, Kashif, and Gary A. Greenberg. *Everything You Better Know about the Record Industry*. Venice, CA: Brooklyn Boy Books, 1996.

Kitwana, Bakari. *The Hip-Hop Generation: Young Blacks and The Crisis in African American Culture*. New York: Basic Civitas Books, 2002.

Lewis, Miles Marshall. *Scars of the Soul Are Why Kids Wear Bandages When They Don't Have Scars*. New York: Akashic Books, 2004.

McCoy, Quincy. *No Static: A Guide to Creative Radio Programming*. San Francisco: Backbeat Books, 1999.

Obst, Lynda. *Hello, He Lied: And Other Truths from the Hollywood Trenches*. New York: Little, Brown, 1996.

Passman, Donald S. *All You Need to Know About the Music Business*. New York: Simon & Schuster, 2000.

Poulson-Bryant, Scott, and Smokey D. Fontaine. *What's Your Hi-Fi Q? From Prince to Puff Daddy, 30 Years of Black Music Trivia*. New York: Simon & Schuster, 2002.

Reeves, Marcus. *Somebody Scream! RapMusic's Rise to Prominence in the After-shock of Black Power.* New York: Faber and Faber, 2008.

Rose, Tricia. *Black Noise: Rap Music and Black Culture in Contemporary America.* Middletown, CT: Wesleyan University Press, 1993.

Runell, Marcella, and Martha Diaz. *The Hip-Hop Education Guidebook: Volume 1.* New York: Hip-Hop Association, 2007.

Shemel, Sidney, and M. William Krasilovsky. *This Business of Music.* New York: Billboard Publications, 1985.

Industry Trades

AdWeek — www.adweek.com

Back Stage — www.backstage.com

Billboard — www.billboard.com

Black Renaissance Exclusive — www.bremagazine.com

Broadcasting & Cable — www.broadcastingcable.com

CMJ (College Music Journal) — www.cmj.com

HITS — www.hitsdailydouble.com

Hollywood Reporter — www.hollywoodreporter.com

Radio & Records — www.radioandrecords.com

TV Week — www.tvweek.com

Urban Network — www.urbannetwork.com

Variety — www.variety.com

Biographies and Autobiographies

Fong-Torres, Ben. *Becoming Almost Famous: My Back Pages in Music, Writing, and Life.* San Francisco: Backbeat Books, 2006.

Gordy, Berry. *To Be Loved: The Music, the Magic, the Memories of Motown: An Autobiography.* New York: Warner Books, 1994.

Jones, Quincy. *From Q with Love.* Van Nuys, CA: Alfred Publishing, 1999.

Turner, Tina, and Kurt Loder. *I, Tina: My Life Story.* New York: HarperCollins, 1986.

Wilson, Mary, with Patricia Romanowski and Arghus Juilliard. *Dreamgirl: My Life as a Supreme.* New York: St. Martin's Press, 1987.

Business Books

Ambrose, June. *Effortless Style.* New York: Simon&Schuster, 2006.

Black, Cathie. *Basic Black: The Essential Guide for Getting Ahead at Work (and in Life).* New York: Crown Business, 2007.

Bridgforth, Glinda. *Girl, Get Your Money Straight!: A Sister's Guide to Healing Your Bank Account and Funding Your Dreams in 7 Simple Steps*. New York: Broadway Books, 2000.

Eker, T. Harv. *Secrets of the Millionaire Mind: Mastering the Inner Game of Wealth*. New York: HarperCollins, 2005.

Evans, Gail. *Play Like a Man, Win Like a Woman: What Men Know About Success that Women Need to Learn*. New York: Broadway Books, 2000.

Frankel, Lois P. *Nice Girls Don't Get the Corner Office: 101 Unconscious Mistakes Women Make*. New York: Warner, 2004.

Friedman, Caitlin, and Kimberly Yorio. *The Girl's Guide to Kicking Your Career into Gear: Valuable Lessons, True Stories and Tips for Using What You've Got (a Brain!) to Make Your Worklife Work for You*. New York: Broadway Books, 2008.

Fry, Ronald. *101 Smart Questions to Ask on Your Interview*. Franklin Lakes, NJ: Career Press, 2003.

Gehring, Abigail. *Odd Jobs: 101 Ways to Make an Extra Buck*. New York: Skyhorse Publishers, 2007.

Gerber, Michael E. *The E Myth Revisited: Why Most Small Businesses Don't Work and What to Do About It*. New York: HarperBusiness, 1995.

Gladwell, Malcolm. *Blink: The Power of Thinking Without Thinking*. New York: Time Warner AudioBooks, 2005.

———. *The Tipping Point: How Little Things Can Make a Big Difference*. New York: Little, Brown, 2000.

Hansen, Mark Victor, and Robert G. Allen. *The One Minute Millionaire: The Enlightened Way to Wealth*. New York: Harmony Books, 2002.

Kiyosaki, Robert T., and Sharon L. Lechter. *Rich Dad, Poor Dad*. New York: Warner Books, 2000.

Levinson, Jay Conrad. *Guerilla Marketing*. Boston: Houghton Mifflin, 2007.

McNeal, Delatorro L., II. *Caught Between a Dream and a Job*. Lake Mary, FL: Excel Books, 2008.

Miller, Dan. *No More Mondays: Fire Yourself—and Other Revolutionary Ways to Discover Your True Calling*. New York: Currency Doubleday, 2008.

Mitchell, Jack. *Hug Your Customers: The Proven Way to Personalize Sales and Achieve Astounding Results*. New York: Hyperion Books, 2003.

Orman, Suze. *Women and Money: Owning the Power to Control Your Destiny*. New York: Spiegel & Grau, 2007.

Pollack, Lindsey. *Getting from College to Career: 90 Things to Do Before You Join the Real World*. New York: Collins Business, 2007.

Ryan, Robin. *60 Seconds and You're Hired*. Manassas Park, VA: Impact Publications, 1994.

Seligson, Hannah. *New Girl on the Job: Advice from the Trenches*. New York: Citadel, 2007.

Shapiro, Cynthia. *Corporate Confidential: 50 Secrets Your Company Doesn't Want You to Know—and What to Do About Them*. New York: St. Martin's Griffin, 2005.

Stamm, Hillary, and Peter Nowalk. *The Hollywood Assistant's Handbook: 86 Rules for Aspiring Power Players*. New York: Workman, 2008.

Stanley, Thomas J., and William D. Danko. *The Millionaire Next Door: The Surprising Secrets of America's Wealthy*. Atlanta, GA: Longstreet Press, 1996.

Weingarten, Rachel C. *Career and Corporate Cool: How to Look, Dress, and Act the Part at Every Stage of Your Career*. Hoboken, NJ: John Wiley & Sons, 2007.

Wolf, Michael J. *The Entertainment Economy: How Mega-Media Forces Are Transforming Our Lives*. New York: Times Books, 1999.

Recommended Resources

Professional Organizations

Academy of Motion Picture Arts & Sciences — www.oscars.org
African-American Public Relations Collective (AAPRC) — www.theaaprc.com
Digital Media Wire — www.dmwmedia.com
National Academy of Recording Arts & Sciences (NARAS) — www.naras.org
National Association of Black Female Executives in Music & Entertainment
    (NABFEME) — www.nabfeme.org
National Association of Black Owned Broadcasters (NABOB) — www.nabob.org
National Association of Recording Merchandisers (NARM) — www.narm.com
New York Women in Film & TV — www.nywift.org

Conferences and Festivals

African American Women in Cinema — www.aawic.org
American Black Film Festival — www.abff.com
American Film Market — www.ifta-online.org/afm
Black Entertainment and Sports Lawyers Association (BESLA) — www.besla.org
Bronner Brothers Hair Show — www.bronnerbrothers.com
Cannes International Film Festival — www.festival-cannes.com
H2O: A Hip-Hop Odyssey International Film Festival — www.h2oiff.org
Handle Your [entertainment] Business Seminar — www.thembisamshaka.com
Latin American Film Festival — www.latinamericanfilmfestival.com
Magic (fashion and apparel trade show) — www.magiconline.com

Midem — www.midem.com

New York Asian Film Festival — www.subwaycinema.com

Outfest — www.outfest.org

Own Your Power Retreat — www.ownyourpower.biz

Pan African Film & Arts Festival — www.paff.org

Radio & Records Convention — www.radioandrecords.com

Reel Sisters of the Diaspora Film Festival — www.reelsisters.org

South by Southwest — www.sxsw.com

Sundance Film Festival — festival.sundance.org

Urbanworld Film Festival — www.urbanworld.org

Winter Music Conference — www.wintermusicconference.com

Endnotes

Chapter 4: Imaging

1. http://brandchannel.com/features_effect.asp?pf_id=203.
2. http://money.cnn.com/magazines/fortune/fortune_archive/2005/11/14/8360679/index.htm.

Chapter 6: Read the Label

1. www.billboard.com/bbcom/news/article_display.jsp?vnu_content_id=1003797885.
2. *Birmingham Post,* business section, June 19, 2007.
3. Patrick McGeehan, "Sex Bias Suit Settled for $74M," www.theage.com, July 14, 2004.

Chapter 8: The Art and Nuance of Production for Script, Stage, and Screen

1. Teresa Wiltz, "Idlewild: A Rap Movie with Rapturous Originality," August 25, 2006, www.washingtonpost.com/wp-dyn/content/article/2006/08/24/AR2006082401903.html.

Chapter 9: President and CEO

1. Nielsen Rating data for the week of June 26, 2007.

Chapter 11: The Revolution Will Be Feminized

1. Apple press release, "iTunes Now Number Two Music Retailer in the U.S.," February 26, 2008, www.apple.com/pr/library/2008/02/26itunes.html.
2. Adam L. Penenberg, "The Right Price for Digital Music," *Slate*, December 5, 2005, www.slate.com/id/2131573.
3. John Murrell, "Universal Test Emergency Exit at iTunes Store; Sets Off Alarm," July 2, 2007, www.blogs.siliconvalley.com/gmsv/2007/07/universal_tests_emergency_exit_at_itunes_store_sets_off_alarm.html.
4. Ibid.

About the Author

THEMBISA S. MSHAKA is a five-time Telly Award winner who has served in the entertainment industry for over seventeen years, spanning the areas of touring, management, magazine publishing, recorded music and technology, advertising, music supervision for film, voice over, and television. As senior copywriter at Sony Music and two-time NARM Award winner, her campaigns contributed to the sale of more than 150 million albums for artists including Lauryn Hill, Will Smith, Beyoncé, Wyclef Jean, Nas, Maxwell, George Michael, Wu-Tang Clan, Bow Wow, Jill Scott, and Babyface. The former *Gavin* rap editor has also written for *Honey*, Essence.com, and Launch.com, and served as contributing editor for theHotness.com and *Blaze* magazine. She contributed to the anthology *Sometimes Rhythm: Sometimes Blues*, edited by Taigi Smith, and *Icons of Hip-Hop*, an academic reference volume edited by Mickey Hess. Thembisa is currently the copy director for BET Networks. A native of Los Angeles and favorite daughter of the Bay Area, the Mills College alumna resides in the Bedford-Stuyvesant neighborhood of Brooklyn, New York, with her husband and son.

790.2023 MSHAKA
Mshaka, Thembisa S.
Put your dreams first :handle your
 entertainment business /
R0112315015   ROSWEL

AUG 1 4 2009

ROSWELL

ATLANTA-FULTON COUNTY LIBRARY